The Complete Advertising and Marketing Handbook

Your Twenty-First Century Advertising and Marketing Manual Is Available Right Now

Herschell Gordon Lewis

Bonus Books, Inc., Chicago

02   01   00   99   98   5   4   3   2   1

Library of Congress Cataloging-in-Publication Data

Lewis, Herschell Gordon, 1926-
     The complete advertising and marketing handbook : your twenty
  -first century advertising and marketing manual is available right
  now / Herschell Gordon Lewis.
        p.   cm.
     Includes index.
     ISBN 1-56625-101-X
     1. Advertising—Handbooks, manuals, etc. 2. Marketing—Handbooks,
  manuals, etc. I. Title.
  HF5823.L528 1998
     659.1—dc21   98-4434
                                                                            CIP

Bonus Books, Inc.
160 East Illinois Street
Chicago, IL 60611

Printed in the United States of America

Contents

Preface

I'd guess I've read as many books about advertising as anyone on this planet; and I've also written as many (this is my twenty-first book, inadvertently coinciding with the twenty-first century).

The problem with many books that either instruct or tell you "How I did it" is that they're fractional. We all know the old joke about experts — "An expert is somebody who knows more and more about less and less, until he/she finally knows everything . . . about nothing at all."

We've seen this in articles and books relating to every facet of what I call "force-communication." They seem to be written for the writer, not for the reader.

Suppose you want to know — *really* want to know — how to maximize the impact of your Yellow Pages advertising. Or maybe you want to take a shot at television. Or, more likely in the twenty-first century, you either are pressed to establish a web site or to make your existing web site effective. To whom do you turn?

Usually, you find yourself in one of two positions:

1. You meet with representatives of the chosen medium. Uh-oh! They're *salespeople*. Their viewpoint is self-oriented. Their purpose is to sell you; if they also help you, that's an incidental benefit.

2. You read articles in the trade publications. These are written for the cohorts of the writer and not for an outsider. Or you read books about the subject. Often, such books espouse the author's singular area of expertise.

These circumstances are natural and not particularly damaging. But what spurred me to write this Handbook was the realization that what most people in business want is a "how-to" approach . . . an impartial dissection of each major medium, neither glorifying it nor damaging it, analyzing the most successful techniques for capitalizing on its uniqueness and strengths.

The comments in this Handbook are deliberately breezy, not academic. We're dealing in hard-boiled professionalism here, not pedantic theory.

So you won't find a lot of technical talk in this book. You won't find stiff exposition. You won't find a lot of "How I did it." And you won't find untested theories. I make my living in the world of force-communications, and I enjoy the battle for attention; I enjoy hearing the phone and the cash register ring. I enjoy having my ad or mailing pull more responses than the other guy's.

So will you.

Herschell Gordon Lewis

Acknowledgments

Rules for communication don't appear by accident. They're the result of picking the brains of experts . . . of having access to the results of head-to-head creative tests . . . of benefitting from discussions with professionals, who share their wisdom.

Some of those to whom I'm indebted for so graciously letting me pick their brains, for sharing the results of tests, and for patiently discussing with me some of the principles that led to their success are Carol Nelson, my close business associate and frequent co-author; Uwe Drescher, the dynamic advertising genius of Hamburg, Germany, the source of much of my information about international marketing; Charles Peebler, the amiable head of True North Diversified Companies, of which my company, Communicomp, is a fortunate affiliate; Treesa Drury, Advertising Standards Director of the American Association of Retired Persons; Bill Keenan, the talented editor of *Selling Newsletter,* in whose pages some of the concepts of effective letter-writing first appeared; Laura Beaudry, the brilliant editor-in-chief of *Catalog Age*; Ray Schultz, the astoundingly astute editor of the magazine *Direct*; Henry Hoke II and Henry Hoke III, the previous and present publishers of *Direct Marketing* magazine; and two UK publishing giants, Peter Peskett, the unflappable publisher of the UK publication *Direct Marketing International,* and Jane Revell-Higgins, the indefatigable editor of *Catalogue and Mail Order Business.*

I'm also indebted to many of those for whom I've created advertising and marketing programs, for their invaluable feedback and advice. Foremost among them are Lori Genk, who directs many marketing programs for American Bankers Insurance Company; Les and Amanda Adams, two of the most astute marketers I have ever met; Richard Pordes, who directs much of the fund raising operation for the United Nations Children's Fund;

Mary Foster and Leonor Lucero, who so perfectly guide the fortunes of Ethel M. Chocolates; Denise Bovo, the marvelously talented creative chief of the Barnes & Noble catalog; the very bright Bob Bernardini and Paul Harrington of Bozell Kamstra Advertising; my good friend Landis Hann of Hann & dePalmer, one of the giants in database management; Dr. Ralph Elliott of Clemson University, a marvelous backboard for creative ideas; David Madigan of CNA Insurance, who in casual conversation drops more profundities than most experts can muster in a formal presentation; Harry Hester of DeeCee Laboratories, whose marketing instincts are uncannily accurate; the remarkable Jennings family of National Mail/Marketing Corporation, as astute a group of marketers as I've ever met, let alone had the pleasure of working with; Eric Greenberg of Intelihealth, the number one expert in catalog copy psychology; Liz Murphy and Rick Ritter of National Geographic, who should be famous for their ability to select details that will excite recipients of their sales messages; Erik LaPrade, who so incisively guides the marketing destiny of Commerce Bank's credit cards; and Bob Dunhill of Dunhill International Lists, whose tennis game is as formidable as his knowledge of mailing lists.

The person to whom I am most indebted is the person who is at once my most alert and clear-eyed critic, my most thoughtful and sympathetic proof-reader, my most effective source of both ideas and inspiration, and my lifetime partner — my wife Margo, whose patience and understanding still surprise me after all these years.

I thank you all and love you all . . . and Margo, especially you.

1

The Nature of This Book

This is the only chapter of *The Complete Advertising and Marketing Handbook* that isn't a "How to . . ." instruction. Instead, it's a quick recitation of opinions and prejudices I hope you either share or will come to share.

Advertising is just about as inexact a "science" as exists. A television program will lead all others in its time period; the sponsor sees no upward movement in sales. A Christmas test-mailing in June, when no one is thinking about Christmas, will outpull the "roll-out" in October. An airline loyalty program will spawn more complaints than accolades.

These aren't phenomena; they're standard operating procedures. Throughout this text I comment on successes and failures, highs and lows, strengths and weaknesses, obvious brilliance and obvious stupidity; therefore, I use the first-person approach. As Harry Truman so bravely said, "The buck stops here." I use "I" because the opinions and conclusions expressed in this book are mine. But don't dismiss them unless your own experience contravenes their advice, because they're based on hard results, on testing and research, on prejudices founded in fact and not in preconception nor prior bias.

In one sentence: This text is based on reality, not conjecture.

Reality = the mad battle for a) attention, b) sales. So:

If you regard the subject of this book as a gentlemanly or ladylike way to build a career, that's fine . . . so long as you realize that gentlemen and ladies often have to battle against those who aren't so gentlemanly or ladylike.

The nature of advertising and marketing is implicitly competitive. Just as fund raising professionals recognize that theirs is a competitive business (because most contributors establish a finite amount of money they will give to *all* causes), so do advertising and marketing professionals realize that their messages compete for attention — and for money — with all other such messages.

Depending on whose research you believe, the average individual in the United States is exposed to 1500 to 2500 selling messages every day. What chance does your message have, competing within all that clutter?

Well, it has a pretty good chance, because most messages have next-to-zero impact. We all have seen television commercials for automobiles that show us everything but the car. We've seen commercials for beer that make the brew seem the choice of foolish, infantile people.

Keeping score the wrong way.

Why do advertisers create messages such as this?

Two reasons: First, the imperfect means of keeping score — how many viewers "notice" the message, not how many viewers respond positively because of it.

Second, the nature of too much of the twenty-first century advertising philosophy: The creative team wants recognition for its cleverness, not for results. When a writer or art director interviews for the next job, on the next-higher plateau of income and authority, what matters is the "reel" of television samples and/or the folio of attractive ads. Did the messages pull response? In the past that hasn't been a major factor.

But we're wallowing in the Age of Skepticism. "Image" advertising has to share its position with "Go-for-the-jugular" advertising. Car dealers, franchisees of fast food restaurants, and computer retailers have staged organized rebellions against parent companies whose approach to marketing has emphasized image over salesmanship.

Can you succeed on the World Wide Web?

The Internet has proved itself to be a huge conglomeration of niche markets, rather than a single mass market. Those who lack an understanding of Internet-surfer attitudes are already dropping from the overcrowded, overcompetitive web site milieu. "The Web just isn't for us," they claim in bewilderment.

Opinion: The Web *is* for every consumer and business marketer, subject to three factors: 1)an understanding of who the surfers and visitors are and how to stop them and motivate them; 2) the realization that an offer on the Web has to be specific, clear, and instantly valuable; 3) sufficient links and banners to attract a constant flow of new surfer-visitors.

A twenty-first century imperative: Don't run on tracks.

One purpose of this book is to clarify marketing avenues with which you may not be familiar or with which you haven't experimented.

Are follow-up mailings, for example, worth a full chapter? You bet they are! You've converted an inquiry into a customer. Wonderful. Now you've added the buyer name to your database. Wonderful. Does the name just sit there? Not so wonderful.

Recognizing that your most recent buyers or donors are the best prospects for whatever your next offer might be is in itself an adequate reason to consider a follow-up mailing. This isn't parallel to consistent media advertising, because it carries the advantage of one-to-one.

For example, mailing a dollars-off or percentage-off certificate — with an expiration date, of course — a week or two after the original sale will result in solid business. Can you afford a 10 percent discount? Easily, if you equate the proportion of anticipated response to the cost. Media advertising may result in a response of .002 percent to 1.0 percent; a follow-up mailing, with an offer the recipient feels is logical, will generate a response of 5 percent to 15 percent.

The follow-up needn't be a discount; it can be an allied or ancillary product or service. I've bought vitamin E from you. You have two mandates: First, you absolutely, positively have to enclose a catalog or price-sheet of vitamins and supplements with my order, whether it's in a bag over the counter or in a package sent by mail or a parcel service. Second, to hold me as *your* customer, you initiate a series of follow-up mailings.

A point to remember if you want maximum response: Put an expiration date on all follow-ups.

And how about telemarketing? Are you using it? Or, more to the point of effective marketing, are you using it properly?

Telemarketing has tumbled from its lofty position in which, not that long ago, we could predict with confidence that using it would increase response by 200 to 300 percent. That was before overuse and abuse and the ubiquitous and predictable "How are you today?" opening inflicted near-mortal wounds.

Telemarketing *does* work; but the rules of the early 1990s no longer are valid. Yes, telemarketing is worth a chapter.

Classified ads and yellow pages are the common denominator in advertising and marketing; yet, they seem to have had the least amount of attention in books describing advertising techniques. They're worthy of a chapter.

Card decks? Free-standing inserts? "Magalogs?" You may never have need of any information about them; but then again, you may.

What this book isn't:

If you're looking for a self-congratulatory book larded with "How I did it" success stories that make marketing sense only to the person recounting the episodes, this isn't it.

If you're looking for descriptions, but not for suggestions, of how to improve response, you have the wrong book in your hands.

The intention of this book is to provide an up-to-the-moment, hard-boiled "How to" Handbook you can start using today and continue using at least through the first decade of the twenty-first century. How effective and how realistic it is in accomplishing that goal depends on both of us.

Before we go any further . . .

I suggest you check any advertising or direct response messages you create and distribute against three criteria. Each of the three is structured — and guaranteed, for that matter — to improve the effectiveness of a message. Improved effectiveness = greater response.

The first criterion — The Clarity Commandment:

When you choose words and phrases for force-communication, clarity is paramount. Don't let any other component of the communications mix interfere with it.

The second criterion — The Rule of Negative Subtlety:

The effectiveness of your message decreases in direct ratio to an increase in subtlety.

The third criterion — The Concept of Reader Dominance:

The *writer's* knowledge of colorful words and phrases is inconsequential. What matters is whether the *reader* knows them.

With these imperatives in place, you might not create brilliant messages, but you also won't create stupid ones.

And one last warning before we get into it: Don't look for stiff-necked, stilted language in this book. I'd be a total hypocrite if I followed up my own Clarity Commandment with a pile of obfuscation.

2

Positioning and Loyalty Programs

Why give a customer a reward?
To generate more business, that's why. Loyalty is not only fragile, it's almost extinct. And some "loyalty programs" are so complicated, so complex, or — ugh! — so feeble, they have all the impact of a wet sponge.

Keep The Clarity Commandment in the foreground.

A reward is as subject to The Clarity Commandment as a conventional mailing. If the recipient can't penetrate the benefit . . . or if the benefit doesn't seem beneficial . . . you may be better off not offering a loyalty "bonus."

Under the umbrella of that Commandment, this chapter offers some logical rules for implementing and profiting from a loyalty program.

Be as loyal as you want your customers to be.

For years I've had "Priority Gold Plus" status with one of the airlines. But then . . . uh-oh. The airline sent me a letter, signed by the "Vice President, Marketing Services," telling me "I am pleased to be able to present you with the privileges of Preferred."

Hmmm. *Preferred.* Is that an upgrade or a downgrade? No explanation accompanies the category-change. A spartan descriptive brochure tells me Preferred is "Designed for the exclusive benefit of members who achieve 25,000 miles with us each year." I *think* that parallels Gold Priority Plus, but without some sort of cross-reference I hang in limbo.

My suggestion to this airline and all whose loyalty programs are murky and apparently equivocal . . .

Heed The Clarity Commandment. I'll repeat it in case you missed it in the previous chapter:

> *When you choose words and phrases for force-communication,* **clarity** *is paramount. Don't let any other component of the communications mix interfere with it.*

Should you reward all customers equally?

Sophisticated marketers laugh at the notion of equivalence in any reward program. They point to the success of the Neiman Marcus "InCircle" award, which establishes levels of membership.

InCircle's payoffs openly — no, *proudly* — admit to a tie to total purchases. Here is a store whose patronage covers every stratum of society. A customer may spend $200 a year . . . and another may regularly spend $20,000 a year. Should the benefits to each be an InCircle Card, plus regular mailings offering subscriptions and free samples when a member calls a toll-free number on a certain date?

Without the elitist potential, the program has no goad. This would parallel an airline offering two free first class tickets to anyone who paid for a flight. No! Without goads, a loyalty program is a simple parallel of an open announcement of "Sale!"

But the question of whether *loyalty* is the right word hits hard at our twenty-first century culture. Airlines, department stores, and restaurants *buy* loyalty. This gradually becomes an Arabian bazaar. One chain of restaurants decides to offer a Frequent Diner program, awarding points for each dollar spent. It isn't a casual decision, because establishing the program requires computer hookups and membership cards. Validating the program means establishing a hierarchy of rewards . . . ranging from free desserts to a trip to Europe.

The competitive nature of business plugs in. So another restaurant, catering to a parallel demographic group, establishes a parallel frequent diner program, with parallel rewards.

What does the diner do?

Loyalty isn't any part of the decision. The diner's decision is just as much a cold-blooded business decision as the restaurant's. Apparent losers are restaurants that haven't created frequent diner programs. But are they losers? Avoiding the colossal bookkeeping any loyalty program demands, they can compete on a more traditional level — space ads with coupons, direct mail to the neighborhood, free glass of wine or dessert, or an uncomputerized certificate.

The sliding-scale of awards — dollars spent or miles flown — has become totally acceptable, and, for that matter, totally expected. Hypercompetitiveness causes restaurants to award ten points per dollar, so the total seems to build faster even when it doesn't.

Offer alternatives

The gym where I occasionally work out offered a reward for an early membership renewal — a "New Age" CD.

That was it. I happen to like New Age music, but a lot of folks don't. In fact, the young lady on the next exercycle machine — cassette player strapped to her arm and earphones plastered to her head — was listening to rock music whose clamor leaked out of the earphones at a level that had me moving to a different section.

Opinion: When the target-group isn't homogenized, offer alternates. The gym probably would have initiated a greater number of early renewals by offering the choice of rock, golden oldies, and a classical CD in addition to the New Age disc.

Similarly, an airline offers not just a choice of destinations for a milemilestone reached but alternatives — upgrades and companion flights.

Which credit card will you use?

Credit cards have begun to offer a huge menu of perks. They recognize that a shopper doesn't really care which card he or she uses and will brandish the one that may offer side benefits.

This, in fact, is the total marketing philosophy of the Discover Card, which carved its niche by offering merchants the lowest fee and by offering cardholders rebates on purchases.

The American Express Platinum Card has the most sophisticated reward program going. In fact, bonuses are so heavy the typical cardholder easily justifies paying hundreds of dollars for this card when the same wallet holds free credit cards that actually are accepted at more establishments.

Platinum cardholders can use their card to buy an airline ticket to Europe and have a companion travel free. Every dollar spent with this card is translatable to frequent flyer miles on a number of airlines. Toll-free numbers abound, for every kind of executive-level service, from dining reservations to transportation in the event of illness or an accident overseas.

(On a recent trip to New York City, I wanted to have dinner at a famous steak house. "Sorry, we're full. No openings until 10 p.m." I went to the phone, called Platinum Card, waited five minutes, and went back to see the head waiter. "Of course, Mr. Lewis. Your table is ready." Even as such experiences breed cynicism, they also breed card loyalty on a level far beyond any frequent flyer miles.)

Cards now regularly sponsor sweepstakes. They offer "Twofer" discount coupon books. Their statement stuffers extend discounts on dining, cookware, books, and subscriptions, not from outside third-party marketers but from the card issuer. Awareness is universal: Loyalty isn't to the card issuer; it's to the added perks and values.

The changing face of marketing

Those added perks and values have become the basis of heavy promotion, in all media. Television and direct mail are the principal outlets because these are the most emotional media, but we also see space ads. The phone is likely to ring in the evening with a pitch from a credit card company.

Long distance and cellular telephone companies have flooded the mails with "deals" tied to loyalty programs. Frequent flyer miles are the most common incentive, so much so that the very multiplicity of such mailings threatens to undermine the value of frequent flyer programs.

Airlines, quite rightly seeing free-seat overload on the horizon, have begun to back away from their promises. Some have appended an expiration date on mile use, where no such expiration existed before. Others keep raising the number of miles necessary to reach a goal and offer few seats. Some eliminate peripheral awards from hotels and businesses from usable mile totals.

The result is a well-deserved *disaffection*. Passengers whose fragile loyalty is tied to the anticipation of the award promised in the original brochure react with scorn and hatred to the announcement of award "streamlining" that cancels the original commitment or skews it.

Whether the result of panic or greed, loyalty programs that change their benefits for the worse deserve the desertion some of them are experiencing. Adding grist to the Age of Skepticism is not only unstatesmanlike and damaging to the credibility of all marketers, it is, in a competitive ambience, ultimately self-defeating.

Continuity marketers have to be smart!

My wife buys coffee by mail. One of the early perks was a name-brand coffee-maker, sent after a certain number of shipments.

When my wife switched to another brand of coffee, the original source quickly responded to her cancellation with a letter thanking her for past patronage. Then, after a respectable wait, this company came back with an offer she couldn't refuse. A lost customer was regained.

Open-ended series of collectibles and subscriptions employ careful database-fed resuscitation programs, often reinforced by telemarketing. Without these spurs, waning subscribers would be lost in far higher numbers.

The shrewdest approach to loyalty marketing lies in the hands of computer software producers. Often, they'll send an early version of the software at a giveaway price. Then upgrades begin.

Even the most unbelieving individual seems to be at the mercy of computer software upgrades. These become loyalty programs, although they never are presented as such. (See chapter 17, "Follow-up Mailings.")

Some Logical Rules for Loyalty Programs

The aggressive and astute marketer can avoid the pitfalls and many of the unnecessary costs of loyalty programs by acknowledging and following a handful of logical rules. The most obvious (and easiest) dozen of these are:

1. Honor the Clarity Commandment. This Commandment has to ride serenely above all the other factors of the program. Without clarity, you're firing blanks.

2. Offer obvious benefit. Some marketers allow a slide-rule mentality to govern the program. Without apparent benefit, such approaches are not only useless, they can generate a negative image.

3. Establish an easily reached first plateau. If you require ten visits or a $200 expenditure to qualify for free desserts or wine for two, you're less likely to induce frequent visits than if the original goal is five visits or a $90 expenditure. Traditionally, most members use the lowest rung of the loyalty ladder as a touchstone, not as a goal, so this becomes a psychological weapon rather than an end.

4. Establish easily reachable additional plateaus. The plethora of loyalty programs has built a competitive marketplace. The formula is reasonably simple: You estimate the lifetime value of the typical participant, estimate the difference in lifetime value without a loyalty program, and allocate a tolerable percentage of the difference to the program. This will give you a total budget from which you extrapolate the various plateaus. Each should be apparently reachable from the previous one.

5. Demonstrate stability. Don't change the rules after participants have signed up, unless you change them to make them — temporarily or permanently — more favorable.

6. Stay in touch. The more you regard your members as family, the more they will regard themselves as family.

7. Reward frequency. This is, after all, frequency marketing. Loyalty programs lose value in direct ratio to the extent of time participants take between uses.

8. If points will expire, state this clearly. Adherence to the Clarity Commandment should cover this, but you cannot overstate the rules of the game, except by adding the deadly ingredient of complexity.

9. Offer at least partial reinstatement of expired points. Human psychology is predictable. When a participant realizes that points have expired, disgust is aimed at you, not himself or herself. You not only can blunt this reaction, you can exploit it by offering reinstatement within a limited window of time. The member's failure to reinstate then turns the disgust inward, where it belongs.

10. Treat expired members as current members. This does not differ at all from a classic marketing technique. You can benefit from an individual's fickleness, disgust, or indolence just as much as you suffer from it.

11. If you charge a membership fee, waive or rebate it for members who reach a high level. Nothing inspires loyalty so much as recognition . . . and this move guarantees a renewal.

12. Keep the pot boiling. We call this "Frequency Marketing" . . . and not just frequent contact, but frequent incentives and positive surprises are a major force in keeping the program active and healthy.

The rules are simple enough. If you don't like them, the alternative is equally simple: You don't have to play in this arena.

Figure 2-1

Omaha Steaks is one of the most alert and astute direct marketers. Customers constantly receive "special" loyalty-based offers, both from the parent company and from the company's local retail stores.

An exclusive offer for IBM Stockholders.

Figure 2-2a

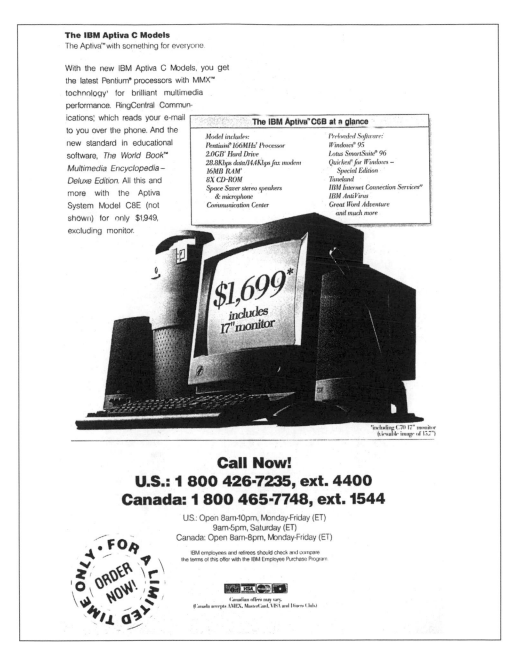

Figure 2-26

A public company's stockholder list is an even stronger base for loyalty mailings than a customer list. This "exclusive" offer for IBM stockholders is a computer. The price isn't remarkably favorable, but the technique avoids the inevitable negative retailer reaction to parent company promotional moves the retailer feels are competitive.

Outdoor Advantage Program™

17955931450 QS53
Herschell Lewis
340 N Fig Tree Ln
Plantation FL 33317-2561

Your Preapproved§ Credit Line is up to $20,000

Offer expires July 14,
and is nontransferable.

FREE Regular FedEx®
delivery of L.L.Bean merchandise

Valuable Points
toward L.L.Bean merchandise

Exclusive Previews
of L.L.Bean sale merchandise

Introductory 5.9% APR
on purchases, cash advances,
and balance transfers†

No Annual Fee

Dear Herschell Lewis:

At L.L.Bean, we are always looking for ways to help you enjoy the outdoors and provide you with superior service. We also seek meaningful ways to say "thank you" for making purchases at L.L.Bean.

With this in mind, we created a way for you to save with every L.L.Bean purchase—the **Outdoor Advantage Program.** This program offers the quality and lasting value you have come to expect from L.L.Bean, along with special savings like **FREE regular FedEx delivery on L.L.Bean orders.**

You have been preapproved for the L.L.Bean Visa® credit card—the key to the Outdoor Advantage Program. With this credit card, you will enjoy the many exclusive benefits of being an Outdoor Advantage Program member.

I have enclosed a brochure that fully explains all of the membership benefits, but let me highlight a few of the exceptional savings:

- Receive **FREE regular FedEx delivery** anywhere within the contiguous United States. You save $3.95 to $5.95 every time you use your L.L.Bean Visa to place a catalog order at L.L.Bean. Take advantage of this offer to order for yourself or to send gifts to friends and family.**

- Earn **valuable L.L.Bean points** every time you make a purchase with your card. Each point is worth $1 toward future L.L.Bean purchases. Points will be issued to you as coupons in $20 increments. Coupons can be redeemed in our stores, through the mail, or over the phone.†

- Receive **exclusive previews** of sale-priced L.L.Bean merchandise throughout the year.

- Enjoy a **5.9% Introductory Annual Percentage Rate (APR)** on purchases, cash advances, and balance transfers. And of course, the L.L.Bean Visa comes with **No Annual Fee.**

(continued on back)

Here's an Example of What You Can Save with the L.L.Bean Visa

Regular FedEx Delivery	If you place five $100 orders at $5.95 per order	SAVE $29.75
L.L.Bean Purchases	If you make $500 in purchases with points worth 5%	EARN $25.00
Other Purchases	If you make $3,000 in purchases with points worth 1%	EARN $30.00
Potential Savings Per Year		**TOTAL $84.75**

For illustration only. Your savings may vary.

To apply, call
1-800-545-7898
or complete the enclosed
Preapproved Request Form.

Figure 2-3

Note the first sentence of this letter. It cleverly presents an offer—parallel to many others, but a step ahead because of the tie to loyalty.

Sample A. Sample
123 Any Street
Anytown, MT 12345-6789

ACCOUNT STATEMENT

Replay Member Number:	99999999	Expires:	07/01/96
Beginning balance for next $15 Award:	138 Pts.	Replay points since enrollment:	573 Pts.
Replay points this period:	135 Pts.	Total award certificates earned since enrollment:	$45
Points needed to earn next $15 Award:	27 Pts.	Award earned this statement:	$15

Activity period 04/29/96 through 06/18/96

MEMBER ACTIVITY SUMMARY

Date	Store Location Source of Points	Total Purchases	Regular Points	Bonus Points	Total Points	Description of Activity
04/29	One Main Street	29.34	30		30	Purchase
05/06	One Main Street	38.94	39		39	Purchase
05/06	One Main Street	65.99	66		66	Purchase
05/30	One Main Street					

Purchases made with AT&T True Rewards coupons cannot earn Replay points.

REPLAY CUSTOMER SERVICE CALL 1-888-REPLAY1 (1-888-737-5291) TOLL FREE

$15 *Award Certificate* $15

Sample A. Sample

SAMPLE CERTIFICATE

Is Awarded Fifteen Dollars

to redeem at any Musicland or Sam Goody.

Redeemable for merchandise only. No cash refunds or change back. This certificate will not be replaced if lost or stolen. Valid for one year from date of issue

Issue Date: 07/02/■

12345678 15

Figure 2-4

Loyalty programs can become complicated. For some "members," the complexity is proof of stature. The concept of reaching goals through awarded "points" is completely sound. Use of a certificate, with an expiration date, assures maximum re-visits to the issuer's place of business.

3

How to Write Effective Business Letters

What's so dear about "Dear"?

The English-speaking world has staggered, over a period of more than two centuries, into a standardized greeting: "Dear Joe," or "Dear Mr. Jones," or, in the case of bulk mail, "Dear Friend."

Good or bad?

Neither. It's invisible. From childhood we've written and received that greeting. It's a puzzlement because many well-educated non-English speakers adopt that greeting even though it bewilders them. Webster's first definition of dear is "Loved and cherished." Ha! We've corrupted the adjective so thoroughly we ignore the corruption. (A more recent replacement: "Dear Colleague.")

Until the 1970s, the two standard closings were "Yours truly" and "Sincerely yours." Proof that we do have the power to upgrade our correspondence is the disappearance (good riddance!) of "Yours truly"; and "Sincerely yours" in its twenty-first century version is tightened to "Sincerely."

Not so with "Dear." We become automatons. Brain out of gear, we write — and the recipient accepts —

Dear Mr. Jones,
I really enjoyed our meeting yesterday.

At a more personal, one-to-one sitting, I might vent my spleen about that opening sentence, recognizable by all parties as one of the Great Lies of our time. But in these pages we're discussing the greeting.

The danger of experimentation

The problem with replacing "Dear" with *anything* is the upset-factor we generate whenever we break a mold. It's recognizable as what it is — a deliberate attempt to be different. Occasionally we'll get such a message:

I really enjoyed our meeting today,
Mr. Jones,
and . . .

See the problem? The recipient identifies the greeting *as a greeting,* and that identification casts a pall of artifice over the entire message. Our target's eye doesn't slide over it the way it would with a "Dear Mr. Jones" opening.

You can see the two edges of this sword: The person we're contacting, *if he or she is a stuffed shirt,* may react negatively to your entire letter just because you tried to cast off the gray sameness of "Dear"; conversely, *if the person we're contacting is an aggressive businessperson,* he or she may react positively just because you aren't following the tired old formula.

So all of us in the advertising/marketing profession have another decision to make, on top of the 3,450,987 other decisions we make every day. Should we play it safe or take a chance? Are we helping or hurting ourselves by beginning with an artifice that will get us noticed?

Another option

If you don't have any "From the desk of . . ." forms with your name on them, it might be worthwhile to have some printed.

These forms, by their very nature, are both personal and terse. What a blessing that is for the salesperson whose message — which might be one or two paragraphs — looks lost on a full-size sheet.

It's both normal and logical to avoid a formal greeting altogether on a "From the desk of" page (typical size = 4.5" x 7.5", or 11.4cm x 19cm).

After the date, the writer can launch directly into the message, with the recipient's name as the first word:

> *John, as we discussed in our meeting this morning, my company is able to deliver . . .*

If it's "Mr. Jones" instead of John, no problem on a memo. The same type of opening is in order. These forms add the dimension of personal relationship without appearing to be presumptuous.

Good Morning, John!

I sometimes use "Good Morning" as a greeting, anticipating a twenty-first century overall loosening of traditional communications.

This (note: *opinion*) works well when you're comfortable addressing the recipient by first name:

Good Morning, John,
and I'm counting on being able to make the rest of the day good
for you as well. . . .

Some yahoo asked me, "What if he doesn't open the letter until afternoon?" So what? It's morning in Hawaii. The effect, I've found, is brightening without seeming brash.

If you experiment with this, you have the option of capitalizing "Morning." Use a comma after the individual's name. Don't consider an exclamation point unless you're tennis buddies.

Should you try "Good Morning" on people you've met just once or don't know at all?

That depends on two factors: a) the image you want to cast, and b) your position relative to your target's. I'll explain:

I'm chairman of my company. If I'm writing to someone lower in his company's echelons than I am in mine, *and he knows he's lower in his company's echelons than I am in mine,* I have far greater latitude than I'd have if I was communicating as an unknown. So in that circumstance "Good Morning" not only is safe, it underscores my conviviality and my acceptance of my target as an equal. If my target hasn't the foggiest notion who I am, departing from "Dear" can be a game of Russian Roulette.

Winning at Russian Roulette

Now, understand, please: Winning at Russian Roulette means the gun hasn't blown your brains out. It isn't a comfortable, exhilarating diversion.

As we open this Pandora's Box of greetings options, the point I want to make is that letter-writing isn't automatic. The thought process has to enter the creative mix, just as it does for a head-to-head sales call. "Dear" isn't sacrosanct, nor is its use a symbol that you're an unimaginative fuddy-duddy.

As you sit down to write a letter — an introductory letter, a thank-you letter, a clarification/explanatory letter, or a hard- sell letter — before you turn your fingertips loose, close your eyes for 15 seconds and visualize your target as he or she reads what you've written.

Do that and the right greeting will pop into your mind . . . and onto the paper.

Start Off in High Gear. Then Accelerate.

What an easy litmus test we have for effective business letters:

All we have to do is ask ourselves: If I were reading this letter instead of writing it, would it spur me to lift the phone and call this guy?

We see case after case in which a silver-tongued salesperson loses both image and tempo when writing a sales letter. We all have received (and, consciously or casually dissected) many a letter (especially a follow-up letter, a "re-up" after a sales call resulted in a moderately receptive reaction) that has all the impact of a wet sponge. Why can't the letter-writer pretend he or she is sitting head-to-head? Would the tongue excrete the same pap the keyboard does?

If letter-writing were an art, the process would be reserved for an elitist corps of scribes. But letter-writing isn't an art; it's closer to a science, on a plane far below nuclear physics or gastroenterology. "I can't write an effective business letter" is a cop-out.

What do you say for starters?

How many letters do *you* get that open with a yawn? One of the most useful tips I, or anybody, can transmit to you is: Start off in high gear.

For example, the typical post-call letter begins something like this:

Dear Mary,
I very much enjoyed the opportunity to meet with you today and tell you how Acme Industries can offer a complete construction service.

What's wrong with that? Nothing, if you're the type who will settle for water instead of wine at dinner.

Visualize Mary getting this letter. It doesn't quite cause her eyes to glaze over, but neither does it get the adrenaline pumping.

So what might we say as a substitute? It depends on a) the personality you project, b) the amount of guts you have, and c) the image your target has of herself. Before you write one word, analyze those three elements.

The three faces of Heave

Let's suppose both you and she are extroverts. You might start your letter:

Wow, Mary! Some meeting! Are you as enthusiastic as I am?

One step down, if you aren't sure of her reaction:

Wow, Mary! Some meeting! I hope you're as enthusiastic as I am.

Another step down, if you want to project your personality without including hers:

Mary, that was some meeting! You really know how to challenge a prospective supplier.

Now, suppose Mary is aggressive and you aren't. You have a couple of options. You can fake a move up to her level; you can be businesslike and "correct"; or you can stroke:

Mary, I don't ever recall meeting as dynamic an individual as you seem to be. I can't begin to compete with your personality.
So I guess I'll have to compete on the basis of being able to supply exactly what you want, when you want it . . . recognizing that my company is under the gun.

The point I'd like to hammer home is that when you write a sales letter you *do* have a multitude of options. Ask yourself: Who am I supposed to be? Who does my prospect think she is? How can I establish or reinforce that marvelous and elusive link, *rapport*?

Get to the point.

About a hundred years ago, somebody introduced what was then a logical progression for a sales letter — the venerable "AIDA" formula. AIDA isn't the opera; it's a sequence: 1) Attention, 2) Interest, 3) Desire, and 4) Action.

That was a hundred years ago. The twenty-first century is here, and attention-spans are gnat-thin. Well, yes, the niceties of business courtesy still demand a polite or semi-polite opening. So open. Then start blasting. Get to the point.

I've read hundreds of business letters that don't seem to have a point. They sum up laundry-lists of equipment. They glorify premises and personnel. They seem to be happily ignorant of the great differential between seller and sellee:

> *The seller's concern = What it is.*
> *The sellee's concern = What it will do for me.*

Get to the point.

If you think the alpha-to-omega of a sales letter is a repetition of "Thank you for meeting with me" or "I enjoyed our meeting today," you aren't thinking like a salesperson. You're thinking like a clerk. Look at that computer screen and ask two questions: 1) "Who do I want to be, in the prospect's eyes?" and 2) "What action do I want this person to take?"

Answer those questions and your letter won't be just another blather-filled throwaway.

Is an aggressive attitude damaging?

A mysterious force exists in the world of one-to-one salesmanship. The force is called *chemistry.*

We hear salespeople say, "The chemistry was just wrong. We might as well have been on different planets." We also hear them say, "Oh, boy, was the chemistry between us churning away! All things being equal, I've got the deal."

No letter can have as profound an effect on the mutuality of chemistry, or lack of it, as a personal call can have. The letter is the result of a guessing game. Whether your guess is educated or uneducated depends on your own talent for perception.

But a follow-up letter, dynamically constructed, is more likely to rescue a teetering deal than it is to destroy it.

Which means what?

I'd better qualify this as an opinion, although my personal experience tells me it's a fact: A forceful, energetic, convincing business letter is far more likely to generate a positive response than the standard "Umm — what we have to offer you" or "May I introduce my company?" or "I enjoyed our meeting" blandness.

Some Easy and Underused Weapons: Punctuation Marks

Two punctuation marks can be powerful allies to the business letter writer — the question mark and the exclamation mark.

They also can be saboteurs.

How can punctuation be a saboteur? One obvious way is misusing punctuation marks . . . an indication of a literacy-gap. The most common mistake is linking two sentences with a comma instead of separating them with a period or a semicolon. Example, from a letter that came to me the day I'm writing this:

We are experts at setting up Internet sites, you won't find better service anywhere.

Execrable second half aside, you can see — I certainly hope — the negative impression this misuse of commas makes on anyone with even a moderate grasp of grammar. The writer might have chosen one of three options:

We are experts at setting up Internet sites. You won't find better service anywhere.

Or, a slightly more sophisticated version using a semicolon:

We are experts at setting up Internet sites; you won't find better service anywhere.

The third option? Dump the second half and replace it with information.

Of the two punctuation marks we'll look at here, the question mark is the more valuable. Why? Questions are automatically reader-involving. They can draw a reader into a letter without blemishing the message the way a declaration might. An example:

Dear Mr. Jones,

As I began to write this letter, I suddenly asked myself: Why are you contacting this man?

A more prosaic example:

Dear Mr. Jones,

Do I dare ask how your Internet site is doing today?

I still remember a letter that came to me years ago . . . and resulted in a business relationship that profited both parties:

Good morning, Mr. Lewis . . .

Want to play a game of "Travel Agent" today? Okay. You be the customer.

I also point out that it's more difficult to bore and/or insult a reader with a question than with a statement. Want proof? Try it in conversation, a logical parallel to a sales letter. A statement is a point of view. A well-worded question asks for a point of view. Which involves your target more?

Careful, though. Don't get cute. In my opinion, more sales letters are damaged by cuteness than by any other misstep . . . possibly excepting bad grammar and spelling.

And here again the question can be your salvation, because you flat-out have a more difficult time being artificially cute when you ask than you do when you announce.

If you want to achieve a one-to-one impression, avoid "boiler plate" questions that betray the mad desire to sell, lurking just under the surface . . . questions that become obvious precursors to a pitch, such as . . .

- *When was the last time you . . . ?*
- *What if I told you that . . . ?*
- *Are you interested in . . . ?*
- *If you could foretell the future, would you . . . ?*

Opening with questions such as these might make sense in a speech or a mass mailing whose greeting is "Dear Friend," but in a purported or actual one-to-one communication they're a turnoff. They not only don't build the rapport a question is supposed to construct, they disable it.

A well-constructed question should parallel the wording you'd use in a head-to-head conversation, immediately after a prospect has said to you, "What is it you want to talk about?" — itself a question.

On to the most dangerous punctuation mark — the exclamation point.

Dangerous? It can get you kicked out the door. (For a sales letter this means tossed, not kicked, into the wastebasket, instead of out the door. The result is the same.)

A lot of exclamations don't exclaim. They're phony, an obvious artifice. In a marketing situation *any* obvious artifice is a shot squarely into your own foot.

I'd better point out an exception . . . one you might try if you're a consummate expert at communication: the obvious artifice you yourself quickly acknowledge *is* an obvious artifice. It becomes charming because *you're* the one who decides the exclamation is an obvious ploy. That makes your target — who *can't* form the conclusion because you've already admitted it — your ally.

An example:

Shazam!
I admit, Mr. Jones,
that was just to get your attention. Now that I have it, I hope
you'll let me hang onto it for another twenty-five seconds.

I once sent a follow-up letter that began with a one-word exclamation. It was so successful I continued using it for years:

AWESOME!
That's the only word to describe my reaction to the dynamic
meeting we had today . . .

Shazam! and *Wow!* and *Awesome!* and *Unbelievable!* are one-word exclamations. Much more trouble attends a multi-word exclamation. (An absolute rule: The more words in the sentence, the less exclamatory power it possesses.) Compare these exclamatory openings:

What an exciting challenge!

Or . . .

What an exciting challenge you've given me!

Or . . .

*I don't remember when I've ever worked on a challenge as excit-
ing as the one you gave me today!*

With each additional word-grouping, some of the pep vanishes. That's
because the power dilutes itself as it spreads among more words. That's not
necessarily bad, because you might not want the most aggressive exclamation. Why not? Because the amount of exclamation should diminish in ratio
to either a) your target's unfamiliarity with you, or b) your target's personal
stuffiness. In such circumstances, a milder exclamation may well be better.

You can see the possibilities and the pitfalls. Make punctuation your
partner and your letters will sell more. Or — make punctuation your partner and your letters will sell more!

Little Things Mean A Lot.

Too many writers of sales letters are either in awe of formal stylebooks
or just forget the purpose of the communication — to sell.

The significance of a communication *increases* when the recipient of
the letter senses importance; it *decreases* when the writer consciously and
obviously attempts to claim importance.

A beginner or an unsure letter-writer looks at a business letter and concludes, "Since that letter was written by a business executive, it represents
the kind of style I should follow." Naah. The result can be stilted
prose . . . or pomposity . . . or, *worst of all,* projection of an arm's-length relationship, instead of the magical ingredient *rapport.*

We walk a rhetorical tightrope and sometimes do fall off, because we
don't know enough about the state of mind of the person receiving our
message. The purpose of analyzing, experimenting, and absorbing letter-
writing principles is to give us as sure a footing as possible, under circumstances which can be both unpredictable and uncertain.

Here is a mini-supply of tips that should increase impact without
lapsing into stilted prose, pomposity, or distancing.

• Capitalization is an easy and effective tool. The value of capitalized
letters is their quiet statement of importance without using the word itself
or thumping the chest for all to see. For example, unrelated to selling:

Which suggests greater importance?

Sent direct to you from the United Kingdom

or . . .

Sent direct to you from The United Kingdom

I told you it's a quiet statement. In fact, you may have read through it without noting the difference: The word "The" is capitalized in the second version. Somehow, capitalizing the word adds consequence to what follows.

• A second invisible rapport-builder is substitution of a comma for a colon after the greeting. What (if any), in your opinion, is the difference between these?

Dear Mr. Brown:

or . . .

Dear Mr. Brown,

You probably noticed that the colon brings the reader to a dead stop, while the comma is a momentary pause. Oh, sure, I know that manuals on letter-writing have suggested, for the past hundred years or more, beginning a personal letter with a comma and a business letter with a colon. But doesn't that make my point?

You're trying to establish rapport. You dare not cross the line with someone whose attitude toward you — and toward life in general — is an unknown factor. The comma is your invisible agent, opening an invisible crack in the attitudinal wall.

• Another little trick is one more letter-writers should use. Which of these has the greater potential of generating a little rapport?

Sincerely,
Joseph A. Demento
Joseph A. Demento

or . . .

Sincerely,
Joe Demento
Joseph A. Demento

If you chose the first version you're betraying some insecurity. Ever wonder why you're annoyed, even subliminally, when a lawyer adds "Esq." to his or her signature? It's an artifice that not only widens the gulf between message sender and message recipient, it widens that gulf *deliberately*.

This mini-trick has surprising power, because it's the denouement, the finale. Here I am, Joseph A. Demento, but to you I'm just plain Joe. A barrier has been knocked sideways. Visualize an even more profound example:

Sincerely,
Joe Demento
Joseph A. Demento, Ph.D.

Good old Joe has abandoned his academic title in favor of conviviality. Now, suppose the signature had been:

Sincerely,
Joseph A. Demento, Ph.D.
Joseph A. Demento, Ph.D.

Wouldn't the recipient feel the sender was emphasizing the title, claiming artificial superiority, establishing his turf on a plateau higher than that of the person getting the letter?

Please, now: I don't want a flood of letters from people who have "Esq." or "Ph.D." or "III" or even "Jr." and use it in a signature, even when the title is typed below. This text ties itself to *selling*; we aren't denigrating a title somebody may have gone to school an extra three years to achieve, nor are we damning Jrs. and Srs. We're dealing in that elusive element, rapport.

• If you want to stretch the envelope, here's a procedure that not only will positively get your envelope opened on the busiest day, but get it opened by the person you're sending it to and not a secretary or administrative assistant.

The mystic ingredient: sealing wax.

Stationery stores sell this stuff. All you do is drip a splash of it in the center of the sealed edge of the envelope flap.

If you're especially inventive, find a small embossing or intaglio item with your initial or some sort of design (cufflinks often work). Just touch that item into the seal.

Phony? You bet it's phony. But it isn't objectionable-phony. In fact, before the development of modern glues, most people sealed their letters that way.

The idea behind it is to persuade your target to notice and open your letter. It does work, because it's unlikely that any other letter in the stack of mail is sealed with wax.

Mechanical suggestions, not brain-twisters

What's so delightful about all the devices we've discussed here is that none of them require a lot of thought . . . and will initiate the right kind of thought by the person who gets them.

THE OXFORD CLUB

U.S. MEMBERSHIP OFFICE • 105 WEST MONUMENT STREET • BALTIMORE, MD 21201

Dear Fellow Investor:

You have been chosen from a select list to receive an invitation into what must be the world's most remarkable—and profitable—financial alliance.

It's an alliance that includes many wealthy investors, financial experts, and extremely successful entrepreneurs.

There's an excellent reason why you were among a select few chosen to receive this invitation—a reason that will become very clear to you in a moment.

But first, let me come right to the point.

By focusing our efforts on creating a legacy of PRIVATE WEALTH for ourselves and our families, we have established a long history of finding extremely **safe investments** with far **higher yields** than you are probably getting now.

In fact, there's one investment we regard as the ultimate SAFE and PROFITABLE investment for 1996 and 1997:

✦ It's a utility bond, offered by a company in a major developed nation, with annual yields of **15.5%** to maturity in the year 2008...

✦ It's the most liquid and highest-quality bond that this nation's government guarantees...

✦ It yields *twice* as much as you get with 30-year U.S. treasury bonds...

The fact is, very few Americans are even aware this investment exists.

But it's just one of 10 outstanding investments we've uncovered from around the world to boost your income with SAFE, SUPERCHARGED YIELDS ranging from 8.25% to 15%.

What's more, they're all covered in a special briefing called *UltraCash Today—10 Easy Ways to Supercharge Your Income*—one of **five FREE special reports** we'll rush to you should you decide to join our unique alliance.

You'll learn all about the profits you can earn from these invaluable reports—as well as the multiple other benefits of membership—a little later in this letter.

A Long History of Grand Profits

You'll also learn about some of the astonishing 200% to 1,300% gains we've pocketed investing in unique stock selections over the years—and come to understand the reason why *every stock recommendation the Club makes* is *virtually guaranteed to make a profit.*

But first, you should know that we are <u>not</u> in the business of selling investments. Nor are we brokers or financial advisors.

So why do we exist?

Our Club was formed for one purpose: **to ensure that each member grows substantially wealthier** by seeking out safe, high-yield investments while eliminating the major threats to our capital that we face every day—inflation, taxes, currency

over, please...

Figure 3-1

This letter begins with stroking — "You have been chosen from a select list . . ." — then says, in its fourth paragraph: "But first, let me get right to the point." The letter runs 16 pages. Will a recipient read a 16-page letter? Wrong question. The proper question: Will a recipient *respond* to a 16-page letter? Yes, if the information seems relevant. Note the writing technique: "You have" is formal, as a proper exclusivity-based opening; then the writer uses contractions for conviviality and easier reading. Suggestion: Test letter lengths. Results run both ways.

The
SECOND AMENDMENT
AMERICA'S FIRST FREEDOM

N A T I O N A L   R I F L E   A S S O C I A T I O N   O F   A M E R I C A
CHARLTON HESTON
First Vice President

Dear Hershell Lewis:

I need to know if what they're saying about you is true.

When I first heard what they said, I brushed it off. I thought it was one gun-hating journalist looking for a sound bite she could twist to paint me as a lone, anti-American lunatic. But then I heard it again on a talk show. Then again from a newspaper editor. Then again from a network anchor.

If what they say is true, it could destroy our crusade to save our constitutional right to keep and bear arms.

I must tell you, Hershell Lewis, I'm outraged. Their lies and deceit threaten our crusade to restore the Second Amendment and relay it to a generation ready, willing and ABLE to defend it.

And there's no way I can step back onto the national stage, fight our fights and win our battles until you tell me the truth and set the record straight.

The anti-gun media claims I do not speak for you. They claim my celebrity gives me exposure but the views I advance are purely my own. They say they have polls, surveys and statistics **that prove you support gun control**...that you're 100% in favor of certain gun and ammunition bans...

...that you don't believe the Second Amendment is worth saving.

Now I'm left with no choice but to ask you myself in the privacy of these pages: Is what they say about you true? Yes or no?

Have you ever answered a media poll saying you support gun control? Do you favor gun and ammunition bans? Do you believe the Second Amendment should be ripped right out of the Constitution? Do you support our crusade to save your right to keep and bear arms?

Yes or no?

I've written down these questions on a separate page of this letter. **Will you please, for the sake of the Second Amendment, take a moment to answer them today?**

With your answers, I can blast the anti-gun media right out of the water.

I can expose their cowardly campaign to undermine, deride, degrade, dilute and redefine the Second Amendment. I can challenge their manipulation of manufactured statistics spoon-fed to them by Handgun Control, Inc. and other organizations that wouldn't know a semi-auto from a sharp stick. I can shame them for wanting to leave our friends and families with little more than a rolled up newspaper to thwart the advances of a criminal intruder.

Figure 3-2

The misspelled first name destroys the credibility of this letter, but it isn't the fault of the wordsmith; it's the fault of the list compiler. The first sentence is a strong "grabber," immediately reader-involving. Note the second personalization (also misspelled, a computer-personalization consistency) in the fourth paragraph. Generally, one-to-one letters seem less distant if paragraphs are indented.

Consumer Reports

Remember Consumer Reports?

The magazine you used to think of checking
before you bought a car?

Well, please <u>rethink</u> Consumer Reports. Because
now there are even more important reasons to
read it.

Yes, we can still save you hundreds of dollars
on the products you buy.

But now, more than ever, we can also save you
<u>thousands</u> of dollars on the <u>services</u> you buy.
And help you make the high-stakes financial,
health and safety decisions that affect the
quality of your life for years.

You need Consumer Reports more than ever.
Here's how you can get it on very special
terms.

Dear Friend:

    I'd like to make you an offer I think and hope
you'll find irresistible. I'd like to send you:

    1. <u>A sample issue of Consumer Reports</u> ($2.95 at the
       newsstand).

    2. <u>A free copy of the 1997 Consumer Reports Buying
       Guide</u> (regularly $8.95) with hundreds of brand-
       name product ratings.

    3. <u>A free copy of our $11.95 book, How To Clean
       Practically Anything</u>. Updated, fourth edition.

                                        (over please)

Figure 3-3

The boxed text above "Dear Friend" is called a Johnson Box, after Frank
Johnson, inventor of the device. Many mailers now prefer a less formal,
handwritten overline.

"Come... join me!"

LEFTY'S LITTLE LIBRARY OF FLY FISHING

You only think you've enjoyed fly fishing up to now.
LK

Dear Fellow Fly Fisherman:

I want to send you a free book. It's a book I <u>guarantee</u> will have a lot more fish fighting to get at your fly. And oh, yes, a free privately-recorded audiocassette.

No. I'm not nuts. Lefty Kreh has been called a lot of things, but not nuts. Well, maybe nuts about fly fishing.

And if you're like me, no joy is greater than picking the right fly, executing the perfect cast, and having one of those big babies grab at that fly before the second hand has gone around your watch dial even once. No despair is greater than moping over a dead line all day, being ignored by fish.

As you probably know, I've been a fanatical fly fisherman for more than 40 years. And as you might imagine, after all these years I've pretty well licked the problem of "fishless fishing." And the whole point of this letter is: <u>You</u> can end "fishless fishing" too.

You will know why never to strike upward when fishing a sinking line . . . how to master a simple hand trick to vastly improve your casting distance . . . what to do when a knot appears in your fly line and a fish is escaping . . . how to avoid forever the world's most common casting mistake . . . thousands of secrets that translate <u>immediately</u> into more fun and more fish.

For you: Free Book ... Free Cassette

What I propose to do is this: My techniques are packed into a series of easy-to-read books we call *Lefty's Little Library of Fly Fishing.* I want to send you the first book <u>free</u>: *Lefty Kreh's Modern Fly Casting Method.*

(Please keep reading. I'm just getting started.)

Division of Odysseus Editions • 2100 Southbridge Parkway • P.O. Box 530065 • Birmingham, Alabama 35253

Figure 3-4

A contemporary technique with considerable power is the handwritten overline, above the greeting of the letter. A caveat for this technique: The overline has to grab and shake the reader's attention, but positively should not synopsize what's in the letter.

4

Telemarketing: How to Sell Over the Phone

"Anybody can answer the phone. Anybody can make a phone call." Marketers who take this position suffer from lack of information. And whose fault is that? Why don't they have better information on the difference between sophisticated telemarketing and somebody answering the phone?

Actually, telemarketing is a much more precise and more disciplined profession than buying media. Do telemarketers say to those who create media advertising, "Anybody can buy space ads and broadcast time"?

A mistake some telemarketers make is assuming total ignorance of telemarketing is the standard position of those who aren't their peers and confrères. It isn't. Oh, sure, some advertisers still live in the stone age, and we have to educate them. But in my opinion the reason telemarketing doesn't show up on more media budgets is that media directors don't regard telemarketing as part of the prime media mix.

The way to correct this is to sell a specific, not a generalization. An enlightened marketer won't react to the naked, unsupported suggestion that he or she include telemarketing in the next campaign. No, if we want a positive response, we have to show that person *how* to include telemarketing in a specific campaign for a specific product or service.

One plus one equals three. That's synergism. It's what a properly constructed telemarketing campaign adds to the media mix. An *improperly* constructed telemarketing campaign won't kill the total but it won't add anything to it . . . except expense. One plus one equals one.

Primary or secondary? Inbound or outbound? Or all of these?

Is telemarketing a primary medium — that is, a basic means of generating business, not a support medium?

Certainly. There's just one "if."

The "if " relates to what we're selling. If the campaign is to generate store traffic for a food staple, be cautious. That isn't telemarketing's strength. If the campaign is for subscriptions . . . or test-driving an automobile . . . or a political candidate . . . or an insurance estimate . . . or employee recruitment . . . or offering new services to a company's existing customers . . . or a free trial of anything at all . . . or best of all, resuscitation of dormant customers or clients . . . telemarketing has top credentials. Telemarketing can't lose. It's the surest media bet an advertiser has.

Telemarketing straddles two different universes — inbound and outbound. These two facets of telemarketing have only one marker in common: the telephone itself.

Don't lump inbound and outbound together when planning a telemarketing campaign.

Enlightened marketers are very much aware of the difference between inbound and outbound. They're aware, too, of the considerable difference in expertise, staffing, and mechanisms of these two separate businesses.

Professional companies abound in both the inbound and outbound spheres; most of these companies claim expertise in both, and some actually do have such expertise, but the disciplines aren't parallel. Outbound requires major scripting talents, constant supervision, and a cast-iron gut. Inbound requires a profound knowledge of database and how to implement it, along with the equipment and determination to cross every "t" and dot every "i."

If you haven't used telemarketing before, you may be wise to employ a professional telemarketing company — at least until you're comfortable with what equipment and bookkeeping you have to have, and what hiring and supervisory procedures you have to implement. Disaster lurks for the marketer who decides to carve an office into tiny sound-treated kiosks and staff it with after-school students, assuming the entire technique consists of inserting a toll-free number in an ad and then simply answering the phone and entering the order on a computer.

The professionals bring three assets into the arena. One: Total experience in the medium. Two: Capability of answering calls without hiring or training new personnel, plus all the benefit packages the advertiser would have to offer new employees. Three: The easy ability to get out without damage if the campaign fails, or, for that matter, when it ends.

Everybody in advertising knows the benefit of a toll-free number. Catalogs that have tried to compete without it have lost market share; in fact, catalogs that don't have a toll-free *fax* number are losing market share.

The percentage of mail order companies that include a toll-free number with their mailings and space ads is well over 90 percent; any mail order executive will tell you that the greater percentage of responses — often between 60 and 80 percent — come in by phone, when the option exists between a toll-free call and a postage-free envelope.

(A higher percentage of mailed responses come from the 55-plus age group.)

In the United States, adding the 888 prefix for toll-free calls also added confusion. One year after implementation of this number, more than one-third of people polled didn't know 888 is toll-free. For that matter, a hard nut of oldsters don't believe 800 is toll-free, and some marketing hi-jinks by borderline companies implement their distrust.

Staffing up for a campaign is a two-edged sword. The advertiser has to ask: Will this be an ongoing department? Will I be able to keep these people busy enough to justify their salaries during the next year? Is it profitable for me to allocate space and equipment? In a fast-moving world such as telemarketing, am I going to be able to stay competitive with outside firms who automatically upgrade to new technology?

Independent telemarketers know many of their clients are companies who originally had in-house capability. They now have gone, if you'll pardon the expression, from in-house to out-house. These are the best clients, because they recognize what capability they have and what capability they don't have. They aren't suspicious of every move and every cost. And they're telemarketing-literate, which can be an advantage or disadvantage depending on the telemarketing company's own ethics.

In-house and outside telemarketing can peacefully co-exist. Many telemarketing companies have consulting and automatic call-overflow agreements with clients who operate their own departments but aren't staffed for heavy traffic times nor after hours and weekends.

For advertisers considering adding telemarketing to the media mix and adding an in-house telemarketing department at the same time, the outside firm has that sensible sales argument: Before you invest in all that equipment and remodeling and hiring, use us to test the waters.

Outbound is a different game from inbound. Equipment is far more sophisticated. Terminology differs. Developments such as predictive dialing and intelligent call processing integration systems, plus the bogeyman of "opt-out" legislation that makes a crime of calling someone who doesn't want to be called — all these mean the decision to use outbound telemarketing is a complex decision that shouldn't be made casually.

Outbound employee turnover is far higher. Legal problems, including those stemming from operator ad-libs, can haunt you. Training and preparation have to be far more exhaustive. Calls have to be clustered within a limited number of hours.

We are witnessing much legislation against telemarketing fraud. The image of telemarketing has sunk so low in some quarters that telemarketing is labeled fraudulent just because it's telemarketing.

Somebody sues, and the courts seem to think: "Oh, this guy is a telemarketer. Rule against him."

Outbound is an iffy business, and any level short of total one hundred percent professionalism has the fast-growing seeds of potential disaster. The advertiser can face legal problems, untargeted sales appeals, personnel not dedicated to the job, insufficient capacity, poor record-keeping, slow transfer of data to the order department, and the worst of all results: You can have a situation in which a customer or even an advertiser is killed off. You'll hear: "Telemarketing? Oh, we tried that, and it didn't work."

A peculiar marriage

Effective telemarketing is a peculiar marriage of the highly technical and the highly creative. Technology is leaping along, and the telemarketer who wants to stay competitive had better know what's out there.

"How are you today?"

Even more pertinent: The marketer who would be a telemarketer had better have a basic knowledge of psychology.

An advertiser decides to go ahead with telemarketing. The marketing department or the advertising agency turns the program over to a junior writer. What we get is boiler-plate copy such as this:

Is this Mrs. John Jones? It is? Mrs. Jones, how are you today?

If ever a sentence were deadly, that's it: "How are you today?" My wife has a standard answer — on those rare occasions when she doesn't hang up. She'll say, "Oh, dreadful, dreadful. The dog died. Yes, the dog died. You see, he was in the barn when it caught fire. I hated to see that barn catch fire, but it happened when flames spread from the house. It wasn't my fault. When I shot that burglar, the kick from the shotgun broke my arm and I fell back against the table. The candle fell on the floor and started the fire. I couldn't put out the candle because my arm was broken, and you probably know I lost my other arm in that accident at the factory. I wish the car hadn't been parked in the driveway, next to that gasoline can." And she goes on until the caller hangs up.

I don't usually hang up on that "How are you today?" opening unless I'm busy, because I like to know what telemarketers are doing. But I fooled myself once. A man's voice said, "Hi, how are you today?" and I hung up. It turned out to be a friend trying to put together a tennis game.

The top floor of the skyscraper

Among nonprofessionals the most expensive pitfall is making random calls to anyone in the pile of prospect names. You may not agree with this point . . . but if you don't, test the concept for yourself.

A professional telemarketer knows that if you're making outbound calls, you call just the top floor of the universal skyscraper — your very best prospects and *only* your very best prospects. Once you start dipping down into the lower floors, you're in dangerous territory.

Using telemarketing for "shotgun" prospecting doesn't make any more business sense than a doctor treating every patient for malaria, whether that patient has any symptoms or not.

A major marketer and an advertising agency instinctively think "mass" — logical enough, because they're mass marketers. Telemarketing uses a rapier, not a shotgun. We choose a target and with an exquisitely delicate thrust, stab it right through the wallet.

So, we offer the advantage of selectivity. Oh, certainly, advertisers understand selectivity in conventional media. They have an academic understanding of the First Great Law of Force-Communication:

Reach and influence, at the lowest possible cost, the most people who can and will buy what you have to sell.

The telemarketer's job is to convert that *academic* understanding into a *force-communications* understanding. Every word of that Law makes sense to the telemarketer.

Telemarketing guarantees absolute *reach*. If you run an ad in a publication or if you schedule a broadcast campaign, no matter how sophisticated your market research might be, you have only the vaguest idea of whether or not you've reached your targets. With telemarketing, the moment that person picks up the phone — whether to call you or to take your call — you know you've reached him or her.

The middle phrase, "at the lowest possible cost," eliminates outbound calls to people on the lower floors of the skyscraper. If those people want to call *in,* that's gravy. In fact, you should make it as easy and as profitable as you possibly can to have them call in. Why? Because once they've called in they join that select group in the penthouse, the top floor where top prospects dwell, and it's both logical and profitable for you to contact them.

Now look at the last phrase: It isn't "the most people"; it's "the most people who can and will buy what you have to sell." That phrase alone should say to you: If you want the gold nuggets, you won't get rich by inspecting each individual stone, scraping it and weighing it to see if it's a gold nugget. Nobody gets rich that way: Finding the gold costs more than the gold is worth.

The old-fashioned concept of "reaching the most people" is the classic bulk-approach advertisers understand. But reaching the most people is fifty years out of date. We don't want the most people. We want the most people who can and will buy what we have to sell.

That imperative is especially true if we pay any attention to the phrase "at the lowest possible cost." Telemarketing isn't just expensive. Compared with any other medium it's *outrageously* expensive. That's the education we have to absorb, a new set of parameters . . . that we shouldn't be comparing the outrageous cost of telemarketing with conventional media. Instead, we should be comparing the singular effectiveness of proper telemarketing with the outrageous cost of personal sales calls.

The basic rules of salesmanship apply here.

Specifics sell. Generalities don't sell. When you're creating outbound telemarketing scripts, ask yourself: Have I been straightforward, clear, *and specific*?

When you're creating inbound scripts, ask yourself: Have I included all pertinent questions and added specific "upsell" suggestions?

But for outbound calls don't forget the most valuable imperative.

Getting attention is not parallel to offering a benefit. So a message which wants to offer a benefit — and get the cash register to ring — has to tell your target what to do. *Tell your target what to do!*

Understand — outbound telemarketing isn't for every ad, nor even for every campaign. But where it makes sense is when we're working inside a database and the advertising manager or sales manager says, "Everybody who sees or hears this message should respond."

If what he or she says is true, you can say with equal truth: Adding telemarketing will add at least 40 percent. It might double response, and don't be surprised if response is twice or three times as high with it as it is without it. Here's where a test is wonderful, because assuming you know your business, you can't miss. You're reaching a targeted group with a targeted message. You're calling the top floor of the skyscraper.

Telemarketing as "reminder advertising"

You have another weapon. It's a subtle one, but it can be the difference between getting telemarketing included in the media budget or not.

Yes, it's a subtle one, and we all know subtlety doesn't work as a sales weapon. But this is subtlety from the viewpoint of power persuasion, not subtlety in your own approach to a conversation. It's this little rule:

In marketing, asking questions can help formulate attitudes. Read this one over a couple of times. You can see another way that bringing in telemarketing to ask questions of those who have been exposed to other media advertising cannot only help shake up results, it can even satisfy those who keep reciting the catechism about image advertising.

Using telemarketing to ask questions about an advertising campaign has three huge advantages for the advertiser:

1. It assures the advertiser that whether or not the respondent has seen or remembered the advertising, from this moment on a powerful image has been implanted. Even the most anti-telemarketing advertiser can't quarrel with the assertion that having a telephone caller ask about a message inserts that advertiser's name firmly into the respondent's consciousness.

2. The advertiser gets totally usable feedback. For those who did see the advertising, reactions are timely and pointed.

3. The advertiser can tack on an incentive by making the phone call a quiz or ballot. The right answer — and you can structure this so every answer is the right answer — wins a discount certificate or sample coupon or small premium. Telemarketing personalizes an impersonal campaign.

But best of all, the way an experienced telemarketer frames the question validates the rule. The question itself can help formulate a positive attitude. This is just one more way in which the most personal of all mass media justifies its existence.

Telemarketing as a solo medium

Now, what about telemarketing as a solo advertising medium? That is, what about the notion of using *only* telemarketing? Will it work?

Using telemarketing alone works for intensive rather than extensive promotions. The marketer has to have a very limited universe in which every contact is pure gold.

Telemarketing works, too, for reviving lapsed subscriptions or goosing donors to support a fund-raising organization. Synergism exists when you combine these with direct mail. One plus one equals three. Direct mail *plus* telemarketing, to limited universes, invariably generates considerably more response than either medium alone, well in excess of the additional cost.

Basic rules for inbound telemarketing

Inbound, we've agreed, is considerably less complicated than out-bound. So not as many rules apply. These are absolute mandates which, if violated, will reduce response, induce hang-ups, and damage record-keeping accuracy:

1. The phone should ring no more than three times before being answered. If you consistently exceed this number, you need additional capacity.

2. If you're understaffed and the phone rings while all operators are busy, don't rush to answer. Lose a "possible" instead of losing an "on hand." But even semi-professional telemarketing will funnel overflows into an answering device.

3. Answer with a smile.

4. Speak slowly, clearly, and without a regional accent unless your market matches a specific region and only that region.

5. Repeat the order, when given.

6. Always be prepared to upsell. Example: A customer orders vitamin E. Be prepared to offer a "special" on selenium or vitamin C.

7. If you advertise more than one item or have a catalog, don't suggest the order is complete until the customer says the order is complete. After each entry, ask, "Next item?"

8. Always thank the customer for the order.

Basic rules for outbound telemarketing

Outbound is where the most peril lies. Ignoring the first two rules not only will cost you response, it could result in litigation. Don't be afraid to use telemarketing; rather, be afraid of turning it over to an untrained team.

1. Every word has to be scripted. Absolutely no ad-libbing.

2. Never allow an individual to start making calls until and unless you've auditioned that person, with you acting as a potential customer.

3. If yours is a professional operation, have supervisors make the first fifty calls, noting "glitches," uneven spots, and unexpected questions and objections.

4. Keep the Clarity Commandment in the forefront as you structure the script: Will the people you call know the terminology? Are you introducing an unexplained concept that should be explained? Test the call on someone who typifies your targets.

5. Make entries simple, either on a computer monitor or in a notebook set up for duplicate copies. One of the duplicates goes immediately to the order department.

6. Check the background of anyone authorized to ask for credit card information.

7. A constant instruction to each operator: Smile as you begin, smile as you end, and smile in between. Regardless of any verbal abuses by people you call — and inevitably this will happen — never loose your "cool" and never raise your voice.

8. Oh, one more thing: When you call, don't start the conversation with "How are you today?"

A Sample Telemarketing Script

(NOTE 1: Capitalize instructions. This eliminates the possibility that the operator will speak the instructions. <u>Underline</u> words you want emphasized.)

(NOTE 2: This example, an offer of flood insurance to someone who has just bought a home and not yet closed on it, is somewhat truncated. Any script is constantly polished and refined as questions are added to the list of most common responses.)

Hello, is this [(Mr.) (Mrs.) (Ms.)] *[THEIR LAST NAME]*? Hi, I'm *[MY NAME]* from Acme Insurance Company. I'm calling because your mortgage company — that's *[NAME OF MORTGAGE COMPANY]* — asked us to give you a quote on flood insurance for your new home.

It turns out your home is located in a special flood hazard area . . . that's an area in which floods are most likely to occur. And if your home — or for that matter <u>any</u> home — is located in a special flood hazard area, the federal government won't let *[NAME OF MORTGAGE COMPANY]* issue your mortgage until you have flood insurance. Did you know that?

(WAIT FOR <u>ANY</u> REACTION)

[NAME], this isn't bad news. Maybe I should explain: When a geophysical *[PRONOUNCED JEE-OH-<u>FIZZ</u>-UH-CULL]* search — that's a study of the natural environment — shows anybody's home is in a hazard zone, the government steps in and requires flood insurance. That's the law, and it makes some sense. For example, if you lived in South Florida you'd know about this because just about every home in South Florida is on a special flood hazard area . . . and every one of those homes has flood insurance. It's a good thing, too, because a really heavy storm can do a lot of damage. And understand: Your homeowners' insurance <u>doesn't</u> cover floods. Floods are excluded from homeowners' policies.

Anyway, it's a federal law, and we all have to live with it. After a flood, when you have a claim, the federal government's money backs it. We're an insurance company, but in this situation we're really just an agent of the government. In fact, they set the rates for flood insurance. We don't.

The cost depends on several considerations, including the elevation of your home — that is, how high it sits on the lot.

Oh, and other factors enter into this. Maybe you can save some money right off the bat. Does the house have a basement? (WAIT FOR ANSWER) Good.

(IF ANSWER IS NO) See, I told you you might save some money. You get a better rate because the house doesn't have a basement.

(IF ANSWER IS YES) Is the basement finished or unfinished? (WAIT FOR ANSWER) Okay, that's the information I need.

[Including the basement] how many floors in the house?

[NAME], most folks want to have as much flood coverage as they have on their homeowners coverage. Do you know how much homeowners coverage you have?

(IF INDIVIDUAL DOESN'T KNOW) Do you have that information there somewhere? I'll wait while you look it up.

(IF INDIVIDUAL DOESN'T YET HAVE HOMEOWNERS COVER-

AGE) Well, maybe I can help you there too. But for now, let's base the coverage on the purchase price of your new home . . . which is how much?

And one last question: Is your house new? Or if not, when was it built? (WAIT FOR ANSWER)

CONTINUATION "A" — IF HOUSE WAS BUILT BEFORE AREA WAS MAPPED

Hey, you're in luck. Your house was built before the government mapped the area, and that means you don't need an Elevation Certificate. That's a form you'd need if your house was built <u>after</u> the area was mapped.

[NAME], I can quote you a rate right now. Based on what you've told me, your premium is $ (SPECIFY AMOUNT), and that's due at your closing. That'll cover you for a whole year. (CONTINUE WITHOUT WAITING FOR RESPONSE)

Let's take a closer look at this, because we might have an opportunity to shave more money off that quote.

First, you don't need an Elevation Certificate. But if you have one, it might — that word is <u>might</u> — qualify you for a lower rate.

I can tell your lender you want an Elevation Certificate. If the Elevation Certificate shows you should be paying more, we can ignore it. And if that Certificate shows you qualify for an even lower rate, we can accept it and take advantage of it. Do you want to do that? (WAIT FOR ANSWER. SAY <u>NOTHING</u> UNTIL HOMEOWNER RESPONDS, NO MATTER HOW LONG THE PAUSE.)

(IF ANSWER IS "YES" OR AT ALL TOWARD THE POSITIVE SIDE) I agree with you. That's the thing to do. You might want to contact your lender to see if a Certificate exists. Or maybe I'd better contact your lender and get that Certificate. Would you like me to do that for you? (WAIT FOR ANSWER) It may or may not be free — I don't know how much it might cost, but your lender probably will be able to incorporate this into your closing costs. Should we go ahead and contact the mortgage company? When we have that information I'll call you back and you can decide what you want to do. At the very worst, your flood insurance won't cost any more than it would without the Certificate. Okay with you? (WAIT FOR ANSWER)

(IF ANSWER IS YES) Okay, I'll mail your quote today, so no matter what we find out you can close. And I'll contact your lender for an

Elevation Certificate. If the Certificate works in your favor, we can readjust the rate even after closing. If not, your only extra expense is the cost of the Certificate.

(IF ANSWER IS NO) No problem. I'll be able to mail your quote today.

Now, we have another way we can save some money, and that's by having a bigger deductible. The standard deductible is five hundred dollars. When you have a claim, you pay the first five hundred and your insurance pays everything above that. We can increase the deductible to a thousand dollars. You'll enjoy a lower rate if we do. What's your opinion? Should we increase the deductible to a thousand dollars? (WAIT FOR ANSWER)

(IF ANSWER IS "NO" ABOUT ELEVATION CERTIFICATE) Well, okay, no problem. Without the Certificate, I can tell you right now what flood insurance will cost you. (MAKE QUOTE)

(OPTION IF PROSPECT LIVES IN RATED COMMUNITY) Let me take one more look here. Hey, you know what? You have a discount coming because of the community your home is in. The Federal Government has qualified your area for a Community Rating Discount, because the community has taken steps toward flood control. (SPECIFY DISCOUNT) Isn't that a nice surprise?

(CLOSE) Okay, I'll outline the process for you. Nothing to it. First, we'll send you a copy of the quote. Second, we'll send that same quote to your lender branch, so it will be in your closing file. That's it. You won't be delayed at closing. All right? (WAIT FOR ANSWER—IF NO OBJECTIONS RAISED, CONCLUDE) That's it, then. Good luck with your new house. 'Bye. (HANG UP.)

CONTINUATION "B" — IF HOUSE WAS BUILT AFTER AREA WAS MAPPED

The reason I asked that question was to determine whether your house was built before or after the government mapped the area. It was built <u>after</u> the mapping. So do you have a survey which shows the elevation of your home? (ANSWER WILL BE "NO.")

I'll tell you what, *[NAME]:* I can't even give you a quote on your flood insurance until you have an Elevation Certificate. That's the law.

The U.S. government says we need it, you need it, and your lender needs it. Now, if you like, I can contact your lender and tell them you need an Elevation Certificate. That Certificate gives us the ammunition to give you the best possible rate for flood insurance . . . and based on where you live, you do need some flood insurance in order to close on your house.

So we have to get an Elevation Certificate. Do you have a relationship with a company that does this kind of survey and issues the Certificate? (ANSWER WILL BE NO) Then, if it's okay with you, I'll contact your lender — that's *[NAME OF MORTGAGE COMPANY]* — and tell them to get you an Elevation Certificate. You can't close on that house without it. They'll send that information to us, and we'll be able to complete the paperwork. It might cost a few dollars — I don't know how much, but it'll be part of your closing costs. Okay?

All right, then, we'll handle it all so you won't be slowed down on your closing. If we have a problem I'll call you back, but I don't think we will. 'Bye for now. (HANG UP)

5

A Ton of Information about Effective Catalog Copy and Layout . . . and Some Easy Rules for Adding Octane

"If I only had more space, I could have. . . ."

Have you ever met a catalog copywriter who hasn't mourned wistfully, "If I had the space Sharper Image or Herrington has to describe what I'm selling, I could *really* write powerful catalog copy"?

Prefabricated short copy-blocks are the bane of the writer whose creative wings beat vainly against their restraining nets. Yet, we should consider two valid points of logic which justify considering ways to boost the effectiveness of short copy.

First, we have as many catalogs set up with tiny, absolute, locked-in, unstretchable copy areas as we have catalogs whose vast open areas invite rhetorical exploration and experimentation.

Second, catalog copywriting *is* a professional job. The test of professionalism isn't adjectival rhapsody; it's maximizing effectiveness within whatever constraints the guy who signs the checks puts on the job.

Can short copy be dynamic copy? Yes, if . . . : The First Rule of Short Copy Effectiveness

The writer who assumes that working within small spaces demotes him or her to a descriptive clerk makes a sub-assumption: "I'm not a writer, I'm just a clerk."

Don't do that.

If your job is filling a small grid with alphabetical symbols, start expanding your articulating muscles. Start looking at adjectives with the same jaundiced eye your copy chief casts when investigating ways to cut copy, and instead look for the more demanding (ergo more professional) solution of replacing nouns and verbs with more colorful substitutes.

The First Rule of Short Copy Effectiveness:

Improvement in short copy comes from replacement of nondescript nouns and verbs with colorful nouns and verbs. Adjectives and adverbs are ancillaries because these are the most expendable.

Oh, certainly some product-types lend themselves to this rule more readily than others. A catalog of videotapes has the advantage of format-standardization, so the entire description can be of content rather than dimensions and operating method. A catalog of novelties may hardly have the space to tell what each item does. To the writer, each should be a challenge: How can I sell this within the predetermined limit?

The Second Rule of Short Copy Effectiveness

The veteran writer always has a mechanical trick or two available to kick into gear on those days when the muse has departed. One of those tricks is The Second Rule of Short Copy Effectiveness:

Pretend you're writing a 10-second radio commercial. Copy is easier to write, and conversion to catalog copy is a snap.

Understand, please: *Conversion* is a snap, but original composition does require positive and disciplined word-control.

The benefit of thinking in terms of a brief radio spot, instead of a catalog description, is that the writer immediately discards all extraneous elements and concentrates solely on the impact of the words. Conversion is the easy part because the cataloger has an illustration as an extra tool.

So which is harder to concoct, the short catalog description or the short radio spot? Right! The radio spot. But name one writer for a tiny copy-block catalog who doesn't think the radio writer's job is not only more glamorous, but easier.

A few examples, from various catalogs

Is this good or bad copy?

The catalog — a wholesale novelty source. The illustration — a stark blue rectangle in which two strange flashlight-shaped objects with bulbous heads appear, plus an inset photo of a box of batteries — obviously requires explanation. This is the total description:

> 7½" Plastic LIGHT-UP WATER GLOBE.
> Flip the switch and watch as the water changes colors. Assorted colors. *Requires two "AA" batteries.*
> **Dozen — $12.00**
> IMPORTED "AA" BATTERIES. (2 dozen per unit) **Unit $1.80**

Now, do you say, "That's about all the writer could do within that space"? Sorry, I don't agree.

If *you* were writing this copy, would you follow "changes colors" with "Assorted colors"? The most inexcusable gaffe in short catalog copy is confusion. Repetition of the word "color," which makes an undefined double interpretation-suggestion, is indefensible.

And how about the word "imported" as the descriptive word for "batteries"? Did you catch this? If you didn't, you aren't thinking in catalog copy terms — which is, after all, thinking in catalog reader terms.

If this were a music box movement or a watch or a silk scarf or a high-fashion garment, "imported" might have some significance. But batteries? When we have terms such as "long life" and "heavy duty" sitting patiently like teenagers at a dance?

Let's try another.

One of the better-known upscale catalogs accompanies a handsome photograph of two women's sport shoes (one black, one red) with this copy in a vertical stack):

36. COMFORTABLE
STYLE AT A PRICE YOU
CAN LIVE WITH: BALLY'S
SPORT SHOES OF NYLON
FAILLE AND NUBUCK.
EASYGOING RUBBER
SOLES. IMPORTED.
SIZES: 5½–10M.
SPECIFY COLOR:
BLACK OR RED.
36. SPORT SHOES
$59.00 (5.00)

This example was peculiar, because short copy here is a deliberate stylistic approach, not a necessity. Lots of unused open space here.

I have a personal prejudice against all-cap copy, which may sour my reaction, but in all fairness this is pretty good use of short copy. I do like matching up seldom-matched words, "Comfortable style." I do like opening with a reason to buy: "Comfortable style at a price you can live with."

What's "Nubuck"? I assume it's an ersatz buckskin, and since "buck" is part of the manufactured word the reader accepts it on that level.

Remember the earlier comment on the word "imported"? Here it's apt.

So we have a bare-bones description which still fulfills both Rules of Short Copy Effectiveness.

Another example:

Here are three adjacent descriptions of rings, within a catalog of simulated precious gem jewelry:

L. Galway — 14K Solid Gold Ring with 4.0 Carats *Emerald Essence*™ Emerald Cut Center. 5.0 Carats in all. Shimmering enticement.
M. Reynolds — 14K Solid Gold Ring with 3.0 Carats *Emerald Essence*™ Oval Center. 3.12 Carats altogether. Deep, rich color.
N. Emerald City — 14K Solid Gold Ring with Emerald Essence™ Oval Center with Melee accents. 1.50 Carats in all. Lovely and lavish.

See the style here? This writer is locked into a tight format; creativity is limited to the final two or three words. How would you rate these examples? — "Shimmering enticement"; "Deep, rich color"; "Lovely and lavish."

No, these aren't barn-burners. Any group of descriptions in which the straightforward "Deep, rich color" wins best-of-show isn't the stuff a writer's sample portfolio is made of. But in defense of the writer, these appear on page 21 of a standard-size catalog which has 12 to 15 items on each page.

These are superior to others on this same page, such as the execrable "You'll be inimitable," but less effective than others in this catalog such as the deceptively simple "Impressive but delicate."

Preparing to write short copy? Do this:

Much short copy is the product of individuals who aren't career copywriters. They feel — with some justification, as we've proved here — hiring a "writer" to extrude a handful of nondescript words is a wasteful luxury.

For them, and for the writers who feel trapped in lilliputian formats, a suggestion:

Make lists. Make lists of picturesque nouns and vibrant verbs. Make lists of unusual synonyms for standard adjectives such as "beautiful" and "lovely" and "valuable."

Then use that list. Sooner or later, somebody will notice.

What You Say Depends on Where It Is.

Good or bad? Strong or weak? Motivational or blah? You're looking at a catalog of women's fashions. The entire description:

DKNY: Garnet acetate/rayon jacket, 415.00. Navy tissue wool skirt, 225.00. White rayon/acetate/silk faille vest, 145.00. White cotton/polyester/spandex bodysuit, 55.00. Navy foulard silk ascot, 45.00. All imported. Leisure Sportswear.

Purists might complain on two separate grounds. First, where's the dollar sign before those numbers? Second, how can they charge $415 for an acetate and rayon jacket in Donna Karan's "popularly priced" line?

This marketer squelches the complaint in two words: "Neiman Marcus."

The dollar signs would seem crass. The spartan copy accompanies a lush full-page photograph. And the ambience makes dollar comparisons insignificant.

The point: Ambience has tremendous control over the amount of sell the copywriter has to inject into the copy. If this were a season-end close-out sale, dollar signs and discount percentages would be in, and DKNY would give way to "Designer label." We might even see some exclamation marks. And certainly the store would be gracious enough to tell us what sizes are in stock.

Now we move to the other side of the street. This fashion copy, in a different catalog, reads:

> Our great ensemble . . . jacket dressing! Our overscaled jacket features lace ties in front, drop shoulders. The easy dress features a drop waist, "pearl" button front, short sleeves. In a fine blend of crinkled acetate and rayon faille. BLACK/ivory as shown. Even sizes 4 to 16. Made in USA. The 2-pc. outfit was $129. **SALE PRICE: $99.88.**

See the difference? The environment has changed, so the approach changes. We have crass, hackneyed words such as "great" and "features." We have the downscale "2-pc." But what the heck, this is a sale, and the writer has to stay in key.

Just who do you think you are?
Just who does the *reader* think you are?

What's the difference between an "adaptation" and a "reproduction?" It depends on the ambience . . . who the cataloger is. In what kind of catalog would you expect to find this description?

> "CH'ING" SCARVES
> The richly colored flowers and scalloped border design on these striking silk scarves are adapted from the decoration on a Chinese (Ch'ing dynasty, early 18th century) porcelain monteith bowl. Imported pure silk *crêpe de Chine*, with rolled hems, 34" square.

Okay, then, if you've guessed that one, then guess where this reasonably parallel description came from:

> Oriental Kimonos were the height of fashion in the Ching Dynasty. Our Oriental Kimono Paintings are reproductions of ancient designs that have been handpainted on hand-loomed silk.

Framed in gold. Each print measures 2' x 3' and comes ready to hang.

Yes, each of these is flawed. But if you recognized the first description as typical of a museum catalog, your analytical powers are blasting away full-steam; and if you saw evidence of a home gift catalog in the second description, you're among the elite evaluators.

The first description carefully puts the apostrophe in Ch'ing and assumes the reader has no translational difficulties with *crêpe de Chine*. One major puzzlement: Why does the writer explain the Ch'ing dynasty and then hit-and-run with monteith (a 17th century silver, *not* porcelain, punch bowl named after its originator — a Scotsman), never telling us how a Scottish motif wound up as a Chinese decoration. Conclusion: The writer emptied his knowledge basket.

The second description doesn't bother apostrophizing Ching. Conclusion: The writer either a) parallels the readers or b) thinks the readers won't know or care about the apostrophe. "Framed in gold" is a throwaway, obviously untrue. Gold leaf? Gilt frame? Whatever it is, again the writer thinks the home giftware reader/buyer doesn't need a puristic interpretation. Incidentally, this description capitalizes Dynasty, which in my opinion gives it an edge over the museum's downplaying. The Rule of Capitalization, already stated in an earlier chapter:

Capital letters add implied importance.

(That goes for the first word "The" in a company or product name too, the [The?] Associated Press Stylebook notwithstanding.)

The source suggests the use.

Here's a comparison that isn't so easy.

You're selling men's sport shorts in a catalog that includes other apparel. Compare these two descriptions, for shorts priced within a few cents of each other:

Affordable Asics
Runner Shorts
There's nothing here to hold you back, especially the price. Lightweight tricot half splits. Mid-cut for maximum movement.

Dyed to match nylon brief and key pocket. Royal, Red, Navy, or Black. Unisex M, L, XL

. . . and here's the other description:

> ***"Bulldog tough" Sport Shorts in regular and volley length.***
> Choose our regular length (3½" inseam) for sports. Or our volley length (6" inseam) for all-around casual wear and a little more coverage.
>   Either way, you get the same "bulldog tough" features. Like 100% cotton twill fabric that's slightly sanded for softness. Elasticized drawstring waistband with four rows of stitching that'll withstand your toughest workouts. Front pockets roomy enough to hold a couple of tennis balls. And for men, a back flap pocket with Velcro® closure. Machine wash. Made in USA. *Colors above.*
> **Men's** M 32–34, L 36–38, XL 40–42.
> **Women's** S 6–8, M 10–12, L 14–16, XL 18–20.

If you identified the difference, you looked for the proper criterion: *emphasis*. The first description emphasizes *you*; the second description emphasizes *product*.

So, assuming both writers had their wits about them — which they did — the first catalog is a sports attire catalog, which assumes its readers take the mechanical aspect of shorts for granted and would be drummed out of the corps for wearing shorts with pockets big enough for a couple of tennis balls.

One major problem with this description: Wouldn't you interpret "Dyed to match nylon brief and key pocket" to mean these shorts are dyed (not a good word for health buffs) to match briefs and a key pocket described elsewhere? The need for re-interpretation is death and destruction in catalog copy.

The second catalog is a general apparel catalog, whose emphasis has to be on product superiority. So "four rows of stitching" — inconsequential to runner-addicts — becomes a serious sales factor.

Still, I wish the writer of this totally professional copy knew he or she didn't have to use the no-impact word "features." "You get the same 'bulldog toughness'" out-impacts "You get the same 'bulldog tough' features."

Think like your reader:
Who is he? Who is she? Who are they?

Demographic knowledge isn't as pivotal in catalog copy as it is in a solo mailing. But every catalog aims itself at a specific target-group. This group *has* to respond or the catalog fails. Sure, some peripheral buyers will order. But if you think casting a deliberate image at buyer-groups depends entirely on graphics, why hire writers at all?

Good question.

Why Not Ask Yourself: "Who Is My Customer? . . . And Why Should That Customer Buy from ME?"

The merchandise manager has just tossed a product description onto your desk. "Sell this to our customers," is the standard imperative.

You look at the photo and description: It's a rocking chair.

Too many journeyman-copywriters shrug and start pounding the keys. They describe the rocking chair . . . and they do it with complete *technical* professionalism. Too often what they don't do is re-ask themselves — as they should before writing every blurb in their catalog — *"Who is my customer? And why would my customer buy a rocking chair?"*

Some catalog writers think of themselves as specialists the way physicians do. To them we should say, "Physician, heal thyself," because in sales writing over-specialization, or super-saturation with corporate lore, can mean withdrawal from the marketplace.

And that syndrome means what? This: The copywriter no longer mirrors the prospective buyers whose motivators his or her copy is supposed to match.

Why would *you* buy a rocking chair?

Would you buy a rocking chair for yourself because of nostalgia? Yes, you would . . . if you were over 55.

Would you buy that chair because it's again fashionable? Yes, you would . . . if you fit the increasingly blurred "would-be" profile.

Would you buy that chair because it's a bargain? Yes, you would . . . if you recognize the source as a bargain-based catalog.

Each of these motivators requires a different description. One of the most effective tests we can give writer-applicants is writing differing descriptions for the same item.

If differing descriptions are logical and pertinent, based on a) catalog ambience and b) catalog-reader psychographics, let's target our copy to the readership.

One contra-indication: DON'T target copy with such pinpointed accuracy that you exclude those on the periphery of the group. Zero-variation pinpointing is profitable only for extremist-group fund raisers.

Comparative motivators

I've seen the same rocking chair in two catalogs. One, whose theme and merchandise strikes a nice balance between the down-home bucolic and the contemporary outdoor-upscale, has this firmly-anchored-in-yesterday description:

Rockers Like Grandma Used to Have
Remember those big, comfortable rockers your grandmother had on her front porch? We've found some just like them. With ample, contoured seats and wide, flat arms, they're comfortable enough for whiling away an entire evening. Made of kiln-dried red oak, they are finished with a weatherproof Indurlux "Yacht" paint. . . .

The photograph shows two rockers (one white and one green) sitting on what surely was Grandma's front porch.

A competing catalog takes a more crisply contemporary copy approach:

PLANTATION ROCKERS MADE FOR YOU
Designed with classic flair these porch rockers were gracefully designed in every detail. Select kiln dried oak is used because of its durability to last for years. Both finishes (white and spruce green) are enamels that were originally designed for the boating industry. . . .

Which description would sell you a rocker?
For me, it's no contest. I'd buy the Grandma version for two reasons: First, the description is thoughtfully charming, and, fuddy-duddy that I am, I'm still a sucker for charm in an increasingly charmless world.

Second, in my opinion the "Grandma" description is a better-written piece of copy. The very headline "PLANTATION ROCKERS MADE FOR YOU" draws almost no word-image, and the almost-hidden suggestion that "made for you" means these are custom-built (nonsensical on its face) is left dangling, unexplained.

Beyond that, the crucial first "Plantation Rockers" sentence is 100 percent nonspecific. And why use boat enamel? I know the reason because of Grandma's copy, but the writer can't assume others have Grandma's competing description at hand. If the writer knows the reason for using boat enamel, why not share it? (Incidentally, enamels are formulated or compounded; they aren't "designed." And they're for boats, not for "the boating industry.")

If this copy is upscale-intended, it needs upscale specifics. Lacking specifics, except for actual technical description, this copy is just loose puffery.

Good "makin's" for the composter

All right, let's try the same litmus test for composters. This time, we have three candidate-catalogs, each of which sells the same "Soilsaver" composter.

The smart catalog copywriter asks himself or herself: "Who reads this catalog? Does the reader know how composters work? Can I assume, because this is a house-and-garden catalog, the reader knows why having a composter might be beneficial?"

All three catalogs handled the question with high professionalism. Each described the composter on a basic level . . . without alienating those whose backgrounds might be considerably more extensive. Yet, each writer was able to develop an individual personality for the composter, and as hawk-eyed critics we can judge the descriptions competitively.

Which composter would you buy?

The first catalog aims itself at "Practical Products for Your Home, Yard & Garden." I'm not enamored of ampersands, but I like the straightforward approach this catalog takes:

The Soilsaver makes composting so simple anyone will have success.

Set up the Soilsaver anywhere on your lawn even close to your back door. This method of composting is not messy and it gives off no unpleasant odors. Put in grass clippings, garden wastes, coffee grounds, egg shells, vegetable and fruit skins. The lid lifts off for easy loading. Heat and moisture are retained as the waste begins to decompose. In 6 to 8 weeks you will have compost . . .

The second catalog, "The Catalog for Home, Lawn, and Garden," has this description:

THE COMPOSTER — EVERY YARD NEEDS ONE

It may seem serene and peaceful there by the garden, but the composter is seething inside. And after a while, you see the benefits. New developments are making the ancient technology of composting look better every day. Here's why: You put stuff in the top that nobody wants — grass clippings, leaves, weeds — anything biodegradable. After a few weeks, out from the bottom comes rich, sweet-smelling compost that is useful in many ways. . . .

The third catalog bills itself as "Products for Country Living." Its writer took a money-saver approach:

Turn Kitchen and Garden Wastes Into Valuable Compost

Why spend good money on fertilizer and soil conditioners when you can make your own for free? Our Soilsaver Composter is scientifically designed to produce up to half a ton of rich, nutritious compost per year without odors or harmful by-products. The slatted sides let air circulate freely, yet keep out rain or snow. The polyethylene walls retain the heat needed for composting . . .

Which one did *you* think had the best "grabber"? Which one gave you the best understanding of what the Soilsaver does?

For me, the obvious third-place position went to the second version. I'm uncomfortable thinking of a composter "seething inside," right there in my peaceful garden.

More significantly, I felt this description was loaded with fat. Example — the second sentence: "And after a while, you can see the benefits." This is a statement best omitted because without a description of what the benefits are, it not only adds nothing to the comprehensional mix, but suggests benefits will not be immediate. Other segments of this copy also hit and run: ". . . out from the bottom comes rich, sweet-smelling compost that is useful in many ways." What are some of those ways? Of all areas of copywriting, catalog writing demands the most specificity.

I'm torn between the other two descriptions. The first headline is superior for those who haven't dabbled in this area before; the second headline is superior for those with a practical or budget-conscious viewpoint.

Assuming that psychographics of the typical catalog reader more closely parallel the first position — and sensing a mild unease about linking budget to an obviously optional item — then the first description becomes my personal winner. I'd choose it, too, for clarity and specificity.

You say you don't agree? Wonderful! That's why competing catalogs are able to exist.

But . . .

If you're a catalog copywriter, and you haven't been targeting your description at a logical *somebody,* look out: Another catalog could steal that somebody right from under your order form.

The Difference Between "We" Copy and "You" Copy: Light-Years

An established standard for exclusivity-based selling is: Only you . . . only from us.

Implicitly, this technique ties sellee (our target) to seller (our catalog).

For the catalog copywriter, including both "you" and "we" in the same copy block has a golden advantage, beyond exclusivity: The implied bond suggests *rapport,* that marvelous bonding agent we covet in direct mail and too often abandon in catalogs. *Suggesting* rapport can actually *generate* rapport.

Do you need big copy blocks to tie "our" to "your"? Certainly not. These two words are adjectives, and including them has minimal effect on copy length.

Unless it appears awkward, why not try it?

A music box company uses the We-to-You Shift on many items it labels "Exclusive." An example:

**Warm your tummy
with the Christmas spirit!**

Our exclusive Holiday teapot warms your guests with a cup of steaming English tea and a music box rendition of "We Wish You a Merry Christmas." Fine porcelain teapot holds 6 cups and is decorated with fired decal and 24K gold trim. Call now and order in time for the Holidays! 6½" H.

Notice the sequence. Most copywriters would *begin* the copy-block with "Fine porcelain teapot holds 6 cups and is decorated with fired decal and 24K gold trim." (I hate that word "decal" in describing art; it has about as much class as "toilet." Why couldn't the writer say, ". . . decorated with bright holiday motif permanently fired into the porcelain"?)

Beginning with the relationship — we to you — reinforces the concept of "Only you . . . only from us." Does it create a stronger stimulus to buy? I think so, if only because "warms your guests" represents *product in use,* always a stronger stimulus than raw product description.

Why does the phrase "Holiday teapot" capitalize Holiday and not teapot? Beats me.

The same catalog sells a snow-globe paperweight with a curious selling proposition:

Stamp out stress!
Hold our European winter village in your hand and watch the snow fall peacefully on the train, tunnel, country path, and houses. Made to our own design, this treasure plays "Winter Wonderland" and makes a soothing paperweight for a busy person's desk. 4½" H.

However you might snicker at "soothing paperweight," you can see the consistency of technique. Copy opens with the We-to-You Shift, then describes.

I suppose anything we can view or fondle contributes to stress-reduction. Choosing this as the key selling proposition does separate it from other items in the catalog; and in a catalog filled with music boxes it's an admirable ploy.

"You" without "We" — is it as powerful?

Does excluding "we" from the mix weaken the impact?

The only possible answer is, "It depends on the catalog" . . . which is no help at all to the writer trying to make a decision about copy-thrust.

I'd narrow the answer, mildly: "It depends on whether the catalog wants to project an image of a) exclusivity or b) 'down home' conviviality."

A solid benefit of "you" without "we": The writer can fill a 96-page catalog without jeopardizing credibility or reader-involvement. That's why some catalogs content themselves by emphasizing the We-to-You Shift in the "President's Letter," inside the front cover. Product descriptions are we-free.

An example is a catalog of general merchandise. Note the tone of the President's Letter: It's filled with We-to-You:

- Our *Flags of the World* will put you in the mood for travel.
- We're very proud of our "Buy-any-2-and-get-1-Free" program. It's explained in detail on page 15. Do take advantage of these bargains; it's one of the smartest moves you could make.
- Many thanks for your continued support of our efforts to bring you the best products for a fuller life. . . .

The facing page displays four items. All four are *you* — not *we*. The first descriptive sentence for each item:

- What do you do with a 3-foot-9-inch panda?
- You and your family can launch your own UFO right from your own backyard, with the Flying Saucer Space Probe.
- A hot number — whether you're entertaining or serving the evening meal.
- Its sole purpose for existence is to help you on your dive.

Transforming any of these to We-to-You is a piece of cake. But do we gain or lose by rewriting those first sentences to add "We"?

- What do you do with our 3 foot 9 inch panda?
- You and your family can launch your own UFO right from your own backyard, with our *Flying Saucer Space Probe.*
- We have a hot number for you — whether you're entertaining or serving the evening meal.
- The sole purpose of our Benrus Centurian diver's watch is to help you on your dive.

Well, I kind of like "our" instead of "a" for the panda and the flying saucer. Injecting "we" into the hot number seems forced. And it makes little sense to claim a proprietary interest in a Benrus watch, unless Benrus makes the watch exclusively for us. (Incidentally, isn't it *Centurion,* not *Centurian?*)

But those are opinions, and if our text leaves out a person, let it be ourselves, not the reader.

A textbook example

Another catalog has built its entire image on We-to-You. Reading this catalog, or any of its type, the dispassionate observer sees why customers think of themselves as family (a major advantage in maintaining customer loyalty and confidence). Copywriting for this catalog has to walk a tightrope over two chasms — straight description, which in this ambience is out of key, and overpersonalization, which damages credibility.

How can a 52-page "down home" catalog walk firmly on the tightrope? This one does it by alternation. Some copy is We-to-You. Some copy is We-to-Them. Some copy is It-to-You.

So one copy-block (We-to-You) begins:

Try our new bed rest/wedge and get the best of both possible worlds.

Another copy-block (We-to-Them) begins:

The last time I slipped while bathing, I vowed that I would never again enter the tub without a safety mat.

A third copy-block (It-to-You) begins:

This will make your dreams come true . . . an anatomical mattress pad for the ultimate in sleeping comfort!

The mixture not only helps avoid the inevitable boredom that accompanies sameness, it also helps credibility, because the reader doesn't sense copywriting as copywriting.

So is it We, You, or both?

If yours is a catalog whose copywriting has to follow a manual of uncompromising stylistic instructions, arguing for introduction (or excision) of a We-to-You Shift may cause too much autocratic hemorrhaging to warrant consideration.

Rigid formats represent rigid attitudes. Flexibility isn't always a good policy, because it can lead to anarchy.

But if your catalog has been groping for buyer-loyalty, for identification, or for an extra touch of brightness, introducing We-to-You might supply a minor lift, without having to retrain even one writer.

Why Sizzle Outsells Steak

In the period between the World Wars, society spawned a man named Elmer Wheeler, "The World's Greatest Salesman."

In his day, Wheeler became famous for a line that now has guided salespeople for two generations:

"Sell the sizzle, not the steak."

Are catalog writers salespeople? If we aren't, we're just sales *clerks*. And you know the difference in income and position between sales*people* and sales *clerks*.

Too many catalog copywriters are clerks, putting in time at their jobs. Oh, of course we have a place for dispassionate, unornamented description. Especially in business-to-business catalogs, some companies feel it's statesmanlike to avoid any trace of hyperbole.

I agree . . . and you know the next word: BUT . . .

Sizzle doesn't have to be hyperbole. Sizzle doesn't have to be exaggeration. Sizzle doesn't even have to be simple puffery.

I'm still looking for the writers (or marketers) who coined the term "Furnace Shirt" and "Blizzard Boots." I was so impressed with "Furnace Shirt" I made a slide of that image-provoking description to use in speeches in which I'd demonstrate what imagination can do to enhance a product. This isn't hyperbole nor exaggeration nor puffery. It sells sizzle, and I admire good salesmanship.

Sizzle is telling them what it's for.

I admire any writer who can tune his or her rhetoric to match the experiential background of the reader. The best computer software catalogs seem to be able to attract writers who are masters of this art.

Except for a few running-in-place clichés, this description of mailing list management software, sale-priced at $49.95, is exhaustive enough to satisfy the most inflexible digit-head — as well as the catalog executive who knows nothing about programming. A formidable feat!

The typical copywriting sales clerk would head the description:

FastPak Mail — $49.95

Logical enough, because *FastPak Mail* is the name of the package. But so what? This isn't a household name like MSWord or WordPerfect or Windows. Visualize the clerk holding up the box. The standard prosaic non-description: "This is FastPak Mail. It's $49.95."

Not the salesperson. The actual catalog heading:

Fast, Simple Mail List Management — Just $49.95

The point: If you are selling something, would you sell it by naming it (selling steak) or by telling what its benefits are (selling sizzle)?

In this example, copy is mildly flawed by a nondescript subhead:

Maximize the Performance and Minimize the Cost of Everything You Mail.

If you ask, "What's wrong with that?" you aren't positioning yourself as surrogate for the typical catalog browser. This line violates *The Rule of Unprofitable Non-Descriptive Puffery*:

Puffery is never as powerful a selling weapon as factual benefit that matches the buyer.

Why does "Maximize the Performance and Minimize the Cost of Everything You Mail" violate this Rule? Here's the simple Subrule of *Unprofitable Non-Descriptive Puffery*:

When your claim has your target asking, "*How* does it do that?" you've violated The Rule of Unprofitable Non-Descriptive Puffery.

Just how does this software maximize performance? Copy quickly tells us (after another awkwardly amateurish violation in the first line of body copy — "FastPak Mail can save you money the very first time you use it"):

FastPak Mail automatically eliminates duplicates from your lists (nothing does that right out of the box, if at all), quickly handles zip-code sorting (a real money-saver), imports names from existing databases (like dBASE, for example) and allows you to perform sophisticated (and very selective) mail-merge with no problems at all. FastPak Mail allows you to print labels of virtually any shape or size, print customized envelopes. . . .

No, it isn't ideal copy. Too many parentheses — a writer trapped in a device — and "allows," a weak substitute for "enables." But this copy builds on what the product *does,* directly related to the user.

Should this description, early on, bring up the amount of memory it needs, which printers it supports, and other technical requirements? Absolutely not. Build the desire to buy. Then fill in with nonselling specifics.

A Fleur-de-Lys on every pot

Suppose you're selling a mundane item — a terra cotta pot with a Fleur-de-Lys bas-relief emblem. If you subscribe to the theory that integrity is endangered when you venture beyond unrefined description, your copy would be something like this:

FLEUR-DE-LYS POT
Made in France, this Fleur-de-Lys pot bears the emblem once used as the coat-of-arms by French kings. Made of unglazed terra cotta in buff color, the pot is 16" in diameter, 13½" high. With drainage holes.

What's missing here? Sizzle. All the writer has to do is ask: "Why would anybody want to buy this pot?" This means adding or replacing a handful of words . . . the handful separating a sales*person* from the sales *clerk* who might have written this first description. So a reasonably competent salesperson wrote this description in a recent catalog:

FLEUR-DE-LYS POT
The elegant and large Fleur-de-Lys Pot from France bears the classic flower-of-the-lily emblem once used as the coat-of-arms of French kings. Its ample size makes it an ideal container for a flowering shrub or a small evergreen tree by the front door. Made of unglazed terra cotta in the buff color typical of French clays, its 16" diameter will accommodate a 5-gallon tree or shrub. With drainage holes. 13½" high.

I said this was written by a reasonably competent salesperson. It is, in fact, the exact wording that appeared in a catalog. But "reasonably competent" isn't Meistersinger.

I'll explain.

Yes, this workmanlike copy does sell some sizzle: It explains what Fleur-de-Lys means and it gives us a reason to buy — "Its ample size makes it an ideal container for a flowering shrub or a small evergreen tree by the front door." But only dedicated gardeners will know what "5-gallon tree or shrub" means; for others, this information — which seems to cancel out the broader "flowering shrub or small evergreen tree" — would have been better-positioned adjacent to the first size reference: "The elegant and large (5-gallon size) Fleur-de-Lys Pot. . . ."

Sheets are sheets . . . except . . .

One more.

Bedsheets have enjoyed the best and endured the worst of catalog copywriting. How do you sell sheets? Too many copywriters pre-decide sheets are sheets. So their copy specifies thread count, fabric, size, and price, all of which are necessary if we're going to sell any sheets and none of which separates one set of sheets from another. If the illustration doesn't sell the sheets, the sheets don't get sold.

Compare that prosaic approach with this lovely copy for some exceptionally expensive bedsheets. Although stiff-necked, this word-portrait mixes romance and imagery into the description . . . which creates a secondary selling predicament:

> *SUMMER'S DREAM SHEETS*
> *Longer days, warm nights and sheets as cool and refreshing as a tall glass of lemonade — that is what summer dreams are made of. A satin-weave finish and 280-thread count make these 100% cotton sheets so lush, you will want to linger in bed. They are made by an old, respected German firm that puts great stock in detail. The water-color floral print bordering the cases and turn-back on the flat sheet is mitered at the corners . . .*

Why do I call this description stiff-necked? Two reasons. First, not a single contraction exists: "That is" instead of "that's"; "you will want" instead of "you'll want"; "They are made" instead of "They're made." This is formal copy. And it might reflect the image the writer intended; but it's mildly out of key with romance.

Second, the sentence "They are made by an old, respected German firm that puts great stock in detail" suggests the existence of a greater specific, unstated. We don't respond to the word "respected" on a *buying level* as much as we would to a word or group of words glorifying the label.

"Puts great stock in detail" is surprisingly blurry in this generally polished description.

Now, what's the secondary selling predicament? Lyricism has replaced extravagance. These are expensive sheets — $300 for twin-size. This copy needs reinforcements for the single upscale word "lush." For example, deeper in the copy the writer refers to "mitered corners." Better: "mitered corners, found only on the most expensive sheets."

So sizzle away!

Take a look at your own screen. Are you looking at nondescript generalizations? Do you see "one size fits all" descriptions? Are you depending on technical facts instead of benefits?

Look out. The Rule of Unprofitable Non-Descriptive Puffery can bury your copy under the brightness of a competitor whose copy actually does sizzle.

golf bags

The Original "FLIP" Bag

Individual club dividers run the full length of the bag. Additional features include: 8½" top, 6-pocket traditional cart-bag design, durable water-resistant poly-duck exterior, quick-release thickly-padded adjustable strap, heavy gauge poly liner, reinforced double stitching on top and bottom cuffs, and a fully functional rain hood that accommodates all oversize equipment.
Specify Color: Emerald, Dark Navy or Black.

No. 6276   Flip Organizer Bag $119.95

The Quazar

The high-tech Quazar pro bag has everything the modern golfer needs in a bag... and more! It's a big 9" (9½" o.d.) pro, yet lightweight at only 8¼ lbs. In addition to all the features shown, it comes with a Velcro® brand secured foam-padded rain hood with full-length zipper, and a padded bottom loading strap. Heavy-duty poly-tube construction.

No. 250   Quazar Pro $127.95
Specify Color:
Black/White/Charcoal,
Black/White/Red,
Black/White/Teal,
Black, Hunter Green.

The Quazar bag features an acrylic-lined shoe pouch with divider (shoes not included).

Black/White/Red

Black/White/Teal

Black

Hunter Green

Blk/Wht/Charcoal

Pockets & holders deluxe!
A) velour-padded, six-way club divider
B) thickly-padded carry strap
C) umbrella holder
1, 2) accessory pockets
3) clothing pocket (accessible both sides)
4) acrylic-lined jewelry pocket
5, 6) nylon net pocket w/tee slots
7, 8, 9) accessory pockets
10, 11) nylon net pocket (both sides)
12) acrylic-lined shoe pouch
13) scorecard pocket

Figure 5-1

◀ **Skins. Genuine Leather. Outrageous Quality. New 9½" Tour Staff Model**

We guarantee this bag to be the best you have ever seen or owned.

Only *Garment Quality* 2½ oz. top grain cowhide, tanned to a soft finish is used. It's aniline drum dyed so color penetrates completely. Then, it's specially treated for water and stain resistance. Fully backed with foam and material backing to give it body, this bag will stand up to years of play.

Choose from 8½" Airliner Design, or 9½" Tour Staff Model, the 3 way dividers are fully lined with synthetic shearling to protect graphite shafts. A full zippered ball pocket, full length pocket for sweaters, zippered glove pocket, and elasticized end pouch gives plenty of room for all the necessities.

Yet, for all its features, this bag is lightweight — only 5½ lbs. (9½" slightly heavier). Its thick padded shoulder strap makes carrying effortless, and it fits easily on all carts and golf cars. This is the finest bag we've seen, it's a bag you'll be proud to own.

#7339 Leather Putter Cover $15
#7341 Leather Headcovers $19
#7344 Leather Valuables Bag $28
#7345 Leather ShoeBag $39 ~~$399~~
#7436 Skins Leather Golf Bag 8½" ~~$350~~
#7347 Skins Leather Golf Bag 9½" ~~$450~~
        ~~$399~~

Protect your putter with this synthetic fur-lined leather putter cover. Oversized to fit most putters, it cushions and protects. Black only.

#7339

White
Black
Tan

The leather shoe bag protects and keeps your golf shoes from messing up the rest of your gear. The leather valuables pouch allows you to keep your personal items together in the bag, and take them with you when you go inside. Choose from colors as shown.

Black   *Tan*   *White*

Our long necked Leather Headcovers combine a leather top to protect your clubhead, and an acrylic neck to protect your shaft. Choose from colors as shown in number 1, 3, 5, or X.

Tornado Extreme Golf Bags. Packed with features that will blow you away.

Black

The Extreme Pouch Bag features a 9" top with 16 full length club dividers. Its water resistant nylon fabric is padded for style, while its solid tube construction adds stability and lets it stand on its own.

Six oversized pockets give plenty of room for accessories and apparel, while a hidden valuables pouch inside it removable for trips into the grill room.

Extra thick padded shoulder strap with heavy-duty hardware and sturdy nylon web handle makes carrying easy, while its umbrella sheath, towel clip, velcro glove attachment and bottom assist strap put all the accessories at your fingertips. Get extremely organized. With the Extreme Pouch Bag. Made in U.S.A..
#EPSB Extreme Pouch Bag ~~$119~~ *$109*

The Extreme 16 way full length divider organizes and protects your clubs.

The Extreme Tournament Bag will turn heads. Its 9" top with 16 full length club dividers organize all your clubs, and its high density polytube construction protects them. Eight pockets including a dual-access apparel pocket, tri-lobal antron pockets and 3 oversized zippered accessory pockets give over 2500 cubic inches of storage space.

Bottom assist handle makes loading easy, while its hidden umbrella cavity and storm flaps make it ready for foul weather play. Tough polyduck fabric body and lifetime bottom make this a big, strong and lightweight bag that will keep your golf game together on and off the course. Choose from colors as shown. Made in U.S.A..
#ETPS Extreme Tour Bag ~~$139~~ *$129*

Black /Red

Royal Forest

Black/Royal Black/Yellow

24

Figure 5-2

Figure 5-3

Figure 5-4

Suppose you're looking through catalogs to find a golf bag. Which of these descriptions would sell you? Figure 5-1 uses numbers to point out clinically, item by item, the advantages of this golf bag. Figure 5-2 uses a superimposed "Sale" and the semi-potent phrase "Outrageous Quality" (semi because "Outrageous" has great power and "Quality" has none), plus the eye-grabbing "Packed with features that will blow you away." Figure 5-3 is a group of no-nonsense descriptions, identification with only moderate "sell" (note the misspelling of "excellent" in the first description). Figure 5-4 is pure benefit, selling a bag many would consider a specialty item. Reading all four, which would you choose?

6

Writing Magalog Copy —
Tricky But Not Difficult

As we turn the corner into the twenty-first century, "magalogs" are surging back into direct response prominence.

And what, you ask, are magalogs? A hybrid — a catalog masquerading as a magazine. Typically, a magalog will sport a cover suggesting it's a magazine. In its pages (typically 16, 24, or 32), text usually appears on the left-hand page and advertising, for whatever was described on the left side, will appear on the right.

For years, health services and newsletters — especially those with a financial twist — have used this medium — a *"trompe l'oeil"* (fool the eye) technique.

And why would they want to fool the eye? Simple: If the recipient regards the vehicle as a *magazine* and not a *solicitation,* not only is the receptivity factor substantially enhanced, the reader, *any* reader, is more likely to accept the promotional thrust of what appears to be a third-party endorsement rather than a typical direct mail package.

Actually, the term "magalog" has become more and more a misnomer. The amalgam no longer is primarily magazine and catalog; it's magazine and direct mail . . . but we don't want to call it "magadim."

More than half the battle: Title and cover

Confusion is usually lethal in the deadly serious business of selling with words and pictures. Yet, some magalogs not only thrive on confusion, they promote it. For example, a magalog with the title *Health Breakthroughs* sells a subscription to a newsletter called *Health Confidential*.

Are some readers confused by one "Health Something" pitching another "Health Something"? Not if the magalog is structured properly (as this one is), because the sales pitch becomes the natural evolution of the text in the magalog . . . and the title of the magalog becomes inconsequential once it has served its purpose — to grab and shake the reader's interest.

The person titling the magalog has an awesome responsibility. Within its supercalendared or even enamel pages of solid text and startling illustrations, a magalog usually is *considerably* more expensive, piece for piece, than a typical direct mail package. A thin, flat, emotionless title cripples interest before the recipient even looks inside.

So the principal criterion governing magalog front covers is *The First Rule of Magalogs:*

> *Pretend this is a genuine magazine and your professional life depends on every recipient opening it to see what's inside.*

Obviously that rule includes cover-text as well as title. So from the viewpoint of sales psychology, a superior magalog has a date, an issue price (average: $6.00, which is considerably more effective than $5.95 for this purpose), and some "Wow!" teaser copy.

What constitutes "Wow" teaser copy?

"Wow!" teaser copy demands one of three lines of astonishment:

1. You could die early for no reason just because you didn't know this.

2. You could lose a lot of money, but this inside information can reverse that ghastly prospect and make you a lot of money.

3. They want to get you, to eat you alive, to take away every dime you have, to destroy your lifestyle. Here's what you can do about it.

If you think all three approaches are too harsh, you have an easy way out: Don't use a magalog. Kinder, gentler sales arguments fit quietly into conventional direct mail packages. So ask yourself before you make the initial commitment: Do I want a magalog? And if so, what content am I going to include that will force *The First Rule of Magalogs* into play?

How to Grab and Shake the Reader

Unlike typical "teaser" copy we all have used for years in book promotions ("What are the three words that can turn your lover into jelly? They're on page 142," or "Which stock defied the 1987 crash, has tripled in value since, and probably will triple again before 2004? It's named on page 230"), magalog cover teaser copy has to pay off within its own pages. So a magalog whose teaser copy teases, "How you can eliminate up to 80% of your cancer risk. (See page 10 inside)" had darned well specify on page 10 how to eliminate 80 percent of your cancer risk. This one cheats, in classic magalog fashion, by transferring the answer to the "Free Bonus Report" that accompanies a paid subscription.

Another magalog has as teaser copy on its cover:

New Herbal Remedy
Cures Poor Memory!
PAGE 6.

This one does give us a payoff: It names the over-the-counter Ginkgo Biloba as the memory-saver . . . then promises "more about this in my FREE Special Report."

A financial magalog, whose intention is conversion to a complicated mutual fund "Shareholder Association," promises on its cover:

3 super safe alternatives to low-yielding CDs and money market funds. (Page 17)

Okay, off to page 17. Here we have confusion. Yes, it's a list of three. But the first item is what *not* to do. The second is too obviously self-serving — switch into this company's municipal money market fund. The third is a genuine tip: Move into a short-term bond fund.

Logical approaches to generate maximum response

I learned long ago, when I was in the movie business: Put your best scenes in the "coming attraction" clip — the trailer, the television commercial. The philosophy of saving these for the feature film itself is flawed, because if the trailer doesn't generate a desire to see the movie, form has triumphed over substance. And invariably when that happens, somebody loses money.

So I offer three suggestions for magalog copywriting. They're based on the emotional scar-tissue that comes from bitter reality, when what the creative team thought would knock 'em dead turned out to be a loser.

Suggestion 1: If you make a promise on the cover, keep it in the text. If you say on the cover, "Vitamins that prevent heart disease, cancer, and stroke, page 13," name those vitamins on page 13.

If you don't, you not only have disappointed the reader by making a promise you didn't keep, which depresses interest and suppresses response; you've made the sale tougher by letting a deluding desire to hold back until they pay something force you into a two-step conversion.

And by the way, while you're blithely damaging your own response, you're damaging the magalog genre for the rest of us.

Suggestion 2: The cover should deal in specifics, not generalities. I'm looking at a financial magalog that has this teaser on the cover:

Inside Learn How to
• *Maximize Returns On Your Money*
• *Earn Tax-Free Income*
• *All With Full Service Advice*

Sorry, no. These bullets are about as exciting as watching the grass grow. The writer had to work to make these as nonspecific as possible. I don't care what we're selling or to whom, *The Specificity Rule* prevails:

Specifics outsell generalizations.

What's the state of mind of anyone who does in fact open this magalog? It has to be blah, because nothing has stirred the imaginative pot.

If you're under the pressure of a deadline and haven't had your daily dose of Ginkgo Biloba, just lean on a venerable can't-miss technique: Ask a question. This same magalog cover might have had . . .

• *How much investment money are you losing each month?*
• *Your neighbor isn't paying taxes on investments. Why are you?*
(The third bullet is beyond redemption.)

And include page references, please. That's how we get them inside.

Suggestion 3: When you give the answers or reveal the secrets, open the reality of a bigger universe of answers and secrets. *That's* how you get your subscriptions and investors and vitamin sales.

One qualifier: If your upward reference to that broader, still-hidden, even more profitable universe of fact and profit adds confusion, all your good words are for naught. Confusion is the lethal enemy of magalogs. And why should this happen, when you have 16 to 32 pages of exposition to blow away confusion by making your point over and over and over until it's clear to even the most obtuse reader?

Codifying the Obvious:
Forcing a Magalog to Succeed

Okay, the cover forced them inside. Cover copy promised revelations. What the reader found inside fulfilled those revelations. But that isn't the end of the magalog's function. Now salesmanship comes into play by proving to the reader that other revelations, even more surprising and more useful, are available to those who respond.

As we slide deeper and deeper into The Age of Skepticism, magalogs can be the saviors for campaigns and promotions that need an extra touch of excitement, extra proof that the reader is not being ripped off, extra leverage to generate the sale.

Just three qualifiers: 1. Specifics, please. 2. No confusion, please. 3. Information, please.

Figure 6-1

The cover of this magalog promises "Three easy ways to jump-start your immune system — and live a longer, healthier, more active life! Page 3 — inside."

"Here's what nobody else
is telling you about how to

Live a longer, healthier, more active life."

- **Sickness Is NOT Natural!** Three easy ways to jump-start your immune system —and live a longer, healthier, more active life!

- **"Old Age" Is NOT Natural!** The #1 cause of premature aging—and a simple way almost anyone can turn back the hands of time and feel years younger!

- **Drugs Are NOT Natural!** Sinister side effects of commonly-prescribed drugs. And safe, natural alternatives that are just as effective.

Dear Friend,

Forget the nonsense you've heard from the drug companies and the media ...

Sickness is NOT your natural state! And you don't need drugs and surgery to make you "better."

The truth is, your body was meant to be healthy.

It was custom-designed by God and nature to survive and thrive in the natural environment we call earth.

And it was given a miraculous immune system... with the power to prevent and reverse illness and disease.

Why, then, do so many of us become sick and old? Why do we succumb to "old age" diseases like arthritis...heart disease...stroke...and cancer?

And why do the healthiest of us often feel tired, run-down, and lacking in energy?

Figure 6-2

This is page 3 of the magalog. The "three easy ways" aren't here. In fairness to the magalog, later pages offer specifics such as cabbage juice for treating stomach problems, garlic to control cholesterol and blood pressure, chromium to treat blood sugar imbalances, and other tips. But not keeping the first promise damages the possibility of a read-through.

7

Structuring Catalogs
for the Internet

This chapter and the next discuss the marketing phenomenon of the twenty-first century — the Internet.

An explanation of sequence is in order: chapters 5 and 6 dealt with catalogs; so logical progression calls for "Catalogs on the Internet" to follow, even though the discussion of Internet marketing *in general* is covered in chapter 8.

So, if your interest is solely in catalogs, this chapter will suffice. If your interest is in the Internet and its marketing offspring, the World Wide Web, absorbing both chapters is in order.

Rough surf

If you were an early 1980s modem-user, you have to be mildly bemused. When the speed increased from 300 bps (baud per second) to 1200, then 2400, you marveled, "Incredible!" Then it went up to 9600 baud. Double incredible! Then 14,400 baud. Triple incredible, with the exclamation point perishing through incredibility-overload. 28,800 . . . 33,600 . . . 57,600 . . . ISDN . . . now, we need superspeed or we wait seemingly forever to see what's being pitched. A lot of people — and I mean *a lot* — don't wait. They go elsewhere.

So the key rule of catalogs on the Internet is: *Have **something** download fast.*

What happens with catalogs is what happens with automobile expressways. As traffic grows, we add lanes. Additional traffic appears, to clog those additional lanes. It's an endless circle. When the typical computer had a 14,400 bps modem, smart catalogers tailored their home pages to that speed: few illustrations, not much color. The page could download quickly.

As modem speed increased, basic concern about downloading time faded. Picture, color, increasing use of motion and sound — all became more complex. In many cases, slow download remains a problem, not because modems aren't faster but because images are geared to the fastest speeds.

You aren't computer-literate? Tough!

The revolving-door syndrome has caused some catalogs to drop off the Web — "We aren't making any money" — as others establish Web sites.

A problem catalogers quickly recognize when they're mailing catalogs seems to be a blind spot on the Web. The company that chooses mailing lists with exquisite care, trying to reach only those who can and will buy their specific merchandise, might blindly establish a "Here we are, come see us" Web site . . . then wonder why nobody comes to their party.

Finding and buying from sites on the Web isn't as simple a proposition as leafing through a printed catalog. Oh, yes, it can be more rewarding, *if the marketer gives the online visitor the option of greater depth of information.* But it also can be frustrating, if availability is poor, if links aren't fast, and if the online catalog is simply a slower-to-absorb version of the printed catalog.

The move to a point at which Internet catalogs can be, to hybridize a computer term, more reader-friendly than their printed siblings is a logical anticipation. More exciting is the Internet as the best and easiest way to establish an international marketplace. From the Wright Brothers to the 777 aircraft required a span of 92 years. Certainly catalogs on the Web are moving faster than that.

Why miss the Web's unique opportunity?

A coffee company ignored a problem. One proper Internet use not only would have solved this problem, but would have given this medium a unique edge. This was one of the company's Internet product descriptions:

THE BETTER BLADE GRINDER
Our exclusive blade grinder grinds evenly with its unique sloped chamber that spins beans throughout the chamber, resulting in a uniform grind.
Applicable sales tax will automatically be added to your order.
SKU #111186
$19.95

What was the problem, aside from using variations of the word "grind" three times in one sentence? One of being able to show the item properly. The "sloped chamber" remains a mystery. So does the size of the item. So does the whole concept of "blade grinder," which might have a science-fiction overtone to those who don't know the terminology.

This marketer missed an opportunity to exploit the unique benefit the Web offers a cataloger — the ability to lead the possible buyer into as much product-depth as might be wanted.

Can conventional print copy work on the Web?

Sure, a cataloger can transfer print copy "whole" onto a Web site . . . if the copy is Web material to start with.

For example, a well-known catalog of kitchen items accompanies a big, colorful picture with this text:

No more soggy foods or messy spatters!
Imagine roasts, chops, chicken, and stir fries moist and juicy on the inside, yet crispy and browned to perfection on the outside. The secret? The unique cone-shaped glass cover trimmed with stainless steel traps condensation . . . keeps food from becoming soggy. Sauteed foods brown to perfection with minimal fat, while the stove top stays clean. Fits most standard cookware 9½" to 11" in diameter. Stovetop, oven and dishwasher safe. Made in Germany.

Brilliant copy? Naw. It's workmanlike copy, which often pulls better than brilliant copy. The picture shows the cover, and all is well. Here we have a photo/copy matchup that fits any medium. So special Web treatment isn't necessary. (I do object to the read-through: The typical reader scans together "trimmed with stainless steel traps.")

The omnipresent First Rule

What's your opinion of this, the total copy on a catalog's Internet home page?

> ### Into the Wind Kite Catalog
> *Choose from over 200 of the world's finest kites, from radical hi-tech sports kites to traditional lazy-day-in-the-meadow kites, plus boomerangs, flying toys, windsocks, and kitemaking supplies. Fast, friendly service with your sky-high satisfaction guaranteed. (Only available in the United States.)*

Yeah, that's my opinion too. This cataloger is unaware of the First Rule of Internet Advertising (an extensive explanation of this Rule appears in *Selling on the Net,* co-authored with Robert Lewis):

> *Stop the surfer in his or her tracks.*

Where's the stopper here? ". . . the world's finest kites" is as standard a cliché as any catalog copywriter could unearth. Nuggets are here, left buried in the soil. What *is* a "hi-tech sport kite"? Leading with even a nominal description would save the page.

(I never did get to find out what the hi-tech sports kites might be, because the only "link" on this page is "Send Free Catalog." So, really, this is more a banner than a home page . . . which makes the not-so-stirring copy even more derelict.)

A catalog such as *Lands' End* has an automatic advantage in the Internet ambience: The company's print catalog copy already is breezy, matching the biggest group of netsurfers. Converting those surfers to visitors and then to buyers isn't as difficult as it is for more sedate catalogs which have to decide: Should we adapt our image to the "Gotta go! Gotta go!" mentality of the skimmer-surfer?

This catalog home page has a cleverly-worded legend (spot the cleverness):

> *Where in the world can you find first-quality classic clothing and soft luggage at Direct Merchant prices?*

What's clever is the "Direct Merchant" reference which somehow suggests discount without saying so. The page has two links: "Out our way" and "The Goods."

"Out our way" becomes the real home page, and that's another clever touch. The spartan first home page downloads in a flash, a spur to moving along. This second page is loaded with links. Click on "Women's Casual," then "Sleepwear," and this site delivers a single item: "Women's Sleep T." Here I disagree with whoever set up this page, because opposite the photograph is the price "From $18.00." Uh-uh. Far down the page (actually on another page if one prints it out) is the explanation of "from" — short-sleeved T-shirts are $18.00, long-sleeved T-shirts are $22.00. The photo shows the short-sleeved T-shirt, which indicates how easy it would have been to dump "From $18.00" — not an effective Web pricing ploy — and replace it with "Short-sleeved as shown, $18.00 . . . also available in long-sleeved model, $22.00."

I'm picking nits here; but, as the Web matures and copywriters adapt their craft to the medium, nit-picking will be more common than finding huge mistakes.

Make a deal.

Ignoring the obvious physical contrast, analyze the differences between a mailed catalog and a Web catalog.

A mailed catalog, even to an existing customer, is *intrusive*. The sender performs an active role; the recipient is a passive recipient. Interaction comes when the recipient decides to contact the sender.

On the Web, the roles are equal. The customer comes looking for you. That's the beginning of an *interactive* relationship. And it's why flat descriptive copy, lifted whole from the pages of a printed catalog, often doesn't compete with dynamic Web-sensitive copy that strengthens the fragile thread connecting visitor and site.

So even though no cataloger can be sure of competitive victory, as the Web stands at the turn of the century a sound philosophy is: Make a deal. Have the visitor feel he or she is rewarded for having tapped and clicked and paid for the time.

That means special offers, limited to Web visitors . . . which in turn means you can't lift all your copy in one piece from the printed catalog, even if the catalog also offers special deals.

And that in turn means . . .

Change that offer! Capture that name!

I'm shaking my head in bewilderment at the number of catalog sites that leave timely messages on the screen *months* after the event has passed. A fashion catalog still has Christmas offers in March. A candy catalog and a flower catalog have Valentine's Day specials in April. A computer catalog pitches Father's Day, and it's close to Labor Day.

How many surfers will re-visit those sites? Letting a site go unchanged for a lengthy period of time is a game of Russian Roulette, and you're gonna lose. Far better is to have a single item — a "Daily Special" — to entice the visitor back, over and over again.

And to let a visitor escape without capturing his or her name is criminal. Offer a monthly prize and visitors will register. Award the prize, publish the winner's name to validate your offer, and award discount coupons to the runners-up. Meanwhile, you have names. But just asking for a name, even an online name, without offering something in return is both arrogant and foolhardy.

A parenthetical comment: The Internet is international. If you want business from other countries, include a box on your home page enabling the passerby to choose a country . . . and if at all possible have text in that country's language. The results not only will far outweigh the cost of translations; international customers often display a loyalty factor unknown within the United States.

Nail 'em. THEN get lavish with words.

The Internet has a huge advantage in its ability to offer options. Suppose you're selling gardening equipment. Once the visitor has clicked on Garden Tractors, you can offer page after page after page, each one with a link to an order form. The visitor can glut himself or herself with descriptive fact or read just enough to convince him or her to go directly to the order form or back to the home page. What an edge over printed catalogs!

If you haven't yet concluded that the Web's characteristics differ from other media and require a distinct copy philosophy, spend more time looking at what other catalogers are doing.

The days when the medium is also the message are waning. To those catalogers who are abandoning the Net even as replacements are pouring in, three questions hang in the air:

1. Did you really use the Web with recognition of what it is?
2. Did surfers/visitors have an easy time finding you, and, once they did, did your home page set up fast?
3. Did you offer them a deal and change it often?

Chances are, if the answer to any of these three questions is "No," this cataloger might have had better luck with messages tailored to this still amazing, grotesquely overblown, overhyped, super-competitive, frustrating, still evolving marketplace.

So catalogers can draw the conclusion that best fits . . . any of three conclusions, surveying their own Web sites (or plans for Web sites) and those of other catalog companies:

1. What nonsense — it's all hype and no sales.
2. This is a niche medium and I'd better start talking to printers again.
3. What a bonanza!

Exhilarating . . . and frustrating: A personal odyssey through some typical Web sites.

> *Note, please: There's no point in trying to duplicate this next adventure in Web-surfing, because obviously so much time has passed that whatever I found won't be there now. Instead of following my footsteps and missteps, if you're a serious cataloger, spend time on the Internet every day . . . not in chat-rooms, but scouting competitors' Web sites, deciding what you'd have done differently if they were your sites.*

If you take an electronic spin around the Web you're bound to absorb a curious mixture of exhilaration and frustration.

An example of frustration is a catalog called *Attitudes*. As early as 1996, one of the catalog industry reports said this catalog has abandoned print media and hereafter will maintain a Web presence as its means of marketing.

This catalog's own copy said it features "unique gifts, home decor, personal care items, electronics, and kitchen essentials." Assuming the usual fragment of online surfers hits the site, how much business can it hope to transact?

To generate a reasonably informed opinion, I clicked on "Come see Attitudes Online Now!" and got the unsurprising message:

Can't Access Document: http://www.attitudes.com/

I did access an "Attitudes" . . . a place in Anniston, Alabama, featuring "Sculptured Nails by Ruby Goldfinger." Any port in a storm. The Web also has an *Attila Attitudes,* but I'm afraid of it.

So, the typical surfer concludes, a plague on all their houses. Not soon will the surfer try this excursion again. But beyond that, someone not of our world will draw a cosmic conclusion about catalog Web sites altogether. We're all injured by shrapnel from the fallout.

In fairness to *Attitudes*: Some months later I did get into the site. The results are figures 7-1 to 7-6 at the end of this chapter. Download was painfully slow and the "Product of the Month" failed to parse. Unquestionably, considerable professionalism went into the site, but — and qualify this as opinion rather than fact — too much attention to technique and too little attention to salesmanship has to cost this company, or *any* company, some business.

Catalogers spend a ton of money finding and massaging lists of potential buyers. The Web is a happy adjunct. A primary medium? As Web sites proliferate, the Web seems to be a primary medium only for those catalogs whose product-mix match the medium. That's logical enough.

How much does a Web catalog have to spend in conventional media, advertising its site, to generate traffic? The laws of economics are stringent and brutal.

As an experiment, I clicked on the next listing after *Attitudes* in the Yahoo search engine — the *Cyber Bath Catalogue.* This home page downloaded with acceptable speed, and although the text wasn't exciting it offered a tantalizing link: "Featured product of the month."

I clicked on this and got: Zoe Washlet Bidet, an item which converts a conventional toilet into a bidet. This page had a small picture, but no price. To find out how much it costs, I had to click on yet another link. Okay, two versions, one $495 and the other, heated, $535. Copy? The $495 model had four short bullets, the $535 model five short bullets.

Now, here's my point: In a printed catalog, spartan copy can succeed because of the ambience. On the Web, each page needs its own dose of romance, or at least a clear link to a dose of romance for those who want that link. So my point is: *Think of where you are and who is skimming past.*

Magellan's voyage: How much does a passenger pay?

One of my printed catalog favorites is Magellan. I decided to visit that company's Web site.

On the home page is an icon with the wording, "Click Here If You

Need A Vacation." Good: See the difference between this and bland, no-meat descriptions? Bad: Capitalizing each word unmasks the message as advertese.

The link, it turned out, is a weak one — a Maine resort called The Bradley Inn, described poetically, but with no specifics. So much for my hopes.

Back to the home page, clicking on "Products."

Uh-oh. The top of the product page says, "Magellan Product Summaries." That's as unsalesmanlike as one can be. Surfers don't want a summary; they want to be sold.

I just don't get it. Here are products — some I'd actually like to have — but no prices. Is this a Web conspiracy?

But what if it isn't their fault?

So what, if it isn't their fault.

The technical difference between print and electronic media is stupendous. We can attend a press start-up and tell the pressman, "Pump some more red into this." We mail our catalogs and start lighting candles once they're in the hands of the post office.

With the Web, a glitch can be anybody's fault. Maybe the *Cyber Bath Catalogue* is blameless. Maybe *Magellan* is blameless. Maybe I hit them just as their server died or was overloaded or blew a fuse and couldn't deliver the proper pages. Maybe a more direct way into actual *selling* pages exists but wasn't publicized.

Hold it! That last one is a potential killer. Unless one knows absolutely what a company's URL ("Uniform Resource Locator," or, more simply, on-line address) is, the generic route is the only way to go: "Catalogs." And that means exposure to competitors as well as our sought-after online catalog.

A modest proposal

Think this through: The competitive ambience increases geometrically, not arithmetically, because if we're looking for hiking shoes or electric toothbrushes or vitamins our search engine easily can give us 20,000 sources . . . only one of which is the one we started out to see.

But worse: We can be derailed along the way by a siren song we hadn't expected. A cunning competitor may have the word "sex" in a link. Another might use "free." A third might say, "Lucky you: Everything listed here half off, this week only" . . . and actually show the prices. Farewell, original target.

Two tendencies aren't coincidental. One is catalogers dropping off the

Web. The other is a growing suspicion among catalogers that turning this medium over to the techies may not have been such a good idea after all. Those two circumstances may be linked.

My modest proposal, for all catalogers who either are on the Web, alternately preening over having a site and wondering where the orders are . . . and those thinking, "We'd better get a Web site going, because our competitor has one":

Think like a *marketer,* not a technician. If technical expertise could outsell intelligent marketing, no catalog printed in fewer than six colors on less than 100-pound stock with less than 200-line screens could exist; and the automobile beginner-salesperson who knows how many ccs are in the engine and what the gear ratios are could outsell the old pro who says, "Settle in behind the wheel and take her for a spin."

It's as simple as this: If you're a cataloger who would rather announce than sell, other web marketers will pass you on the far turn.

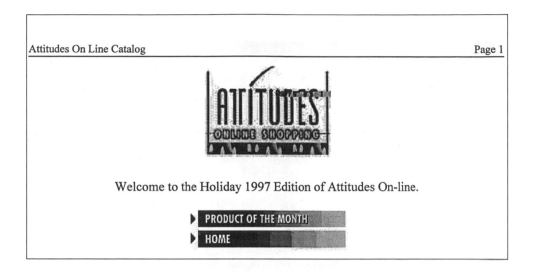

Figure 7-1

Type the URL (uniform resource locator, or address) of this online catalog. The site offers two links — the Product of the Month (an excellent marketing concept) and "Home." We click on "Product of the Month" and get the screen shown in Figure 7-2.

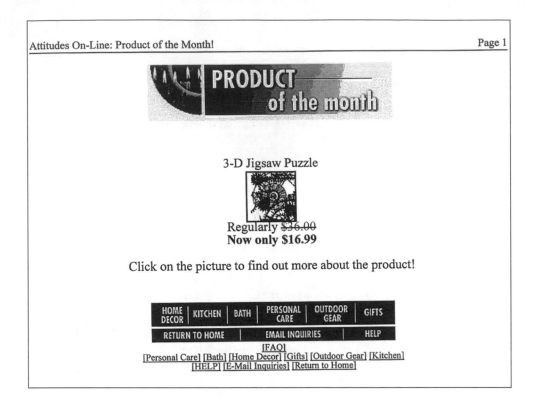

Figure 7-2

The "Product of the Month" is a 3-D Jigsaw Puzzle. Text invites us to click on the picture for more details. We do and get the screen shown in Figure 7-3.

FAILED TO PARSE HTTP

Your request does not appear to be properly formed

Figure 7-3

"FAILED TO PARSE HTTP" means nothing to the typical Web surfer other than an electronic glitch beyond his or her control. "Your request does not appear to be properly formed" cannot apply to the surfer, who simply has clicked on the picture as suggested by the site. Most surfers would leave; in this instance, we return to the main screen and click on "Home," getting the screen shown in Figure 7-4.

Figure 7-4

The online catalog wisely caters to the surfer's equipment and time availability, offering three options. We choose the first and get the screen shown in Figure 7-5.

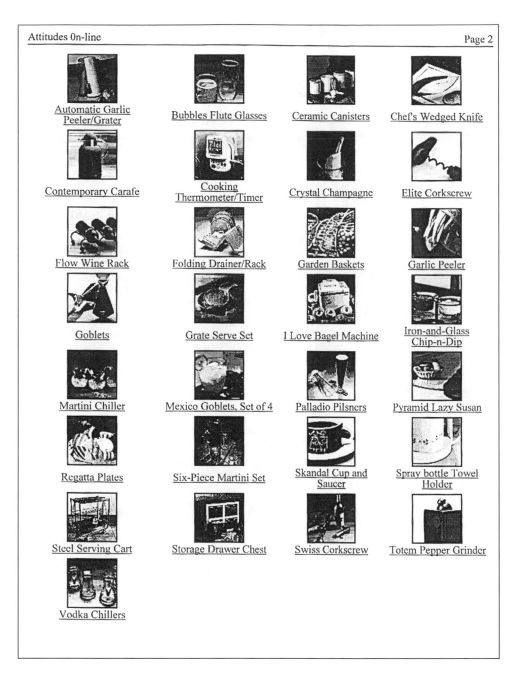

Figure 7-5

Even with a fast modem, this page is a slow download. Compensating is a wide variety of products shown on the same page, a definite plus for a Web catalog. We click on "Automatic Garlic Peeler/Grater" and get the screen shown in Figure 7-6.

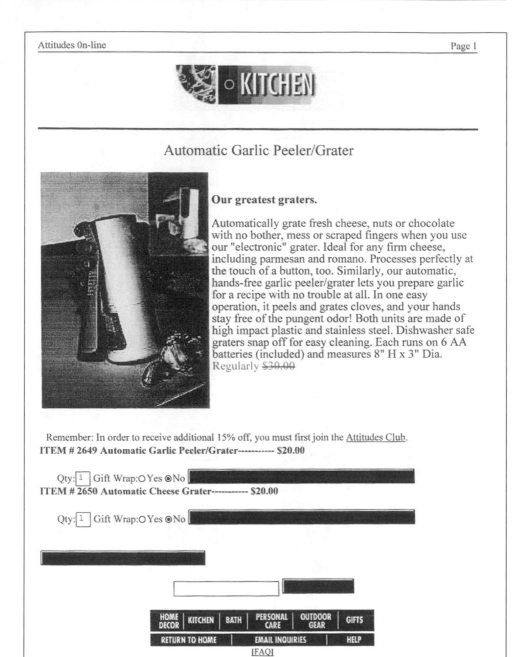

Figure 7-6

Ultimately we have a well-written description that parallels a printed catalog. One apparent misstep: Text says, "Remember: In order to receive additional 15% off, you must first join the <u>Attitudes Club</u>." No link to that
option exists on this page.

8

Advertising on the Internet (Including *The Three Great Rules of Web Site Attraction*)

W hat's new since we last looked at rules for Internet marketing . . . about twenty minutes ago?

Any analysis of Internet progress — or backsliding — reaches obsolescence between the time it's written and the time it appears in print. Add this comment on the "Internet Rush Effect" . . . and the obvious but ignored "Great Rules of Web site Attraction" . . . to the stack.

Printed reports that tell you nothing much changes on the Web, not only from year to year but from month to month, are subject to serious misinterpretation.

The number of magazines dedicated to the Internet is stupefying. Books of Web site listings, obsolete the day they hit the bookstalls, are pouring out of publishers' offices. New web languages, new transmission procedures, new search engines and malls and security devices, and and and and . . . to anyone unaccustomed to the "Internet Rush Effect" these seem phenomenal. To those who follow this phenomenon the way an astronomer follows a comet, it isn't phenomenal at all. It's business as usual . . . or as usual as any procedure can be in a rocketing speculator's paradise that defies the usual.

Careful when evaluating research!

Research, too, is obsolete almost as it appears. If not obsolete, it can be loaded with red flags. For example, in late 1997 MBInteractive conducted a study for the Internet Advertising Bureau. The results couldn't have thrilled the study's sponsor: Exposure to Web banner advertising was shown to be responsible for 96 percent of ad awareness; click-throughs from those banners to actual Web sites were responsible for a minuscule 4 percent of ad awareness.

So research says banners are effective and Web sites aren't effective, right?

Stop, please, and reconsider what we're discussing in this book: advertising *and marketing*. If you want to unscramble that egg, then swallow those results whole. If you want to use the Internet profitably, consider carefully what the study measured — ad *awareness,* not ad *effectiveness*.

Much research exists. As a standard *raison d'être,* a great many Internet publications either sponsor or conduct research programs. But are they really research, when the results are "projections" . . . actually, guesses masquerading as *forecasts*? If that's the case, Nostradamus was a researcher.

Nonetheless, forecasts are fascinating because they give us a look into the unknown. And in the case of Internet forecasting, the unknown may well be science-fiction.

Let's look at some forecasts:

A clever way of overstating Internet size is combining the *Inter*net with *Intra*nets. It parallels adding lead weights to your pockets so you'll qualify for a heavyweight event.

Intranets use the same technology as the Internet, but they aren't a genuine go-for-the-customer marketing medium. They're intramural. The Internet has a horizontal reach; Intranets have a vertical reach. Combining the two is about as realistic as my winning my club's tennis tournament and being listed with the Wimbledon and U.S. Open winners under a blanket category, "Tournament Winners."

Adding additional confusion is a newer term, "Extranet," which refers to an Intranet extended to include outsiders, making it more parallel to the Internet. Huh?

One publication's published research tells us that Internet/Intranet market size was more than $35 billion in 1996; exceeded $53 billion in 1997; and projects to be $100 billion by the year 2000. Those are big numbers. Should we believe them? And if we do believe them, are they of any value in our own marketing programs?

Here's how statistics can skew your conclusions in the wrong direction: A respected and usually accurate report told us in 1997 that by the end of 1996 the World Wide Web had 23 million users (total worldwide, not just the U.S.). The projection: 152 million users in the year 2000. If those 23 million existing users were spending $35 billion on the Web, that's more than $1500 per user . . . and this just wasn't so. As of the publication of this book, more than half the people hooked up to the Web spend zero in purchases through the medium. In fact, that same report said about 46 percent use the Web for shopping. Some 58 percent have initiated a shopping experience at least once; for many, that was it . . . either because of unsatisfactory pricing, poor service, disillusionment with the medium as a bazaar, or simply the result of having shopped once because of the novelty value.

One major success story: Dell Computer, the darling of Wall Street, also was the first darling of the Internet. Even as early as mid-1997 this company was reportedly grossing more than $1 million a month from the Web; later in the year the reported number was $500,000 a week. Those numbers are impressive and significant for Web revenues, but they're peanuts compared with Dell's other direct marketing outlets. And everyone knew Amazon Books as a remarkably successful stock offering, although the company's profit picture is murky.

One surprising note, a huge change from the Internet's earliest days: The biggest percentage of Internet shoppers is the 51-plus age group; the lowest is the 19 to 25 age group. (It's surprising because the Web has geared itself to the youth market. The average age of Web users dropped, between 1995 and 1996, from 35 to 33.)

A more sobering statistic: In 1998, only two of five U.S. households had a computer, let alone a modem and online hookup.

The very existence of a statistic reminds us of two Internet shortcomings compared with other types of direct marketing: a) You can't select your targets; b) You can't reach all your targets. The shortcoming is only on a comparative level and in itself is no reason to bypass the Web. It is, rather, a reminder that no medium — however glamorous — can claim universal dominance.

Suppose, as estimated, we have more than 150 million Web users in the year 2000. Will the ratio of surfers to buyers, of e-mail users and chatroom visitors to customers, have increased? Or might it actually have dropped, as the novelty of the medium wears off?

No problem, because unquestionably the total of Web shopping volume will increase. But so will the number of Web sites, making this medium a Murderer's Row of businesses clamoring for attention like a batch of new hatchlings in a nest.

Example: A meeting planning researcher entered the word "hotels" in a search engine. The search engine listed more than 300,000 Web addresses. Assuming somebody wants to go through the list and can check one site per minute — impossible because of downloading tempo — in 5,000 hours he or she would have hit them all. In full-time 40-hour weeks, that's 2½ years . . . by which time many of those sites will have disappeared, many others will have arrived, and all will have become obsolete.

So it's apparent that for the foreseeable future, attracting *new* surfer-visitors to your site means spending money in other media promoting the site. Are those dollars better spent selling your products or services? Not necessarily. If you can convert surfer to visitor, then visitor to customer, then customer to (the Kingdom of Heaven!) a regular who bookmarks your site or lists it under "Favorite Places," the medium springs to life.

How about advertising revenues on the Internet? Now, *there's* explosive growth! But a study by Coopers & Lybrand, released in early 1997, indicated that 200 sites represented virtually every site grossing $5,000 or more in advertising revenue. Uh-oh. Danger ahead: With millions of Web sites, and 10,000 new sites pouring into the Internet every month, it may be a long time (if ever) before some of these sites become commercially viable. More on that later.

Do you see an indicator?

Do you see any *positive* significance in 300,000 entries under "Hotels"?

You can link that number to a company called Lexis-Nexis, located in Miamisburg, Ohio. Lexis-Nexis is a commercial company, possibly the world's biggest repository of business data. The database contains well over a billion documents, and the entire pile is available on the World Wide Web.

Where else could an individual have access to more than a billion documents (some of which are *many* pages)? More to the point: Where else, by electronic culling, could an individual bypass irrelevant documents, zeroing in on the relevant ones?

The Internet finds its positioning in its ability to provide *depth*. Thus, space ads quite regularly advertise: "For more information, visit our Web site."

And what's on that Web site? Far, far more information than is practical in a space ad. The ad becomes the first half of a two-step conversion; the Web becomes the second half.

Actually, not quite . . . because the Web hasn't proved itself to be a powerful transaction closer. *That's* the challenge for the first decade of the twenty-first century.

Who Are These People?

Who's surfing the Web? In 1998, males, mostly — ⅔ to ⅓. That was changing fast. Even two years prior, in 1996, the ratio was ⅘ to ⅕. Jupiter Communications predicted that by the year 2000 women would represent 46.5 percent of online users.

Average household income for Web surfers was seen to be dropping. U.S. dominance was declining — a natural effect as computer users in other countries were able to effect online connections.

The surfer/visitor gap

The gap between Web *surfer* and specific Web site *visitor* gets wider and wider. I opine — and opinions are as valid as facts as an egg hatches — as novelty wears off, a lot of sites will wither or be left to rot. We already see "abandoned" Web sites sitting within the clutter like untended graves, or old satellites now regarded not as technological miracles but as space junk.

A controversial magazine, *Out*, killed its Web site after two years of waiting for it to pay off. The publisher, Henry Scott, said the site was losing $50,000 to $100,000 each year and had "no hope of profitability." His dire comment, as quoted in *Advertising Age*: "I thought I needed to have it for advertisers who wanted that, but advertisers *aren't* clamoring to get on the Web. We have to beat them up to get on the Web."

The Great Rules of Web Site Attraction

Reigning paramount over every other procedure that can bring action to a Web site is a rule that, even in the first decade of Web awareness, has become venerable: *Stop the surfer in his or her tracks.* Why more Internet marketers don't observe this rule is a genuine mystery. The only possible explanation is that because of infatuation with the medium *as a medium* they lose their analytical abilities. The effect had better be temporary!

For once, critics seem to recognize what practitioners don't recognize. The truism that Web sites enable smaller companies to compete on equal terms with corporate giants isn't a solution; it's one corner of the foundation of a building.

Oh, anyone who surfs the Web can point out million-dollar Web sites that don't have the pulling power of sites costing less than $10,000. Now: Analyze that last statement. If you think it validates the platitude that small sites can compete with big ones, you're still standing on one leg. The point to be drawn is The First Great Rule of Web site Attraction:

Announcements cannot compete with salesmanship.

And The Second Great Rule of Web site Attraction:

Technical expertise cannot compete with salesmanship.

So the days of "We ought to be on the Web because our competitors are on the Web" and "Nothing to it — let's list our items the way we do in our brochures and catalogs" had better go into eclipse or the Web will see wholesale defections.

And a warning to webmasters: (I hate the word "webmaster." It sounds like an evil ruler of the planet Mongo.) Learn the lesson direct marketers learned generations ago. Quit thinking in terms of "flash" and electronic tricks and start thinking of ways to grab and shake surfers who land on your site. Subscribe, instead, to The Third Great Rule of Web site Attraction:

Gadgetry cannot compete with salesmanship.

I doubt webmasters will pay much attention to this Third Great Rule. After all, the proper business objective of a Web site, to attract and hold the surfer, isn't their own business objective. Theirs is to create samples they can show to other potential clients.

Ho hum. Where have we witnessed that attitude before?

(For a more complete exposition on Internet marketing, two books by this author exist: *Selling on the Net,* co-authored with Robert Lewis; and *Cybertalk That Sells,* co-authored with Jamie Murphy.)

Subj: 24 Year Old Finds Secret....
Date: 11-23 06:58:53 EST
From: 71992639@hotmail.com
Reply-to: OpportunityKnocksX@juno.com
To: YourSuccess@aol.com

Learn How A 24 Year Old Man $44,500 In Debt Found the Secret To Filling Your Mailbox with Up To $350 Per Day in Cash Orders!

And He Says to You...
"It's Your Turn Now!"

Learn How To:
* Fill Your Mailbox Daily With Cash Orders!
* Begin a Home Business With Little Or NO Money!
* Use Electronic Marketing Tools To Do Your Selling For You!
* Write Killer Advertising Salesletters, Fax-On-Demands, & More!
* Backend Your Sales For A Long-term Residual Income!
* Build a Business Without Any Personal Selling Required!
* Succeed in Absolutely Any Network Marketing Company!
* Place Thousands of Ads For Little Or No Cost!
* Have 100s of Presentations Being Done For You Automatically
AND MORE!

Fully Explained in An Easy To Understand Sixty-Two Page Step-By-Step Instruction Manual!
This is the One & Only "No Personal Selling" Marketing Concept of It's Kind in the World!

TWO OUTRAGEOUS FREE BONUSES FOR ORDERING WITHIN FIVE DAYS!
10 Mail order How-To Reports With Full Reprint Rights: Including Titles Like...
How To Receive Orders in Your Mailbox 365 Days a Year
A Dozen And One Ways to Reduce Your Postage
20 Major Reasons Why Your Mail Order Business Could Fail
How To Write Irresistable Ad Copy
And More...

Free Dealership To This Manual And A Chance To Fill Your Mailbox With Orders While You Keep Most of the Money!

FULL MONEY BACK GUARANTEE
So, If You Would Like To Take Advantage of Our 30 Day Money Back Guarantee and Receive Both of the Outrageous Free Bonuses that Come Along with this step-by-step 62 page secret manual "It's Your Turn Now", order today!

We Can Accept Checks, Money Orders, VISA, Mastercard, American Express, or Discover!

FOR FASTER DELIVERY CALL OUR 24 HOUR TOLL FREE CREDIT CARD ORDER

Sunday November 23 America Online: HGLEWIS1 Page: 1

Figure 8-1a

LINE: 1-888-820-1731

NOTE: We Will only ship to the Address registered on the credit card so make sure that the correct address is filled out below.

Mail to:
Page Financial Systems
P.O. Box 8072
Richmond, IN 47374

-- --

Name:_____

Address:_____

City/State/Zip:_____

Phone #: _____
(For Problems with Your Order Only, No Saleman will call)

Email Address:_____

[ ] **YES!** I want to set my network marketing business on autopilot. Please send me this Network Marketing Course to explode my bottom line!

[ ] **DOUBLE YES!** I am ordering within 5 days! Please include the extra special bonuses!

Check Payment Type Enclosed:
[ ] Check for $35.00 made out to Page Financial Systems
[ ] Money order for $35 made out to Page Financial Systems
[ ] Visa [ ] Mastercard [ ] American Express or [ ] Discover

(Please Fill Out Below Section and Make sure that the above name and address are listed as it appears on the card) for $35.00

Credit Card Number:_____

Expiration Date:_____

Signature:_____

Date:_____

Note - If ordering outside continental US, please add $5 to S&H to any of above options!

Need more information?
Call our Fax-On-Demand at 1-757-480-4743 Doc# 607

to be removed
click here

Sunday November 23   America Online: HGLEWIS1   Page: 2

Figure 8-1b

E-mail messages have become a separate marketing medium. Controversial and attacked by search engines, e-mail messages have an advantage: A bulk campaign can be mounted quickly, and results can be tabulated within two days. (See Figure 8-2.)

Subj: STARTING A HOME BUSINESS?
Date: 11-23 11:12:53 EST
From: 61676073@AOL.COM
Reply-to: nreach4u@AOL.COM
To: AFRIEND@PUBLIC.COM

500,000 E-MAIL ADDRESSES
ONLY $40.00

How would you let to build your business on the internet exchange? Millions of Home Based Businesses are networking their way to the top. My method of building you business is **100% true.** A business is built with your efforts and hard work that you put into it. It's like a bank account, you cannot take out what you do not put in. As you may or may not know the world is being run through the art of technology.

E-mailing has become the most sophisticated way for advertisement. There are over 100 million e-mail addresses through the internet exchange. In order to sell your products, they have to be advertised. And in order for you to buy them, they have to be advertised. You always need customers. What better way to find customers that you need? Through e-mailing. What faster way to send **Ads, Letters** and **Flyers** to millions of people? Through e-mailing. Facts have proven that businesses who advertise are more likely to succeed than the ones that do not advertise. E-mailing lets you advertise your products to millions with just the push of a button.

Everyone is afraid of taking a chance, even myself. Sometimes you may wonder why some businesses are successful and some are not. The reason is that those were the businesses that took a chance. Advertising is a Billion Dollar Industry, and for only *$40.00* you can get a piece of the pie.

I am offering 500,000 E-mail Addresses for the low price of *$40.00* along with The Mass Mailer Demo that will let you send out your purchase order, *GUARANTEED.* And this does not require any special software. I believe that you must beat your competitors and give your customers **100% satisfaction.** If not, you lose them. I have over 65 million addresses, including yours.(*All Current Listings*). You might be wondering how could this be for real.

TITLE 18 SECTIONS 1302 AND 1341 SPECIFICALLY STATES: PRODUCTS OR SERVICES MUST BE EXCHANGED FOR MONEY RECEIVED. You are also sending to an address, not to a P.O. Box. And Checks or Money Orders are made Payable to a **name** not a company.

This is a one time offer and there is *no need to reply remove.* However, if this offer is for you please use it to your advantage. **Order now and save.** Make CHECK or MONEY ORDER payable to: ALLAN PLOWDEN
6135 N.W. 186TH ST. SUITE 109 MIAMI, FLORIDA 33015

For faster service Please send Money Orders Only!!! **All Products will be send via e-mail, so please include your e-mail address so you can receive you products promptly. If you would like to receive your order on diskettes, please send $4.50 extra for postage and handling.**
THANK YOU FOR YOUR SERVICES.

———————————— Headers ————————————
Return-Path: <61676073@AOL.COM>
Received: from relay14.mail.aol.com (relay14.mail.aol.com [172.31.109.14]) by air18.mail.aol.com (v36.0) with SMTP; Sun,
23 Nov   11:12:53 -0500
Received: from hungary.it.earthlink.net (hungary-c.it.earthlink.net [204.119.177.64])

Sunday November 23   America Online: HGLEWIS1   Page: 1

Figure 8-2

This e-mail sells e-mail — 500,000 addresses for $40. On a cost-per-thousand basis, it's fractional compared with standard media rates. If response is even slightly better than fractional, e-mail offers the benefit of requiring no production, no videotaping sessions, no printing nor postage. Worth checking out? Why not, as long as the advertiser remembers: As is true of all media, if it were a superb buy more major marketers would be using it.

Figure 8-3

This is the home page for Pathfinder, the Time-Warner search engine. Note the links to Time-Warner publications and also, at the bottom, a small Iomega banner.

9

Making Small-Space Ads Pay

Can Small-Space Ads Pull?
Sure, They Can . . .
If They Observe Three Rules.

Space ads aren't a sure-fire source of dollar-producing response. One reason is a misunderstanding of what the reader expects to see in a space ad. When the space ad is tiny, problems are compounded — but not insurmountable. By observing three Rules, you can produce a tiny ad that outpulls a big one.

I'm looking at a one-inch space ad in *The New Yorker*, a magazine often called the most sophisticated publication in America.

This is the ad, in its entirety:

The Kindly Chair
—Discreet, portable, battery powered, highly maneuverable
—Not a wheelchair; not a motorized cart
—Enjoy increased mobility while seated
Call Roamer Technologies 800-544-8566

Okay, let's suppose you're skimming through *The New Yorker* and you see this ad. Somebody in your family has a disability and doesn't walk well. Would you respond to this ad?

"I might" means "no."

It's an unfair question, I know, because your "Yes, I might" would be out of context: You'd respond if this is the *sole* ad you've seen, but in that circumstance you probably would have been exposed to — or aggressively sought out — other sources.

You have to rate the word "might" as a *negative* . . . if only because of The First Rule of Small-Space Copy:

> *The demand for instant specificity increases in ratio to a decrease in ad size.*

Analyze that Rule and you'll see the hole in the fabric of this ad. It's a "teaser": The ad tells you what the item *isn't*; it doesn't tell you what it *is*.

Oh, sure, the bullets aren't parallel, but rules of grammar and procedure aren't applicable to tiny ads.

While we're in the neighborhood, add The Second Rule of Small-Space Copy:

> *Whatever else you include, you **must** include a reason to respond.*

That second Rule can be a bear, if yours is a complex offer. But you can't compress the incompressible: If the offer is too complex to describe in the space you have, switch the offer to a two-step conversion, pointing out benefit resulting from a simple request for more (beneficial) information.

The Third Rule is — or at least should be — a truism:

> *Make an offer.*

You know what? Those three Rules can govern *any* message, and not just small space ads. They become obvious in small space because both observation and analysis are simplified.

Specifics = Clarity

Compare the pseudo-wheelchair ad with this one, in a computer magazine:

WHO SAYS
You can get a Umax Vista S6-E
SCANNER
for just $269?
WE DO.
MacNet 1-800-404-9976

Specific. Clear. No attempt to overcrowd small space. Just one missing element — an expiration date. (Opinion: An expiration date helps any message asking for a specific response when that response brings an apparent benefit.)

"We didn't have enough space" is an invalid excuse for an ineffective small-space ad. Why run an ad you're convinced, in advance, won't work?

Small-space travel advertising

The travel section of every metropolitan newspaper carries a batch of ads three column inches deep or smaller. Some of these are rate-holders. (I pity advertisers who use rate-holders as throwaways . . . *every* ad should be aimed at getting the phone or cash register to ring. *Every* ad should make an offer.)

In the Sunday paper I'm looking at are four typical ads. Recognizing the ambience is competitive, decide which one might get you to lift the phone. The first ad:

**ROYAL CARIBBEAN
CRUISES
SALE   OPEN 7 DAYS
CRUISE RESERVATION SERVICES
966-8500 748-7489**

Any problems here? You bet there are. Principal among these is lack of an offer. "Sale"? What's the deal? The ad violates both Rules.

The second ad:

ESCAPE TO THE KEYS!
CALL 1-800-321-7489
HOWARD JOHNSON / OCEANSIDE MARATHON RESORT
$59.95 + tax
1-4 persons
Subject to availability
POOL & CABLE • 24 HR. REST
Marathon MM54

Any problems here? Not as many. Here we run afoul of our oldest principle, The Clarity Commandment:

When you choose words and phrases for force-communication, clarity is paramount. Don't let any other component of the communications mix interfere with it.

This ad does have specifics, including the bait-and-switch giveaway "Subject to Availability." That's okay. Airlines do this routinely with their frequent flier programs, and travelers are used to it. The problem here is that this ad is aimed at an in-group, those who know the terminology in advance. Probably most — not all — readers know "Rest" means "Restaurant"; but only those already familiar with the Florida keys can decode "Marathon MM54." Others will think it's the title of a Ray Bradbury science fiction novel. (It means mile marker 54, which is at Marathon, a town in the Florida keys. As one drives through the keys, mile markers appear at the roadside.)

The third ad:

LAS VEGAS MAGIC!!
Jan & Feb — 3 DAYS/2 NTS
Delta Air Lines — Day Flights!!
$259 Excalibur $289 Treasure Island
$269 Luxor $319 NY NY (New Hotel)
Air, Hotel, 3 Shows, 3 Day Trips, 2 for 1 Buffet & All Taxes!!
National Travel   1-800-845-5164
Pkg prices pp, dbl air & hotel. Subject to availability, certain restrictions apply.

(I've printed that last line in readable size; in the original it's 2-point mice-type.)

Any problems here? Darned few. Yes, doubled exclamation points suggest the offer isn't 100 percent kosher, and yes, the last line means you probably have to battle to get this original offer. But look at the specifics this advertiser has loaded into a single inch.

Here's another. Take a look and let's see whether we agree on what this ad does right and what it does mildly wrong.

WALT DISNEY WORLD® RESORT AREA
RAMADA
BED AND BREAKFAST
Continental Breakfast Included!
$12.99*
***** **Per Person Dbl. Occ.**
***$1 Extra Fri./Sat. Limited Space**
***** **$5 Extra Peak Periods**
★ **1-800-544-5712** ★

The ad looks tall here, but in print the placement of elements ("Ramada" vertically, for example) fits the message into one column inch.

Opinion Positive: Recapitulating an apparent benefit — free breakfast — is good marketing. Opinion Negative: Using an asterisk, with the references immediately below, unnecessarily calls attention to exclusions.

Can you sell high-ticket items?

Here's a one-inch ad, another from *The New Yorker*:

22k LIMITED EDITION
Gold Filigree Bracelet
Exquisitely Crafted
$595
An investment in gold for generations to treasure.
CALL TOLL-FREE
1-888-445-4554
King's California Gold

The ad includes a shadow-effect low-resolution image of the bracelet.

I'm not privy to the results of this ad, but I wouldn't count on the phone ringing off the wall. Yes, the ad conforms to the Third Rule — it makes an offer. But how about the First Rule and the Second Rule?

Parts of the ad are specific: We know what the item is and we know what it costs. But, the only selling argument presented is that it's a limited edition. How limited? Two? Twenty thousand? The Second Rule, too, suffers here. *Why* should the reader choose this, over whatever offers retail jewelers are presenting? The unexplained hit-and-run is nonspecific, therefore noncompelling.

What would you or I have done? We either would have added a comparative — "Retail value $1,000" (*not* the less-expensive-seeming "Retail value $1000" without the comma) — or priced it higher and added, "Call for free descriptive booklet and $100 Discount Certificate."

Compare it with a simple ad on the same page:

Marble Cigar
Ashtray
Black or Green Marble
$34.95   +S/H
Free Catalog
888•9•MARBLE
(888•962•7253)
Natural Elegance, Inc.
Box 129 Brandon, Vermont 05733

Brilliant copy? Of course not. But this little ad includes a photograph of the ashtray, with a cigar in it, so we know what we're buying.

It's flawed, of course. The ad had plenty of room to give us a specific inch-length. And it pays no attention to the Second Rule. But I can see a few orders resulting, especially since this ad ran during the Christmas season. (Suggesting the ashtray as an elegant gift for the discriminating cigar smoker would have satisfied the Second Rule.)

Selling services in small space

A 1.5-inch ad in an advertising publication shows us how a small-space ad can satisfy all three Rules. The ad (100 percent reverse-type in a TV screen outline):

**Give your
product away
— on television
game-shows.**
It's the ultimate in low-cost, mass
exposure. We provide a complete service
to all TV game-shows. Write for details.
Game-Show Placements, Ltd.
7011 Willoughby Avenue
Hollywood, CA 90038
(213) 874-7818

I don't understand why this advertiser says "Write for details" and then gives us the phone number. But all three Rules are covered.

From a travel magazine, a two-inch ad:

ROMANIA
Exclusive tours
for small groups.
• Transylvania
• Maramures
• Bukovina
• Danube Delta
Private homes, village picnics,
artisans' workshops . . .
Quo Vadis
288 Newbury St. • Boston, MA 02115
(800) 876-1995

Okay, for its market. In a less-specialized publication, this ad wouldn't have a chance, because its specificity isn't universal. A tourist who doesn't know where Maramures or Bukovina is would aggressively ignore the pitch. Yes, I'd have suggested some sort of price reference; but they didn't ask me.

Small Size Is No Excuse.

Publications that accept ads of three inches or smaller (and many don't) tend to tombstone them, piling one atop another. Don't regard this as a penalty. A grabber-offer in the next ad can hold the eye long enough for it to spill over onto yours.

That's your opportunity. If your ad implies, says, or shouts, "Got a second? We'll make that second worthwhile" . . . and then *does* make that second worthwhile by adhering to the Three Rules, you might put yourself in the position of looking at big-space ads and asking, "Why did they spend money on all that space?"

Figure 9-1

Ten ads are stacked together. The biggest is two inches, the smallest is half an inch. Which is the most likely to be read first, especially since this is only part of a section? Chances are it would be either the totally unproduced ad at upper left, which begins with the word "FREE," or the ad which makes a promise not usually associated with schools — "LOSE WEIGHT."

Figure 9-2

Each of these ads — 10 of them one-inch and five of them a little larger —
competes with all the others for attention and interest. Even though the ad
is bigger, does "100% Natural" motivate as some of the others do? If you
think not, what wording would have improved the heading of this ad?

10

Rules for Effective Free-Standing Inserts

Do free-standing inserts pull? Yes, if. . . .
Even if you don't know them as free-standing inserts ("FSIs"), you certainly know what they are. Your Sunday newspaper is loaded with them — extra inserts printed elsewhere and distributed with the paper.

Big free-standing insert companies such as Valassis and News America, and for that matter individually-prepared free-standing inserts from every type of advertiser from Kmart and Walgreens to local furniture stores and insurance companies, are solid test media and often *primary* media. If we use them properly and don't overpay, they represent a reasonably fast and reasonably accurate market indicator . . . as well as a profit center.

What chance does it have?

Here's a Sunday paper with nine main sections, plus comics and Sunday magazine and TV program guide. Oh, yeah — here are two syndicated free-standing inserts, plus other FSIs for Kmart, JC Penney, Target, Sears, and two local stores.

And how about these? A blown-in piece for a local rug cleaner, discount coupons good "This week only" for a chain of pizza restaurants, and a nonspecific discount sheet offering 20 percent off on a specified day at a shopping mall.

So, sure: Some of these die like the dogs they are. But some not only survive; they thrive. What makes the difference?

Start by Keeping Score THEIR Way: The First Rule of FSI Success

I usually have little or no enthusiasm for the way conventional media keep score — indefinable words such as "Noted" and "Recall," only distant cousins of the magical word "Response."

But for FSIs, especially proprietary FSIs, we'd better use these terms *as starters*. If the face of the insert is so flat, so dull, so uninspired it can't compete with all those others, it's a waste of preprinted paper.

So The First Rule of FSI success parallels the First Rule of Internet use:

Grab the eye and shake the complacency.

One profound lesson we've learned from conventional media is that the relationship between eye-grabbing and actually causing the phone or cash register to ring is sometimes tenuous and sometimes nonexistent. So that's just Round One of the battle.

The Second Rule of FSI Success

The Second Rule of FSI Success is just as barbaric and harsh:

Yell, don't just talk.

Remember where you are — sandwiched in a batch of disposables thrown inside a newspaper whose reader-loyalty doesn't extend to you. Want to be sedate? Want to make a straightforward offer, unblemished by the scream of "Bargain!" or "Deal!"? Stay out of FSIs. You're better off adjacent to news or editorial matter in that same newspaper.

An example

A single-sheet FSI has this message filling one side:

**TAKE
WEDNESDAY
OFF**

Let's suppose you see that. Are you inclined to turn over the sheet to see what's on the other side?

If you answered, "Maybe," that's parallel to a "No" in FSI-Land. Oh, it isn't terrible and it does catch the eye. But the flaw — and whether it's fatal or not depends on the individual looking at it — is that it's obviously a gimmick. And an obvious gimmick colors the attitude when someone does turn over the sheet.

On the other side is this headline:

**GO AHEAD! TAKE
20% OFF
WEDNESDAY.**

This is followed by a list of stores in a shopping mall. Down the right edge is a batch of four coupons, which means the user can hit that mall and get 20 percent off in four different stores. At the bottom is a simple map showing where the mall is located.

Now, what if . . .

Pretty good. But don't you now feel those who see the reverse side first (and when FSIs are stuck into a newspaper, who can tell which side will be up) will have a higher excitement-quotient than those who see "Take Wednesday Off?" What if that other side had simply said:

**Ready for
20% OFF
at more than 30 stores?
GREAT! TURN THIS OVER.**

I don't have any way of gauging comparative response because obviously my off-the-cuff version never appeared. My point, though, is that in a simple two-sided FSI, the non-action side should build anticipation for the action side.

The Third Rule of FSI Success

While we're looking at this FSI, consider The Third Rule of FSI Success:

Coupons help response.

That's probably because of the bleed-over from the Valassis and News America FSIs, where our offers are surrounded by coupons redeemable at supermarkets. Nice ambience!

Don't do this:

Here's a one-sided FSI in one color — medium green. The heading and subhead:

Clean Carpet
New System Keeps It Clean

I hope you voted "No" on this one, because the call to action isn't there. Instead, it's in two price-blocks: "Two Rooms $25" and "Five Rooms $49." The piece then shoots itself in the foot with a disclaimer: "Our four step process includes special treatment for visible traffic areas and/or spots. Only $7 additional per room." Huh?

Compounding the weakness is this statement, in 8-point type:

Ask about our **$10 Bonus** for combined carpet and furniture cleaning

Friend, if you're offering this bonus, it shouldn't be "Ask about. . . ." It should be, "This Certificate gives you a $10 Bonus. . . ."

Competing in a Syndicated FSI:

Of course you know the basic rule of preparing advertising for a free-standing insert: Position of the coupon has to be interchangeable, top to bottom, to prevent the possibility of backing up another coupon on the reverse side of the page.

That means no continuous top-to-bottom color-blocks, and it also means you'd better take a look at the way it hits the eye, both ways, before sending it off.

Color, of course, costs nothing extra in a syndicated FSI because every syndicated FSI is printed in full color. But no bleed, please.

The Fourth Rule of FSI Success

The three basic Rules apply, of course. But because of the environment, we'd better add a Fourth Rule:

The more "vertical" and specialized your offer, the less advisable it is to expose it in a free-standing insert.

That's because an FSI is as mass as a medium can get. In fact, because the great bulk of FSI offers are discounts for various food items, the demographic is skewed toward the bottom of the disposable-income scale.

Understand, please: The two most popular trigger-words, "Save!" and "Free!" know no demographic boundaries. But the higher up the economic scale one climbs, the less exciting becomes the opportunity to save 35 cents on Marzetti's Apple Dip by clipping a coupon and handing it to the supermarket cashier.

Typical sizes

Typically, we can buy space in a Valassis insert in the two most popular sizes: half a page (horizontally . . . a vertical half is next to unknown) or a full page. Some of the ads that don't involve a coupon redeemable at a retail outlet have begun to use a technique that has worked well in conventional space ads — instead of a coupon, they put a heavy dotted line around a box in which they place a toll-free number and an address. Careful! If this is not recognized as a coupon surrogate, it might be backed up with a coupon and be forever lost.

The Fifth Rule of FSI Success

For mail order advertising in free-standing inserts, we can add yet a Fifth Rule of FSI Success, one recommended in these pages for other types of advertising:

Adding an expiration date improves response.

Just about every supermarket coupon in these pages has an expiration date, albeit such dates usually are far beyond the logical expiration date of a direct response offer.

My own philosophy — which I'm not superimposing on anyone else, although I repeat it several times in this book — is that an expiration date adds urgency to *any* offer, whether in an FSI, a mailing, a TV spot, or the side of a bus.

If your question is, "What if I want to repeat the offer and have used up the expiration date?" my answer is, "Repeat the offer and set a new expiration date." That should suggest copy, if your ad appears, say, on September 15, 2001, such as "Please respond by October 31, 2001," not "Sorry, we can't process your order if it comes in after October 31, 2001."

In March of one year, I saw a mail order FSI ad with the legend, " 'FREE LABELS' offer good through August 15." That's a deep deadline but (opinion) it's better than no deadline, and the marketer probably can justify it by pointing out the nature of the offer — designer checks, with the extended deadline giving individuals time to use up their existing checks. This ad has run repeatedly, so we have to assume it works.

The Sixth Rule of FSI Success

One of the curses of top-to-bottom interchangeable coupons is the possibility of having the reader scan the coupon before reading the ad. So we have The Sixth Rule of FSI Success, which admittedly applies primarily to coupons in FSI advertising that doesn't require retail store redemption:

*Re-sell . . . **hard** . . . in the coupon.*

This isn't easy because of the space constraint. Try telling a story convincing enough to get an order, in a half-page 7¾" x 5¼", leaving room for a coupon big enough to hold standard response information *plus* a re-sell. That'll teach conciseness to us . . . and it's why the discipline of catalog copywriting adapts itself well to tight-space selling such as this.

Neatness Doesn't Count.

If you're considering invading the FSI world, you must be a consummate negotiator. Dealing in space-buy discounts and end-rates isn't part of the creative process, but if you haven't driven home a favorable deal you have twice as far to go to break even.

But, for the creative team, I suggest discarding any notion of neatness. Discard any layouts you'd like to frame and hang on the reception room wall. Instead, go for eye-impact. Visualize yourself, flipping through the pages of a syndicated free-standing insert . . . or, even more crucial, seeing a batch of pre-printed inserts. Which ones catch *your* eye? Which ones do *you* stop to read?

Go thou and do likewise.

Figure 10-1

Two mail order ads share a page in a Sunday free-standing insert. Coins need little description beyond depiction, but can you sell enough magazine subscriptions in a newspaper insert with such a basic summary to justify the cost? Questionable, unless the space was bought at a "remnant" rate.

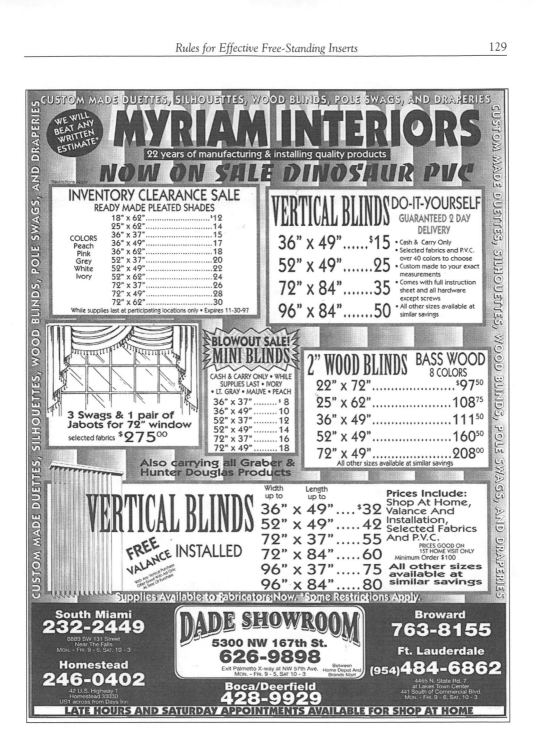

Figure 10-2

This insert, printed on one side only (why?), is a condensed encyclopedia of blinds and shades, complete with specific prices. Type around the borders is hard to read, but the offers are specific, answering many of the questions a prospective customer asks.

11

Creating Effective
Classified Advertising

Too many marketers assign classified copy to those on the lowest rung of their creative department, assuming "Anybody can write a classified ad." A tragic mistake!

Yes, we have a stepchild in our advertising/marketing family, and many of us, in a creative decision-making position, are the evil and insensitive Mr. Murdstone from *David Copperfield*.

Our stepchild is classified advertising. Because (except for display classified, a different phylum) ads are small, with little or no production, creative directors and even some free-lancers take a patrician view: Classified ads are too trivial to bother with, too insignificant a segment of a marketing effort to reduce to rules, too close to mama-papa marketing to be considered professional.

So they waste money on ineffective classified advertising. Serves 'em right.

Classified Categories

Classifieds exist in media other than newspapers. Most trade magazines have help wanted and service classifieds. Some consumer magazines, especially those aimed at specialty target-groups, carry classifieds. A number of broadcast stations, both radio and television, have "Classified advertising of the air." Now the Internet has begun to show dribbles of classifieds, sometimes as a group of stand-alone banners. And e-mail implicitly is classified, although it comes bursting through without the categorization we usually associate with classified ads.

In newspapers, within the genre we have categories. The four main categories: help wanted; goods, equipment, vehicles, and premises for sale or rent; services and personals; and business or investment offers.

Newspapers break down classifieds into a multiplicity of categories, enabling the individual who wants to see offers for computers to bypass household goods . . . and the individual looking for a 4x4 sport vehicle to skip past conventional automobiles. This is no recent concession to contemporary hyperspecialization, because classified divisions have existed for generations. Rather, it is a component of one of the three Rules of Classified Advertising.

Obviously the message has to match the medium. Obviously, too, the message has to be congruent with the Three Rules.

The First Rule of Classified Advertising

The First Rule is one most conventional advertising agencies would reject:

Launch into an immediate hard-sell.

What about courtship, the foundation of most display advertising? What about situational buildup, the foundation of most television commercials? What about rationale for consideration, the foundation of most direct mail?

Remember where you are.

Nah. Remember where you are. The huge difference between classified advertising and other types . . . with the *partial* exception of the Internet . . . is that the potential buyer has come looking for you. Courtship is *competitive,* not absolute; situational buildup is *competitive,* not absolute; rationale for consideration is *competitive,* not absolute.

Conventional advertising is *intrusive*: The prospect is neither expecting it nor seeking it. Classified advertising is *reactive*: The prospect is looking for your business category.

So, the First Rule of Classified Advertising is an attitude match. It's the difference between a dynamic presentation and a limp one.

The Second Rule of Classified Advertising

Compare three classified ads from the same day's "Land" category, in a major metropolitan newspaper. (Capitalizations are as they were printed, probably an idiosyncrasy of the publication.) Ad 1:

WALK TO BEAUTIFUL
RIO GRANDE RIVER!

10AC W. Texas Hunt, Fish, RVs OK. Assume $66.49/mo, $0 Down. Free Map/Info — Call Owner. 800-321-9294

Visualize a casual but obviously interested (or else he or she wouldn't be looking there) reader, seeing that ad and also seeing Ad 2, which appeared in the same group of listings as Ad 1:

COSTA RICA — Large Serviced Lots

*1-5 Acres Sold by Owner. Pacific Side. Breathtaking Views. —
Best Prices. Owner Will Finance 905-238-2663.*

One more for comparison — Ad 3, same group of listings:

17 ac. Wooded, Secluded, El., Tel,
*C.TV, driveway, inground septic approved, pond, 2 mi. shopping.
Must see. Owner. 1-802-362-1635.*

Okay, you're a prospective speculator. Which of these is most likely to get you to lift the phone?

Which ad hits hardest?

Ad 1 has two advantages — a "grabber" headline and dollar specifics. Suppose the headline had been "Rio Grande Adjacency" or "Riverfront Property." The impact would have been lessened. The precision of $66.49 a month is an exact offer to do business.

Ad 2 eliminates all but veteran buyers because a) many people who aren't in the land business won't understand what "Serviced Lots" are and b) in no way can "Best Prices" compete with an *example* of best prices.

Ad 3 suffers on two levels: First, location isn't disclosed. Area 802 is Vermont, but most people outside New England don't know this . . . and even if they do, they have no positive indication that the property itself is in Vermont. Second, "Must see" is a weak substitute for specifics.

So Ad 1 seems to be most congruent with the Second Rule of Classified Advertising:

> *A hard, specific offer will bring more response than image advertising or a promise not tied to specifics.*

For that matter, the Second Rule applies to every form of force-communication; but in classified, specifics-deficiency is more immediately noticeable.

One advantage of being part of a group of listings is the acceptance of condensed terminology because classified advertising, billed by the line, goes as close to the clarity border as it dares. Buyers know *br* means "bedroom" and *ba* means "bath"; *ac* means "acre" (although in neighborhood home classified it also can mean "air conditioned"); *excl* means "exclusive."

The Third Rule of Classified Advertising

That very familiarity lifts classified ads that don't use abbreviations above the standard level, from the viewpoint of impressiveness. From the viewpoint of economics? Better test, and I'll tell you why — the Third Rule of Classified Advertising:

> *The medium is the message, more than any other means of force-communication.*

A benefit for the company advertising a "deal" — a franchise or business opportunity or discount travel — is the very nature of classified advertising. It's tight, brisk, fast, truncated. So exposition isn't called for. Those who don't want to answer questions might well run a display ad worded, "Look for our classified opportunity under 'Business Opportunities'" . . . and maximize the benefit of *not* supplying a complete explanation because classified readers don't expect a complete explanation.

Complete explanation = skewed response

In fact, because a complete explanation is at variance with the medium it can skew response . . . upward or downward. A logical test, if you're planning a classified campaign, is to run a tell-all ad against a teaser ad. Results are unpredictable.

Study the Medium

Don't, as so many arrogant advertisers do, just throw words onto the screen because you're creating a classified ad. Do, as so many smart marketers do, take a look at a weekend paper, or *USA Today* (a powerful classified source).

Which ads seem hokey? Which ones turn you off because they say too much? Which ones tempt you to respond even though you're in the section only as an observer?

From adjectives to apparent logic, classifieds can teach us much. They not only reflect the nucleus of commerce and society, but they entertain, too. So take a look!

MONEYMAKING OPPORTUNITIES

$1,500 WEEKLY mailing our circulars! Guaranteed! Begin now! Free packet!: Mesa-C3, Box 4000, Cordova, TN 38018-4000.

EASY WORK! Excellent pay! Assemble products at home. Toll free: 1-(800) 467 5566, Ext. 2608.

STOP WORKING and retire wealthy! Write: PO Box 10822, Glendale, CA 91209 with self-addressed, stamped envelope.

MAKE THOUAND Recycling! Rush $9.95: Recycling Publications, Box 273, Savage, MN 55378.

LEARN 9 proven methods to success. Send $12.00 check/moneyorder to: Modern Day Miracles, PO Box 1536, Birmingham, MI 48012.

$10,000/MONTH with $10.00 investment. Give away free $10.00 rechargeable 16.5 cents calling cards, or sell them. Earn 15% usage commission. Great for promotions, fundraising. Send $10.00: Community Connections, PO Box 450, Sicklerville, NJ 08081. Free card included. Legitimate, listed company.

EARN THOUSANDS in mailorder. For information package, send $15.00 application fee to: S&J Marketing, 204 Mt. Vernon Drive, Lafayette, LA 70503.

OWN A Bicycle? Make $15.00 hour. Self-addressed, stamped envelope to: Ellsworth, Box 201, Manti, UT 84642.

NO SCAMS and no gimmicks, just an honest way to make big money. Must have car and good health. Send $7.00 and self-addressed, stamped envelope to: Lanny Bianchi, PO Box 18691, Charlotte, NC 28218.

BONANZA BUCKS! Achieve home-based business success. Free catalog/sample: Box GM-22023, Alexandria, VA 22304.

82 MONEYMAKERS! Free details!: Paul Arredondo, 1910 Grant, Wichita Falls, TX 76309.

ADVERTISE YOUR product/service on the Internet. Cheaper than classifieds or displays. You don't need a computer. Call: 1-(800) 530 1190.

BIG DOLLARS in your mailbox daily. Send $3.00, self-addressed, stamped envelope: J.G. Enterprises, PO Box 142, Staten Island, NY 10309.

OFFSHORE BROKERS. Develop huge secondary offshore income. Immediate results - Will train: (405) 720 0425 for free report.

WIN LOTTO Cash almost every draw. Free call shows how! 1-(888) 345 1144.

HUGE DAILY Casino profits. Make $500-$1,000 every day. Very small bets. 100% guaranteed. Impossible to lose following easy, simple, complete instructions. Great way to make living. Absolutely guaranteed. Limited offer $10.00: Lucas, 5632 San Felipe, Houston, TX 77056.

9 MONEYMAKING reports. Bonus with order. For details send self-addressed, stamped envelope: V. Whitney Enterprises, 6471 Northwest 41 Terrace, Pompano Beach, FL 33073.

GET RICH at home. Fast, easy. Large stamped envelope: Products, Box 192, Smyrna Mills, ME 04780-0192.

MILLIONS OF our readers will see these advertisements, and will trigger an effective response from many of our readers.

Figure 11-1

Business opportunities exemplify the strength and the competitive ambience of classified advertising. Strength: Categorization means interested parties are looking, aggressively, for your type of offer. Competitive ambience: In any category, challengers vie for attention and response. You have a choice of appeals, from hyperbole to reserved dignity. In this group of listings, hyperbole seems to be universal, which may reflect the readership of this newspaper. So in effect, the medium *is* the message.

Figure 11-2

The magazine in which these classified ads appeared gears itself to individuals looking for money beyond their regular employment. Note how the ads cater to that readership.

CLASSIFIED
OPPORTUNITIES

RATES
Based on 300,000 Mailed Each Issue

Minimum of 15 words—$85.00. $5.70 per additional word. First four words in first line set in CAPS. Name, ad and numbers must be included in word count. Payment with order unless placed by a recognized advertising agency. No cash discount.

Advertising which is objectionable or misleading, in the opinion of the publisher, will not be accepted. First-time advertisers: please include response material (copy of offer) and your telephone number with your order.

Classified section closes 45 days preceding date of issue. For example: October issue closes August 15. Cancellations not accepted after closing date.

⬧ *Send ad copy to:* ⬧

Classified Advertising Dept.

SPARE TIME Magazine
5810 W. Oklahoma Ave.
Milwaukee, WI 53219

ADDITIONAL INCOME

EASY WORK! EXCELLENT PAY! Assemble products at home. Call Toll Free 1-800-467-5566, Ext. 2444.

WE PAY $200.00 WEEKLY! You mail circulars! Send large stamped addressed envelope: National-20, POB 526, Bowmansville, PA 17507-0526.

$200 DAILY! ADDRESS LETTERS at home. Need typewriter or good handwriting. Free details. National-A, Box 73164, Houston, TX 77090-9998.

$400 WEEKLY ASSEMBLING PRODUCTS from home. For details send SASE: Home Assembly-ST, Box 216, New Britain, CT 06050-0216.

$800 WEEKLY! PROCESSING MAIL! Easy! Free supplies/information! SASE: ABM, Box 201892-ST, Denver, CO 80220.

SPARE TIME CASH. FOR Free Watkins catalog or home-based business information package call Joyce 1-800-SPICE-49.

INTERNATIONAL CO. SEEKS PT/FT people—Work at Home up to $700 / week possible, no experience necessary, will train: 800-813-6063.

LEARN PIANO TUNING AT home. Free brochure. American Piano School, Dept. 6-A, 17050 Telfer Dr., Morgan Hill, CA 95037.

$800.00 PER WEEK Possible...Send "LARGE SASE" to: Kring Publishing, 610 4th Street, Devils Lake, ND 58301-2565.

ALCOHOLISM, STRESS, DEPRESSION, A.D.D Rehab proven, patented, MLM exploding, tremendous business opportunity, free booklet. 1-800-900-7028.

HERBATOL MAKES MLM HISTORY! 84% payout three levels. Write: Marketplace, Box 973, Champaign, IL 61824.

BIG PROFIT WITH 3,500 item catalog. Details send $1 to: Rogers Unlimited, 2741 S. Jamestown, Tulsa, OK 74114.

AMAZING HOME MAILING PROGRAM that pays you fast profits two ways. Details free! Rush self addressed stamped envelope Today to: Q.U.E.S.T. Marketing, P.O. Box 340287, San Antonio, TX 78234.

HOME EMPLOYMENT OPPORTUNITIES! EARN excellent steady income—call toll free 1-800-442-1754, Ext.841. Guaranteed!

BECOME A MYSTERY SHOPPER. Start immediately. Professional training manual teaches you how. Send $24.95: CPP, Box 53942-S, Irvine, CA 92619.

SECRET BANKING SYSTEM! Open bank accounts and make millions automatically! Amazing recorded message reveals details 1-800-935-5171 Ext. 1875.

ADVERTISING SPECIALTIES

DO YOU WANT TO be able to sell the ten Hottest Best Priced advertising specialty items in America today? Lowest Selling Prices on Bic Pens, too! Write to: Alix-Anne, Dept. A, 803 Moore Rd., Mansfield, TX 76063.

WE OFFER BETTER VALUE! Tower Products, 14869 W. 95th Street, Room 892, Lenexa, KS 66215.

BIGGER ISN'T NECESSARILY BETTER! Dave's Advertising Gifts/Business Printing, RR 3, Box 291 ST8-97, Owensville, MO 65066 —Always a personal touch!

AGENTS WANTED

BIBLE, ENCYCLOPEDIA, PORTRAIT PLAN sales. 60% on Financed Sales. Opportunity, Box 721, Morehead, KY 40351.

EVERYONE A PROSPECTIVE CUSTOMER. Show our line of fast selling belt buckles, badges, lapel buttons, tie tacks, tie clasps, name identification badges, money clips to Truckers, Police, Firemen, Paramedics, Medical Technicians, Ambulance Drivers, Postal Carriers, Taxi and Bus Drivers, and others. Personalizations available. Over 8000 emblems available. Free Information Packet. Hook-Fast, Box 1088-ST, Providence, RI 02901.

AUTOMOTIVE

CARS FOR $100! Trucks, boats, 4-wheelers, motorhomes, furniture, electronics, computers etc. by FBI, IRS, DEA. Available your area now. Call 1-800-513-4343 Ext. S-20067.

ALTERNATOR/GENERATOR REBUILDING BOOK. Box 26044, Las Vegas, NV 89126. www.hhtechnology.com

BOOKS & PUBLICATIONS

FREE "BOOKS FOR YOUR BUSINESS" CATALOG. Mail-order, retailing, marketing. 516-754-5000. Forum, 383 Eastmain, Centerport, NY 11721.

CABLE DESCRAMBLER! BUILD FOR $12 with 7 Radio Shack parts! Instructions $10: F.A.S.T., Box 369-MS78, Pt. Salerno, FL 34992-0369.

SMALL BUSINESS RESOURCE GUIDES. Free catalog. D.S. Worley, POB 189, Slaton, TX 79364.

CABLE DESCRAMBLER! BUILD FOR $12 with Radio Shack supplies! Instructions $9: Townsend, 4501-ST, Linda Lane, Anniston, AL 36206.

BUSINESS OPPORTUNITIES

NEW! GROW EXPENSIVE PLANTS. 2,000% Profit. Free information. Growbiz, Box 306-A8 Seminary, MS 39479.

BECOME AN OSHA (OCCUPATIONAL Safety and Health Administration) consultant now. Valuable training secrets revealed. High income. Free exciting details. Write ARCA, 705 2nd Ave. SW Suite S, Altoona, IA 50009.

DISTRIBUTE BUSINESS, PROFESSIONAL "HOW-TO" books, tapes, software. Free catalog. Call for recorded message (219) 295-8220.

$500.00 FROM SACK CEMENT. Picture Proof! Send LSASE to: Brinco, Box 401092, Hesperia, CA 92340.

$1,800 WEEKLY RECORDING VIDEOTAPES at home. No copyright violation. Free startup information. CMS Video, 210 Lorna Square, #163-F20, Birmingham, AL 35216.

(Continued on page 46)

SPARE TIME

Figure 11-3

Newspaper classified advertising alphabetizes the ads. Notice how much less promotional these — just a segment of the many in a typical Sunday newspaper — are than classifieds in special-interest publications.

12

Creating Effective Yellow Pages Advertising

Where are you? How do you adapt your message to the medium?
No, you aren't where you can make an outright aggressive comparative claim of superiority. But you *can* rise above the no-sell boiler-plate copy Yellow Pages representatives will too often try to foist on you. Remember where you are, and make the most of that recognition: You're in a *totally* competitive marketplace.

The Three Basic Rules of Yellow Pages Advertising

The three most basic rules of Yellow Pages advertising haven't changed over the last generation:

1. Don't just sell the category. Sell YOU.
2. Be professional, not cute.
3. Specifics outsell generalizations.

Just in case I've engendered confusion by placing those rules at the head of this chapter, I'll explain and justify.

The First Rule

The first rule is one that applies to *any* form of force-communication:

Remember where you are. The medium affects the message.

If you were sending a solo mailing to a list of people who never heard of you or what you're selling, you'd have a double selling job — generic and specific. The generic selling job would explain the value of the category; the specific selling job would cover the value of *you* within that category.

If you were running a space ad in an industrial publication, you'd bypass generic sell; the publication's readership already accepts the concept. You'd emphasize your competitive edge, perhaps with hard-hitting comparative ads.

Here we have a medium whose use is limited to those already looking for what you have to sell. People don't open the Yellow Pages to have a good read; they open the book to find a supplier within a specific category. If you're selling window shades, and your sole listing is under window shades, you can't expect someone who is looking through the furniture listings to think of you.

The point:

The Yellow Page directory is a compendium of *vertical* business listings, each category unrelated to the others. "Automobile dealers — new cars" and "Automobile renting" may be physically adjacent, but the person looking for a new car won't cross the border into the next category. The person looking for a rental car may want the car model you sell, but interest is confined to car rental listings and doesn't extend beyond.

Which means what, relative to the First Rule?

It means you're wasting money by generic advertising, selling only the category. If yours is a business in which you want to attract the first-time user, then, yes, you'll build reader-confidence by stating categorical benefits; but please don't stop there. Sell *you* with full recognition that every ad in this section is designed to take business away from you.

The Second Rule

Ordinarily sane marketers seem to go berserk when planning ads for the Yellow Pages. They'll use photographs of their children. They'll use a cartoon. They'll use a goofy slogan they think is clever.

What they're doing is ignoring the state of mind of the typical Yellow Pages user. The homeowner battling a leaky pipe is looking for a savior who takes the problem as seriously as he does. So "Splish, Splash!" in no way is competitive with "Service within 30 Minutes, 24 Hours a Day."

Some advertising agencies that handle Yellow Pages advertising for their clients (usually as a courtesy, although we have a $10 billion medium here) will assign a recently-hired copywriter/artist team to create the ads. The result is a message parallel to many television commercials — amusing, droll, sardonic, entertaining.

Big mistake.

The Yellow Pages customer isn't looking for entertainment. In fact, projecting the notion that you think carpet cleaning or computers or package designs are funny can point your hot prospect — "hot" because he or she entered the arena looking for a source — toward a competitor whose message says, "We take you seriously."

So the Second Rule is the governor on the creative throttle:

You can't make a mistake being serious. You can make a big one being cute.

A prime example of the difference between classified and Yellow Pages advertising is the category "Mailing Lists." In advertising publications, list companies know they're reaching a sophisticated buyership. They can, in the pages of publications aimed directly at their targets, substitute attention-getting for an actual offer to do business.

In the Yellow Pages? Don't try it. You're reaching a different state of mind.

Notice, please: I didn't say you're reaching a different person. The individual may be the same, but his or her attitude is a victim of the medium. Cater to the medium. Deal in specific offers and you can't make a fatal mistake.

The Third Rule

Need I repeat this basic tenet of outselling the other guy?

Specifics outsell generalizations.

Yes, this is true of all media, all messages, all instances in which you want an individual to perform a positive act — and that's what advertising and marketing are supposed to be and do, distilled to their essence. But the more "vertical" the medium, the more profound the rule becomes.

The Most "Vertical" of All Media

Except for the Internet as it evolves into its twenty-first century incarnation, no medium is more vertical than the Yellow Pages. So if I'm looking for mailing lists in the Yellow Pages and one list company's headline is "Full Service • Since 1986" and another is "Quality That You Can Afford" and a third is "Top Quality Mailing Lists," my finger keeps walking until it reaches a specific offer. The finalists would be "Free 72-Page Catalog, Over 11,000 lists with state counts" and "We're Local, We're Fast, and We'll Give You a Deal: 10 Million Businesses and 50 Million Residences Nationwide."

In any category, specifics outsell generalizations. I'm looking at my local Yellow Pages, under a prime category — hurricane shutters. Some of these ads are huge, a full ¾-page. On facing pages are two giant ads. One proclaims:

FOR OVER 40 YEARS ONE OF
FLORIDA'S OLDEST
Our reputation is our strength.

The other has this heading:

The Customer Is Always #1
A LEADER AND INNOVATOR
Local Family Owned and Operated Over 70 Years

Which one might I pick? Neither. Longevity doesn't drive the decision; longevity is a pleasant peripheral. Instead, I'd probably call the company that placed a one-incher, sandwiched between the titans. Its headline:

Direct from the Manufacturer:
No delays, no middle-man markups.
Fast, dependable, best price — guaranteed.

Here's a no-nonsense approach, distilled and terse, carrying the salesworthy seeds of specificity.

(As a curiosity, looking at the entire section, I have the feeling most of the ads are generated by the desire to say what the others say, not by sales logic. Almost every one has a longevity reference — "25 Years Experience" . . . "Over 30 Yrs Experience" . . . "Family Owned and Operated Since 1948" . . . "16 Years Experience in the Shutter Industry." Many play up a personal reference such as "Shutters Are Our Exclusive Family Business" or "Family Owned & Operated.")

One ad is a grabber because under the heading "BUY FACTORY DIRECT & SAVE!" is this semi-impressive list of bullets:

- *Our exclusive 'HOOK LOCK' Storm Panels*
- *Save Hours on Installation (Just Hook & Lock)*
- *Passes 210 MPH Wind Load!!! • Catagory 5*
- *Eliminates Hundreds of Seam Bolts*
- *Meets All 1994 Impact Codes*
- *⅓ the Weight of Steel*

The ad even includes a mechanical drawing of the "hook-lock" interlock. It shines with power, compared with the generalizations in the ads of so many of its competitors. So why is it "semi"-impressive? First, the three exclamation points transform "image" into "pitch." Second, the "1994" reference is dead wrong. Even if the codes were changed to a tougher set of standards in 1994, proper wording is "Current Impact Codes." Each passing year makes 1994 more of a historical reference, not contemporary. Too, "Category" is spelled "Catagory." Ungood . . . but still far superior to "We Specialize in Satisfied Customers."

Words with power, not neutral ho-hum

The one rampant word infecting Yellow Pages copy is "Needs" as a noun. What does it mean? From an impact point of view, it means "Please write my ad for me."

Here's the first line of a Yellow Pages ad for insurance:

For All Your Automobile Insurance Needs

Has any information changed hands? Has any compelling reason been transmitted? The same ad has the subhead: "Buy what you want, not what we want!" How can this company think it competes with another company whose ad screams:

UNBEATABLE
RATES!
NO ONE REFUSED!!
Tickets or Accidents?
NO PROBLEM!!
✓ *Young drivers*
✓ *Safe drivers*
✓ *Hard luck drivers*
✓ *Sports car drivers*
✓ *Commercial & multi-car discounts*
FREE PHONE QUOTES

Yes, it's "pitchy" and yes, it violates the multiple exclamation point principle. But it's congruent with the concept of a vertical medium. Who, after all, is looking through the Yellow Pages, searching for insurance coverage? It's much more likely to be a driver who has a problem getting favorable rates and coverage than the driver who expects and gets automatic renewals at favorable rates.

Next to "needs" the word we can most easily do without is "available." This word adds unnecessary weakness to whatever went before it: "Most extensive and reliable paging system available." What does the word add to either comprehension or motivation?

Speaking of pagers, here's a dynamic section — beepers. A huge ad leans on size and bulk as its reason to sign up:

OVER SIX MILLION
PEOPLE HAVE
CHOSEN US.
WHY HAVEN'T
YOU?

What follows is a standard laundry-list of features, followed by a ghastly slogan:

"Providing Quality and Value to
Every Customer Every Day"

(The quotation marks are theirs, weakening the statement a bit more.)

Most of the ads in this section position themselves with headings such as "Wider Coverage, Lower Prices!" or (a puzzler) "Be Sure You Know MobileComm" or the generic "Get more for less."

One smart competitor seems to have asked himself, "Who will be plowing through the Yellow Pages looking for beepers? Aha! I know who — somebody who doesn't have one and wants to be sure it's a logical investment." So, placing the company squarely in the path of a prospect with that attitude, this ad is headed:

Pagers . . . for people
who can't stay put.

Following is this line:

Be in constant contact with a pager and voice mail from Air-Touch. Even when you're out, you're in.

Does this message violate the first rule? It does sell the concept rather than the company. But we not only accept this deviation, we admire it because it aims itself at a specific market segment. Reading the entire ad, we lose some of our admiration because this company doesn't cash in on the message by pointing out how quickly and easily they'll have a live, activated pager in our hands. Instead, the ad lapses into standard boiler-plate copy such as "A leader in wireless communication" and "Unparalleled customer care." Pity.

How Does a Small-Space Advertiser Compete?

I've long preached that the use of brains is a more-than-effective substitute for the use of dollars. Competing in the Yellow Pages is a good test of this concept.

Years ago, companies would re-name themselves to get the first listing: "AAA-Aaron Auto Repair" or "AAAA Able Movers." Even today we have such artificial out-to-grab listings as "A Ability Attorney" and "AAA Memorial Funeral Home."

But the first listing no longer has the edge it once had. Some Yellow Pages publishers are limiting the number of "A's" and others are demanding evidence that the listing is, in fact, a legal name. Yeah!

In smaller space, integrity and a quiet statement of superiority are the ways to go. A great many Yellow Pages shoppers arc afraid of giant advertisers who, they feel, are either overpriced or impersonal.

If your Yellow Pages ad isn't just a simple listing (in which case your advertising is limited to presence), consider condensing into one or two inches the main claims the huge ads make that you can parallel. Some who scan or skim the section will choose you because you apparently offer the same benefits without the suggestion that a customer is a unit within a giant machine.

Should you list your company in the Yellow Pages at all? My company doesn't because few of our clients are local and the calls the Yellow Pages generate aren't from companies whose business we can handle economically. This is a decision individual companies have to make for themselves, based on the type of inquiries they can handle.

One imperative:

If you're in the Yellow Pages, don't settle for boiler-plate copy because the Yellow Pages salesperson presents you with a prefabricated ad with generic wording. Check the ad against the three basic rules, and your Yellow Pages ad is more likely to pay off.

Figure 12-1

Suppose you need a plumber. Bill's Plumbing dominates this page. But even though the ad calls itself "Bill's," it's signed "A-Aaland." And that picture of two children playing with the toilet — ugh. Impact generated by the powerful heading dissipates as we read the ad, which may drive us to one of the less boisterous plumbers listed in the column at right.

13

How to Use
"Card Decks" to Sell

Many marketers who themselves have responded to cards from decks don't recognize decks as a medium. That isn't as big a problem as participants in decks who, misusing them and lacking an understanding of where they are, conclude: "Loose deck cards don't work."

They do work . . . if your message matches where you are, if the deck itself circulates to the right targets, and if other cards in the deck don't ruin your response by killing off lookers before they've gone through the entire deck.

Card decks were in a mild eclipse for a couple of years. Now they're back. (Issuers of these decks deny that a renaissance exists; they've never been away.) Some users say they're pulling well; others say results are spotty.

What are some keys to strong response from a card buried in the bowels of a deck?

Not a major medium, but a potentially effective one

Cards usually are regarded as "alternative media." What makes them attractive to marketers is the combination of low per-thousand cost, no

149

postage, and a card issuer's occasional willingness to accept a p.i. (per-inquiry) deal.

At the Mercy of the Top Card

Card issuers often place their own "cover" card on top. This can be a blessing or a curse.

It's a blessing if the cover card promises a reward — some sort of mini-sweepstakes or prize secreted somewhere in the stack — or a partial listing of the treasures to be found — or provocative copy and/or graphics.

Business-to-business decks often have no cover card. They'll either pack the cards into a glittering mylar sleeve imprinted with the issuer's name or imprint a loose imperative on a neutral card carrying the recipient's name and address.

Are these business-to-business deck techniques good marketing ploys or poor ones?

Opinion: Poor ones. The mailer certainly knows that a businessperson, looking at a card deck, has a decision to make: Shall I open this and flip through the deck, looking for something that may interest me . . . or not?

That very decision should force deck issuers to *sell or make a promise of reward* on the top card; and, if the deck is encased in a glassine sleeve, be sure the bottom card offers the most enticing offer in the deck. If you're leading the deck recipient by the hand, don't let go and allow your target to make an uninfluenced decision.

Get that deck opened!

The obvious first conclusion: If the deck isn't opened, the response from that recipient is zero.

Typical of no-impact decks is one whose top card is the address card. Illustration: The most common cliché in marketing, a handshake. Text: "Local companies providing products & services you need!" Impact: Nil.

Another deck has a double-size card on top. Illustration: a man who, accompanying text says, "shares the secrets of direct mail success inside." Text: A huge word "FREE" followed by "Sample Newsletter" and some bullets. Impact: Favorable, because to almost everybody the word "Free" still has clout, even after having been wounded by decades of abuse.

So a suggestion: When looking over prior decks by an issuer you're considering, attention to *getting the deck opened* should influence your decision.

One-Step or Two-Step Conversion? The Three Rules of Card Decks

A two-step conversion — that is, using the medium to get an inquiry, not to try for an immediate sale — is usually the best use for a card. That point illustrates both strength and weakness. The strength lies in The First Rule of Card Decks:

Make response a no-brainer.

If you object to this Rule, consider: The individual flipping through the deck probably has just looked at another card and is about to look at another card. A challenge is out of order. (Replace the urge to challenge with adherence to The Second Rule, coming up.)

Typical skimming time, depending on which expert you're quoting, is one to three seconds. If you want to stop a skimmer cold, cleave to The Second Rule of Card Decks:

Make a powerful promise.

The Second Rule eliminates such weak cues as "Mail this card for additional information." Oh, certainly, "additional information" is *the* classic two-step conversion; but today's impatient, short-attention-span marketplace demands tying "information" to a more aggressive partner — a discount or a free mouse-pad or a "Confidential Report." At the very least, use terminology such as "Private Offer" or "$25 Value" to add power, however artificial, to the proposition.

The Third Rule? It's a venerable one you've seen before in these pages, one we should apply to every message we print or broadcast or send over the Web or put on the sides of buses or on matchbook covers or sky-write: The Clarity Commandment:

When you choose words and phrases for force-communication, clarity is paramount. Don't let any other component of the communications mix interfere with it.

That Third Rule (or better, that Commandment) can save a marketer a lot of grief.

Additional rules for a "one-step" conversion

A one-step conversion involves four additional rules:

1. *No asterisks or footnotes.*
2. *No qualifiers, no "if" phrases relating to your willingness or ability to deliver.*
3. *A reward — whether monetary or psychological — for a fast reply.*
4. *Clear, non-obfuscatory rhetoric unadulterated by intentional cleverness or unintentional confusion . . . describing a clear, unequivocal offer unadulterated by conditions.*

So a card combining a toll-free number with this text qualifies under these rules as a one-step conversion:

2 Magnetic Door Signs
1 Color on White 30 mil Magnet
4 line max, 12"x18" signs
$50.00

Complicated? No. "If"-phrases? No. Clever? No. Clear and straightforward? Yes. It qualifies.

Here's another:

Turn A Fun Hobby
Into A Profitable Business

The card, reasonably copy-heavy, then spells out the exact deal. If this were a two-step conversion these specifics would help eliminate wastenames. It's a one-step conversion, and that means specifics are mandatory.

Effective or ineffective? It depends on which deck the card is in:

To a list of business opportunity seekers, right on. To a list of sophisticated individuals whose homes cost $250,000 or more, probably not. (Yes, I know lists are full of surprises, and that's why we test lists in the first place; but in low-response media such as cards, we have to go with percentages.)

Just one problem here: Because it's a one-step conversion, the card asks for a credit card number . . . which many will not want to expose on a mailed card.

What About "Image" Advertising?

I'll risk the wrath of card producers by offering a firm opinion — and understand, please, it's an *opinion,* although to me it's a fact — that card decks are the wrong medium for image advertising.

First of all, image advertising is necessarily rhapsodic, semi-poetic, not a fast "better grab right now or miss out" pitch. It's out of key with the whole concept of card decks.

Second, the deck skimmer doesn't expect to encounter image advertising in this milieu. The mind-set isn't tuned to receptivity.

Third, the self-limiting nature of a card is an automatic restriction on size and format. Rhapsody gives way to a predetermined, standard shape.

An analysis of card copy isn't the forum to attack the *concept* of image advertising, but what genuine marketer could quarrel with having this as the purpose of *any* message: getting the phone, fax machine, or cash register to ring?

Don't do this:

I'm looking at a 3½" x 5⅜" card printed vertically. It asks me to fax my reply on the card.

My fax machine is a new one, and I'm not going to risk having an undersized card hang up inside its guts. Anyway, the number isn't toll-free, a mistake when competing in a deck; and "Fax today for information" is a grievous violation of the Second Rule of Card Decks. Don't do this.

I'm looking at another card with this heading:

No Business Plan? Call Us.

Here's a "Huh?" message. "Business Plan" covers acres of possibilities. "Error!" flashes all over the Clarity Commandment. Don't do this.

I'm looking at another card with this heading:

Buy 500 Get 500
FREE
with this postcard only.

The card has a printer's name on it, so we know, generally, what the offer is. But specifically, 500 *what*? We turn the card over and there we see:

*BUY 500 OF ANY PRINTED ITEM AT REGULAR PRICE AND GET AN ADDITIONAL 500 OF THE SAME ITEM. Call For Your Estimate Today!

Uh-oh. The accursed asterisk strikes again, because at the bottom, in mice-type, is:

*Some restrictions apply. This offer applies to any item printed on paper only. May not be used with any other offer or discount. Expires [DATE].

Many will read only through "Some restrictions apply" and stop: "I knew it." Others will wonder at the need for spelling out all those exclusions, as though this were a sweepstakes. And others won't have thought to turn over the card. This message offers too broad a challenge. Don't do this.

I'm looking at another card. Next to a color photo of a field of daisies is this headline:

Want To Get Found?

Uh-oh. Subtlety at work. Even if the text clears up the mystery, we *know* the creative team had a clearer way of initiating the point. Now the subhead:

We have helped large multinational corporations, like Pepsi and QBP do it!
We have also helped small local firms do it too!

These guys either never heard of The Rule of Negative Subtlety or don't believe it:

The effectiveness of a direct response message decreases in direct ratio to an increase in subtlety.

What are they selling? Deep, deep in the copy is a mini-explanation: "Let us show you how the Internet can work for you."

Nah. This semi-specific tries — weakly — to beef up the subtlety, but it's far too loose a generalization for a card. Don't do this.

I'm looking at another card. This is the heading, at the top of the card (the reverse is standard business reply card indicia):

YES! Please send this entire United & Babson Investor's Package for ONLY $9

So this card tries to close before making a promise. Don't do this. I'm looking at another card. The heading:

*FREE VIDEO
ON EXTERNAL DEGREES*

What's an "external degree"? Something to do with the weather? (I'm being wry. Apparently an external degree is a college degree one can earn without having to go to college. But how many targets of this mail order school will understand the term . . . and, if they do, think of it in positive terms?)

Why not, "FREE VIDEO shows you how to get a college degree fast, without setting foot on the campus"? Or, "Want a college degree, but don't have time for classes? FREE VIDEO can change your life." Or, "Get your college diploma at home."

However you might word it, recognizing The Clarity Commandment eliminates "External degrees." So don't do this.

Remember, please: Your card has two sides.

Direct mail veterans, who quite rightly expect recipients to look at both the front and back of their brochures and enclosures, are sometimes dumbfounded by the quick one-side-only rejection rate that so often attends card decks.

"But I explained that on the reverse side. Didn't they see it?"

No.

If you want them to read the reverse side, tell them — in a box or reversed line — to turn the card over. And give them a reason.

The traditional card of the 1980s and early 1990s reserved the reverse side for name, address, and business reply card indicia. The majority of latter-day cards say "Place stamp here" or use most or all of the second side to continue the sell.

If you have a toll-free number, experiment with total sell on both sides of the card. Note: I said *experiment with,* not *switch to.* Results run both ways if the prospect has the option of mailing your card postage-free. If it's a "Place stamp here," putting a coupon-type dashed border around the toll-free number and using the space you otherwise would dedicate to a mailing address probably will produce higher response. The only possible exception: a consumer mailing to seniors.

A Credible Offer Counts

Here's a card headed:

DARE TO SUCCEED!
WORK FROM HOME
350 Billion Dollar Industry!

Notice anything out of key here? Aside from throwing down a blatant challenge/cliché, the concept — however sound it actually may be — is out of sync with itself. Three hundred fifty billion dollars and "Work from home" just don't fit together. What's wrong isn't the concept; it's the copy.

Now, how about this one?

YOUR BUSINESS CAN ENJOY THE SAME SAVINGS AND BENEFITS PREVIOUSLY RESERVED ONLY FOR MAJOR CORPORATIONS!

Yeah, that's okay. Not great, but okay. The headline pushes the reader into a positive attitude as that reader moves into the text.

Following the Second Rule has to result in increased response. Tailor your message to the fast-flip medium. The heading has to make a big promise, present it fast and clearly, and be credible.

These four headlines (from actual cards) are effective:

1. SAVE UP TO 44% ON YOUR PHONE BILL
*2. 500 **FREE** BUSINESS CARDS!*
3. 250 Personalized Business Envelopes
    *Special Introductory Offer only **$9.95***
4. Are Parasites Eating You?

These four headlines (from actual cards) are weak:

1. Your Own Business Today!
2. Are You Interested In . . .
   ★ *Your Own Business?*
   ★ *A New Car?*
   ★ *A House In The Suburbs?*
3. Join War On Crime — A Business Opportunity
4. Dispensa-matic label dispensers will save you time and money!

Get the idea? Using the Three Rules of Card Decks as your litmus test will save you time and money.

Figure 13-1

This is the double-size cover card for a deck. Note the box at lower left — "Free offer inside from: Alamo Rent-a-Car." Devices such as this help improve the percentage of recipients who actually open the deck.

Figure 13-2

This card typifies the two-step conversion. Based on a hard-hitting basic exhortation on the card, the individual asks for a free cassette and report. The complete selling effort accompanies the free items.

Figure 13-3

This card typifies a clear, concise, quick message instantly recognizable by the proper targets at whom it's aimed.

Figure 13-4

Will the card-flipper know what "Voice Activated Home Automation" is? Nothing on this card explains it. The tiny photo of the company's staff (or whoever) adds nothing and, in fact, may damage response by suggesting the company is a family-type operation.

14

DRTV: Direct Response Television and Infomercials

*W*arning: *This chapter contains some outrageous opinions.*
Until the Internet happened along, television was far and away the "glamor medium." The statement, "I'm in television," even when spoken by an usher, could spawn and spur romance.

Until the Internet happened along, television was the most misused medium. The aura of having one's words, one's created images, or even one's face on the screens of thousands or millions of homes was and is irresistible.

What no longer is irresistible is wasting money on non-communicating commercials.

Direct Response Television

Now that so many major players in the world of advertising are moving into direct marketing, attention is increasingly focused on DRTV — direct response television.

The reasons are simple enough:

1. Billing to clients is bigger, cleaner, and easier than is true of direct mail.
2. Television-oriented advertising agencies feel more comfortable with DRTV than with result-specific space ads and mailings.

Just one problem with those reasons: Neither one is valid.

Basing a marketing program on familiarity with individual media rather than maximized penetration is almost as despicable as masking billing. Worse: It's unprofessional. And DRTV *should* be the medium with the most carefully analyzed results, because television response is the most immediate of any medium except out-call telemarketing.

The Major Creative Difference

The difference between the creativity driving conventional television commercials and the creativity driving direct response commercials stems from the way each keeps score.

Conventional television advertisers deal in two catch-all terms: "Noted" and "recall." Direct marketers deal in a single word: "Response."

If you're writing a television spot whose purpose isn't to get the cash register to ring, you might put form ahead of substance. That's what advertised brands such as Coors Light and McDonald's and Burger King and MCI and Coca-Cola and Infiniti automobiles have done . . . with mixed results. When McDonald's and Burger King use television to present a *specific offer* — a temporarily reduced price on a hamburger, or a toy premium for children, for example — store traffic invariably goes up.

I propose (without much hope of acceptance from those quarters) Lewis's First Law of Television Creativity:

Cuteness doesn't increase market share.

As evidence I offer all those screaming spots featuring guys with baseball caps on backward (don't instructions come with those caps?), little girls singing strange Druid melodies on a rocky beach, and expensive computer animation whose point is lost in the convulsive throes of production.

Oh, sure, because television spots usually run in clusters ("pods"), if a spot doesn't get attention it fades into the pile. But if all the spot does is get attention to *itself instead of what it's supposed to be selling*, can anyone claim that the result is maximized use of an advertising budget?

How to structure a direct response television commercial

Rather than lapse into a philosophical diatribe, let's examine our nest. What creative/mechanical procedures can help ensure an effective direct response commercial?

First of all, a direct response television commercial runs in a straight line. No diversions. No sidebars. Some of the grand masters of direct mail packages stumble when they write television spots, forgetting that the viewer can't go back for a second look, the way readers of space ads and direct mail packages can.

One of our basic rules of marketing becomes an injunction when creating a direct response television commercial — The Rule of Negative Subtlety:

The effectiveness of a direct response message decreases in direct ratio to an increase in subtlety.

However you structure your commercial, one creative approach to avoid: Don't challenge the reader's ability to comprehend what you're selling and why he or she should respond.

That means showing what you're selling early and often. It means showing product-in-use. It means including a "super" (textual superimposition) over key scenes of product-in-use, validating what the viewer is seeing.

Don't stint on the supers.

Supers are a direct marketer's dream in television commercial production. Use lots of them. Supers reinforce the image in the viewer's mind. Because they do, the supers have to validate what's on the screen. Don't mix (and confuse) the message by thinking you can double up the message through delivering two blows at once.

More Quick Tips

Television is the most "mass" of all media . . . and DRTV is an arm of direct marketing, the most targeted of all media. If you're after response rather than image, beware of the mismatch-trap. Don't lapse into a "something for everyone" appeal just because you're on television. Aim your commercial the way you aim your mailings and space ads — at the most people who can and will buy what you have to sell. Forget the others; if they're offended, they wouldn't buy from you anyway.

Include a guarantee — a powerful guarantee. Direct offers suffer because so many predecessors schlocked up the medium, and many of our best targets are afraid of a TV pitch. An absolute, unmistakable, un-hedged guarantee can knock an uncertain prospect off the perch.

Keys to response

One of the classic keys to response-generation is a reason for responding *right now*. What is that reason? Something free for a fast order? Perfect. A discount certificate good for a future buy? Not so perfect (because it may be obfuscatory or too long-range), but better than no incentive. Two for one? Usually perfect, but sometimes it denigrates the basic offer.

I don't have to point out the need for a toll-free number and the credit card icons. At least, I hope I don't.

You say including all this — showing product early and often, including validation, generating excitement over an incentive for a timely response, and asking for the order, allowing the viewer enough time to understand the means of response — is a tough assignment?

Sure, it is. If it were easy, others could do it.

Information on Infomercials

Advertisers are increasingly hot on infomercials . . . so much so that the "fringe" time, at one time available at incredible discounts, has tightened to a point at which infomercial producers fight and bid for time on some of the cable channels as well as standard broadcast stations.

And why shouldn't advertisers love infomercials? If they're produced properly, infomercials are better than a personal demonstration, for two reasons:

1. No glitches or inadvertent mistakes stain the presentation.
2. You can load up with testimonials.

The key to a successful infomercial

Testimonials are crucial to selling the viewer anything — and I mean *anything* — he or she regards as beyond the comfort-zone of personal experiences. That means they're especially crucial to two types of infomercials — those selling a product whose use replaces what we might call an "earlier generation" product (such as a convection oven, shown to perform better than the trusty kitchen range), and the "I made a ton of money and so can you" programs, in which testimonials by live (and, please, not overly attractive) folks-just-like-us overcome our implicit skepticism of all Get Rich Quick pitches.

How about a celebrity?

Celebrities serve a potent purpose for *some* infomercials: They'll hold a random viewer who interrupts his or her channel-hopping *because* gee, here's a celebrity on the screen. But a negative: a celebrity can double, artificially, the production cost. Folks-just-like-us testimonials don't.

A well-known infomercial producer has said flatly:

"Other than the product you're selling, the single most important element in *every* successful infomercial is a string of testimonials from satisfied customers or users. Testimonials are so important that without them your chances of producing a profitable infomercial diminish hugely."

How long and how strong

The classic infomercial is 30 minutes long. Some, who jump into the waters without testing for depth or temperature, produce a 30-minute drama that peaks at about 25 minutes, then goes into its close.

Uh-uh.

Direct marketers know a Great Truth outsiders don't know: Most viewers won't watch the whole show. This isn't *I Love Lucy* or *NYPD Blue*. It's a 30-minute direct response sales pitch. They'll watch enough to either sharpen or dull their initial mild curiosity.

The triple close

So if we're smart we try for the close three times. To make the point an easy one, we divide the show into three 10-minute segments (oh, by the way, don't go for a full 30 minutes; allow for station-breaks). Each segment should be self-sustaining, like individual pages in a catalog. Each concludes with a hard go-for-the-jugular close.

The logic is unassailable: If the viewer doesn't pick up the phone, you've entertained without purpose. And a stupefying number of infomercial dilettantes do just that: They're afraid to ask for the order or they think asking for the order isn't part of what the infomercial is supposed to do.

That's fine for General Motors, but it isn't so fine for the direct marketer who decides the company's computer software or single-payment homeowners insurance or laser cosmetic surgery or body-building equipment needs explanation and demonstration. The demonstration *has* to lead to a sale, or the company paying for it and the executive okaying the script have produced an ego-piece instead of a powerful sales weapon.

What Sells and What Doesn't

Every veteran infomercial user I know agrees: Anything priced below $40 to $50 faces a tough future. That's because the cost of production, added to the cost of fringe time on cable or broadcast stations, demands a bigger dollar response than any $19.95 item can bring.

For that reason, if your item just doesn't seem to be worth more than $19.95, bundle it into a group of three and sell the batch for $49.95. (Suggestion: "Buy two for $49.95, get one free.") Is your markup four to six times the raw cost? Fine.

Exclusions

Exclusion from this analysis: 900-number infomercials such as psychic hotlines and sex-related shows. These average $2.95 to $3.95 per minute, and calls can go on and on. The reason for exemption isn't call length, but rather the sale of a non-product: No shelf-life problems, no overstock, no warehousing, no shipping, no back end . . . and often multiple calls from the same buyer with no additional overhead.

A terrifying statistic: Eight of 10 infomercials fail. Why? The answer might be mechanical: The producer has paid too much for the broadcast time, is reaching the wrong viewership, or has underpriced or overpriced what's being sold. From the creative strategist's viewpoint, the failure might be because the offer doesn't connect with the viewers, doesn't convince the viewers, or doesn't perform one of two mandatory functions: a) illustrating a previously unavailable solution to a problem, or b) illustrating easy superiority over a previous financial, social, or physical condition.

It ain't QVC or the Home Shopping Network.

Entrepreneurs look at QVC or HSN and see stratospheric sales of trivia. This drives them to infomercials.

Hold it, fellas! Shopping networks and infomercials aren't parallel. Home shopping junkies watch these channels and bite occasionally. They deliberately tune to the shopping channel. It's like attending an auction: We never know what we might carry home, but we know we're at an auction.

Infomercials catch the viewer unaware. That's why celebrities often can rescue a colorless offer. It's also why a properly-produced infomercial includes repeated toll-free numbers (I'm for "supering" those numbers at the bottom of the screen for minutes at a time) and multiple closes.

The info two-step

No home shopping network has any two-step offers — that is, an offer whose point is to get the viewer to call for more information. A two-step makes no sense in a total shopping ambience. But high-dollar infomercials, paralleling high-dollar direct mail offers, can thrive on "no obligation" and "free details" offers, which dump solid leads onto telemarketers for aggressive follow-up. (For a discussion of telemarketing, see chapter 4.)

A two-step offer has a big positive and a big negative. The positive is that you can apparently relax the pressure (note the word *apparently*, please) because you aren't asking for a commitment. All you're doing is giving the viewer a chance to examine a limited-time opportunity.

The negative is the standard two-step negative: You have to sell twice. Veterans of these marketing wars know getting an inquiry is making a sale. Then they have to sell again. The reason they're willing to put up with a double obstacle is because they never would be able to land the fish with a single hook, no matter how richly-baited.

If you decide to aim for an inquiry, two mandatory recognitions are in order: First, realize that your closure rate will be fractional. Television responses are impulse-responses, and the denials are fierce ("I don't remember asking for that"). Second, follow up *fast* — and by fast I mean the same day if possible. Don't sit on leads, because they age faster than a slab of butter on a boiling-hot day.

Mandatory Inclusions

If you don't repeatedly point out what a terrific bargain this is, you're a loser.

If you don't repeatedly point out that this is a limited offer, you'll lose sales and leads you should have.

If you don't hammer home that toll-free number, you're costing yourself business.

If you sacrifice clarity for arty lighting and strange camera angles, you'll lose viewers.

If you succumb to the MTV hand-held, jouncy-image, multiple cuts approach to camera-work, you'll alienate those most able to buy.

If you use humor only to establish rapport and become totally serious about what you're selling, you'll increase response.

If you have an "expert host" and don't have on-camera acolytes saluting him or her as an expert host, you're wasting the opportunity to add credibility.

If you lump all the testimonials into one corner of the infomercial, you risk missing potential buyers who would believe a testimonial far more than they'd believe your own claim.

Finding the gold pavement

Not every Infomercial Street is paved with gold. But some are. Oh, sure, some of the cream is out of the bottle. But we're not yet down to skim milk. Even with soaring rate costs and viewer-numbness caused by a plethora of same-looking half-hours, infomercials are just emerging from infancy. The infant is aging rapidly: Already abuses and uninformed invasions are damaging the medium.

Remember the golden days of telemarketing, in the mid-1970s? What spoiled the broth was the rancid pepper added by too-greedy, too-pugnacious telemarketers whose lack of manners and lack of grace stimulated a corresponding lack of manners and grace among people being called.

If you want to share in the gold, promise what you can deliver. Couch that promise clearly. Don't let some production maniac divert your message into a mélange of disconnected arty shots. Sacrifice ego-messages for credible testimonials. And ask yourself: If I were watching the television screen instead of shoveling this pap onto it, would *I* be convinced enough to lift the phone?

Then lean over and pick up the gold.

Figure 14-1

Veteran infomercial star Carleton Sheets, host of a long-running series showing viewers how to buy property with no down payment, talks on-camera to Bill and Patsy Hicks, a couple who have profited from using his techniques. User testimonials have great strength in infomercials.

Figure 14-2

Carleton Sheets discusses his "no money down" real estate program with Mark and Tonya Figg, another successful couple. Can an infomercial have too many testimonials? In this author's opinion, if they're pertinent and credible, no.

15

Easy Rules for Effective Radio Advertising

From its once-lofty position, radio has become an ancillary media choice. The glamor of television and the Internet has caused many to ignore and others to misuse radio. For many marketers, radio has become an afterthought: "Oh, yeah, throw a few bucks into radio."

So a copywriter who has little familiarity with the medium adapts a space ad. Spots run and produce little. "Radio doesn't work," the advertiser and his agency agree, retiring from the medium.

Properly exploited, radio can be the most economical and most flexible mass communications weapon. Radio does work, if one uses it properly. And using it properly begins with language.

Television has two implicit comprehensional advantages over radio. As words are spoken, the viewer can see either the speaker's lips, the product he or she is describing, or superimposed words validating those words. With radio, words (plus occasional music and sound effects, both accessories) have to carry the message without assistance.

Infomercials have returned to radio, where the genre began considerably longer than half a century ago. The marketer who simply lifts the audio from the television version of an infomercial has to be making a mistake in one of the two media.

An absolute rule for a radio infomercial: Lacking the possibility of a startling or "grabber" opening, begin by making a big promise. Consider the multi-voice technique, especially a question/answer format.

Clarity über alles.

What's wrong with this sentence from a radio commercial?

When Bob's partner's working, he's red in the face from this sale and ready to bruise again with the next.

What's wrong? Just about everything. Two contractions in a row. "Red," which has to be reinterpreted quickly as the next word is the catalyst, changing the listener's first impression of "read." "Bruise," which many will hear as "brews." Total incoherence.

The radio writer would know the difference between "he's red in the face" and "his face is red" . . . and probably would know enough to avoid this strange construction altogether. No, it isn't as disastrous as "Look into a new gas oven," but the Clarity Commandment had better be in high gear with every radio sentence.

What's wrong with this one?

Alfred D. Strong personally, who's president and general manager of our restaurant, will welcome you.

This one is more subtle. "Alfred D. Strong" might be heard as "Alfred the Strong." "Who's" is the principal offender, because the primal reaction to the word is to "whose," a possessive; reinterpretation has to follow. Not as obvious is the positioning of "personally," which modifies "welcome." Radio's demand for straightforward exposition suggests the modifier be closer to the word it modifies. Better:

Alfred Strong — he's president and general manager of our restaurant — will welcome you personally.

Are these minor changes? Certainly. Are they improvements in clarity and comprehension? Certainly.

A Few Rules for Radio Writing

If we have any reverence for clarity, we'll follow eight very easy rules when generating radio messages:

1. *Place the subject before the verb.*
2. *Short sentences are clearer than two sentences tied together with "and." For example, "They've done this. They're considering that" is clearer than "They've done this and are considering that."*
3. *Use music as a mood-setter, not as an end in itself.*
4. *Narration followed by a jingle is clearer than a longer jingle alone.*
5. *Give ample instructions, within the script, to the announcer. Instructions should be all caps, and nothing else in the script should be all caps.*
6. *Come to an inflectional stop before starting a new concept. (Inflectional doesn't mean temporal. Time is precious, and a long pause lets the listener's interest sag.)*
7. *Spell out numbers. This prevents stupid mistakes and is your assurance the performer will read the numbers the way you want them read. So it's "eleven-twenty-nine," not "$11.29." The year is "twenty-oh-four," not "2004." The amount is "a thousand dollars," not "$1,000."*
8. *Don't leave pronunciation and emphasis to the announcer's imagination. Your script might read: ". . . headquartered in Chickasha [CHICK-A-SHAY], Oklahoma" or "Ask for John Taliaferro [TOL-LIVER]." It might read "Call <u>right now</u> and be a hero to your family," or you might prefer "Call right now and be a <u>hero</u> to your family."*

The very simplicity of these rules demonstrates one advantage of radio as an advertising medium: Changes can be made within minutes of actual air-time, and the need for technical knowledge is minimal.

Multiple voices to prevent "ear-fatigue"

For concepts requiring explanation/education, a two-voice approach can add clarity and reduce listener fatigue. This is especially true in long formats. One voice asks questions: This voice represents the typical listener. The other voice answers the questions: This voice is the happy voice of authority.

If the long format introduces a third voice, that voice should be identifiably different from the other two. In a short radio commercial, three voices can be confusing.

Twin dangers: Cleverness and confusion

An absolute rule:

Don't let the desire to be clever override clarity.

Many inexperienced radio writers think of entertainment first and "sell" second. Cleverness becomes the message instead of the carrier, and what happens is that sell never does enter into the mixture. Marketing messages of any type, for any product or service, in any medium, should tell the reader, viewer, or listener what to do. Never is this more true (and more valuable) than in radio.

Would you have written this?

One of the marketing magazines reprinted this radio continuity, a spot for an athletic shoe, featuring an athlete named Jerry Stackhouse. Your opinion (recognizing that in print we can't "feel" the music)?

The way I feel,
You know the love is real,
With your leather and lace,
You got a tongue but not a face.
Left and right,
I like all the things you do.
Just show me that you love me,
'Cuz I love the both of you.
Chorus: Jerry loves his Fila shoes.
I'm takin' off my socks, baby.
Chorus: What is Jerry talkin' 'bout?
You want a double-know, dontcha?
Chorus: I think the man is freakin' out.
Ooh, I love it when you make that
little squeaky noise.

Five obvious conclusions:

1. The concept is better designed for television than for radio. *Reading the script,* we can imagine a logical visual for each line; in radio, we're well into the spot before we have any idea what it's about, and we never are quite sure.
2. If the listener doesn't know Jerry Stackhouse, the spot makes little sense.
3. If the listener does know Jerry Stackhouse, the spot has a recognizable image.
4. Without multiple exposures even those who do know Stackhouse will have difficulty understanding what's being sold. Nowhere does the lyric mention the name of the shoe — "Stack II."
5. The call to action is zero.

Don't misunderstand that last conclusion. This advertiser wasn't after a call to action. That's why repetition is mandatory in "image" commercials, while each exposure demands immediate replies in direct response commercials.

Which one pulled better?

Compare the Stack II shoe commercial with this hard-boiled, go-for-the-jugular spot selling Las Vegas vacations (I've changed the phone number because the offer no longer applies):

MUSIC: BRASSY MARCH TEMPO, QUICKLY UP AND UNDER
ANNC.: Las Vegas! Your dream vacation in this exciting entertainment capital of the world is about to come true. Listen carefully to this offer from the Las Vegas Holiday Club: <u>You</u> can have a three-day, two-night vacation package for yourself and a companion in glamorous Las Vegas, virtually free. Yes, you heard me right. Your Las Vegas getaway is virtually free. Join the fun . . . see the sights . . . take in the fabulous shows. They're all part of this vacation package for two. Unbelievable but true! But you've got to call right now — one-eight-hundred-three-two-Vegas. In numbers, that's one-eight-hundred, three-two-eight, thirty-four-twenty-seven. You'll stay at Vegas Inn, right on the Vegas Strip. See big-name entertainment. Enjoy free drinks and the twenty-

---

four-hour excitement only Las Vegas can give you. But space is limited. You must call now. Lift that phone and call one-eight-hundred, three-two-eight, thirty-four-twenty-seven. Don't miss out. Call the Las Vegas Holiday Club *now* for your virtually free Las Vegas vacation: one-eight-hundred, three-two-eight, thirty-four-twenty-seven. One last time: one-eight-hundred, three-two-eight, thirty-four-twenty-seven.

A second version of this commercial uses two voices, not as question/answer but as an emphasis device:

MUSIC:	BRASSY MARCH TEMPO, QUICKLY UP AND UNDER
ANNC. 1:	Listen carefully to this offer direct from fabulous Las Vegas:
ANNC. 2:	Why wait? Your dream vacation in this exciting entertainment capital of the world is about to come true.
ANNC. 1:	<u>You</u> can have a three-day, two-night vacation package for yourself and a companion in glamorous Las Vegas, virtually free.
ANNC. 2:	Yes, you heard right. Your Las Vegas getaway is virtually free. Join the fun . . . see the sights . . . take in the fabulous shows. They're all part of this vacation package for two. Unbelievable but true!
ANNC. 1:	But you've got to call right now — one-eight-hundred-three-two-Vegas. In numbers, that's one-eight-hundred, three-two-eight, thirty-four-twenty-seven.
ANNC. 2:	You'll stay at Vegas Inn, one of the biggest and most luxurious hotels and casinos right on the Vegas Strip. See big-name entertainment. Enjoy free drinks and the twenty-four-hour fun and excitement only Las Vegas can give you.
ANNC. 1:	But this offer is <u>extremely</u> limited. <u>You</u> <u>must</u> <u>call</u> <u>now</u>.
ANNC. 2:	And get this: Even if you can't come now, call now to reserve your vacation for later on.
ANNC. 1:	Lift that phone and call one-eight-hundred, three-two-

> eight, thirty-four-twenty-seven. Don't miss out. Call the Las Vegas Holiday Club <u>now</u> for your virtually free Las Vegas vacation: one-eight-hundred, three-two-eight, thirty-four-twenty-seven.
>
> ANNC. 2:   One last time: one-eight-hundred, three-two-eight, thirty-four-twenty-seven.

The two Las Vegas commercials show another beneficial facet of radio — the ability to test one concept against another. (NOTE: When testing, be sure the demographic mix, time of day, and total audiences of all test outlets are parallel.) The first is a straightforward single-voice progression. The second is a relentless multi-voice. Both hammer the phone number. The goal is immediate response.

Which one pulled better?

In premium time, the one-voice version pulled better; in fringe time, the two-voice version pulled better. This may have to do with the personal tensions that negatively affect listener response to a more complex message during drive-times.

The same commercial in two different lengths

Which length produces the most responses per dollar? The smart marketer tests. Usually, if a two-minute commercial fails to produce response it will be a miracle if shorter versions produce response.

So a sensible approach is to air the longest version. If response seems satisfactory, shorter versions then test their comparative pulling power. If a marketer produces 120-second, 90-second, and 60-second versions, the 120-second would air first; based on its success, the 90 comes next, then the 60. Because stations tend simply to increase cost in exact ratio to spot length, twenty-first century lengths seem to be 90, 60, and 30; the 120-second version has priced itself out of the market in many situations.

Here are two versions of a commercial for a cosmetic surgery clinic. Notice the elements in the 120-second version that aren't in the 90-second version.

[120-second version]

MUSIC:	UP AND QUICKLY UNDER
WOMAN 1:	You look marvelous . . . twenty years younger!
WOMAN 2:	I'll tell you a secret: I had a little nip and tuck done on my face and neck.
WOMAN 1:	You did? When?
WOMAN 2:	Last week.
WOMAN 1:	Oh, come on. If you had a cosmetic procedure last week, you'd still be swollen.
WOMAN 2:	(LAUGHS) Hardly. At Beautiful You Centers I got rid of my double chin and all those wrinkles on Tuesday. And while they were at it they got rid of that ugly mole I had on this cheek. Steve and I went out Thursday night.
WOMAN 1:	I can't believe it!
ANNC.:	Believe it! Forget old-fashioned cosmetic surgery. Beautiful You Centers, Bolton's own world-class home of twenty-first century cosmetic procedures, uses the miracle of lasers to give you back your youthful, healthy look.
WOMAN 2:	And no one has to know.
ANNC.:	Absolutely right. Healing is so fast no one has to know. Within a couple of days you'll be looking at your mirror and asking . . .
WOMAN 2:	Why did I wait so long?
WOMAN 1:	Is there any way I can tell how I'll look afterward?
WOMAN 2:	Oh, sure. They have "computer imaging." That means . . .
ANNC.:	Computer imaging means you'll see yourself on the computer screen, the way you'll look afterward. Want a smaller nose or a stronger chin? The Beautiful You computer literally lets you select your own look!
WOMAN 1:	What does it cost?
ANNC.:	It's surprisingly affordable. And consultation is absolutely free, including your computer imaging.
WOMAN 2:	Why wait, when you can look younger next week? Your friends won't know — they'll just say . . .
WOMAN 1:	You look marvelous!
ANNC.:	Beautiful You Centers are at seven hundred Craxton Boulevard, in Bolton Hills. Call for your free consulta-

tion and computer imaging: nine-one-six, four-six-five, five thousand. Men, call too, to find out about hair transplants that let you go back to work the next day: Nine-one-six, four-six-five, five thousand.

WOMAN 1: Give me that number one more time:

ANNC.: Beautiful You Centers, nine-one-six, four-six-five, five thousand. You'll be glad you made that call.

WOMAN 2: And how you will!

MUSIC: UP TO FINISH

[90-second version]

MUSIC: UP AND QUICKLY UNDER

WOMAN 1: You look marvelous . . . twenty years younger!

WOMAN 2: I'll tell you a secret: I had a little nip and tuck done on my face and neck.

WOMAN 1: You did? When?

WOMAN 2: Last week.

WOMAN 1: Come on. If you had a cosmetic procedure last week, you'd still be swollen.

WOMAN 2: (LAUGHS) Hardly. At Beautiful You Centers I got rid of my double chin and all those wrinkles on Tuesday. Steve and I went out Thursday night.

WOMAN 1: I can't believe it!

ANNC.: Believe it! Forget old-fashioned cosmetic surgery. Beautiful You Centers, Bolton's home of twenty-first century cosmetic procedures, uses the miracle of lasers to give you back your youthful, healthy look.

WOMAN 2: And no one has to know.

ANNC.: Right. Healing is so fast no one has to know. Within a couple of days you'll be asking . . .

WOMAN 2: Why did I wait so long?

WOMAN 1: Is there any way I can tell how I'll look afterward?

WOMAN 2: Oh, sure. They have "computer imaging."

ANNC.: Computer imaging means you'll see yourself on the computer screen, the way you'll look afterward. The Beautiful You computer lets you select your own look!

WOMAN 1:   What does it cost?
ANNC.:   It's surprisingly affordable. And consultation is ab-
           solutely free, including your computer imaging.
WOMAN 2:   Your friends won't know — they'll just say . . .
WOMAN 1:   You look marvelous!
ANNC.:   Beautiful You Centers are at seven hundred Craxton
           Boulevard, in Bolton Hills. Call for your free consulta-
           tion and computer imaging: nine-one-six, four-six-
           five, five thousand. That's Beautiful You Centers,
           nine-one-six, four-six-five, five thousand. You'll be
           glad you made that call.
WOMAN 2:   And how you will!
MUSIC: UP TO FINISH

The shorter version necessarily dropped some details and the reference to the men's clinic. The message is intact. Notice how the commercial
transfers its "sell" to an announcer, enabling conversation to remain a credible dramatic unit.

Argue with the Time Salesperson

Each station follows its own drummer. Some regard the rate card as
sacrosanct; others regard it as a point of departure.

The smart marketer knows implicitly, for all media and all production:
Negotiation is never a total waste.

How about p.i. (per inquiry) deals? (A p.i. deal is an arrangement in
which the advertiser pays the station for each response rather than paying a
predetermined per-spot fee.) Many stations reject them; but that p.i. deals
exist at all adds to the fascination of this most misunderstood and misused
of all media.

For image, for retention-value, or for instant transactions, radio is a
medium not to be dismissed . . . and not to be mishandled.

16

Marketing to Seniors

This will be one of the shorter chapters of this book, but certainly not because marketing to seniors is unimportant. Rather, it's because a complete book covers this subject on its own (*Silver Linings: Selling to the Expanding Mature Market,* Bonus Books, 1996).

Seniors are in command, and they know it. They command the power to buy luxury items. They command primary attention from stockbrokers, banks, and the world of finance. They rapidly are becoming a primary group on the Internet. And marketing to seniors — if one has the *chutzpah* to lump this huge, polyglot assortment into one bunch — isn't complicated, unless you're a brave and hardy soul who's willing to depart from the trusted path.

Coddling terminology

One of the horrors of trying to communicate in an era of political correctness is having to coddle terminology while trying to put together a cogent sales argument.

Older folks aren't different from any other groups that share *some* characteristics — women, gays, people of color, religious denominations.

Terminology depends on which segment is speaking or being spoken to. Some political pressure groups call themselves *seniors*. The mammoth American Association of Retired Persons (AARP) calls its legions *mature persons* (actually, "mature Americans," but I'm universalizing). *Golden ager* is mildly poetic, but someone tagged with that phrase seems ancient. We still hear the term *older people,* although this term has assumed a pejorative overtone over the past few years.

Some Basic Rules of Communications

Here's a quick primer describing reasonably foolproof techniques for marketing to — well, let's call them seniors, even though the preferred term is mature persons.

Do you know what the major cause of seniors not bothering to look at your message is? Sure, you do: Small print. For that matter, small print can be deadly in any appeal, but with this age group "small" is any size under 9-point. Make that 10-point. (For the uninitiated: 72 points to the inch.)

Problem: Seniors also want every "i" dotted and every "t" crossed. This isn't a major problem on the Web or in direct mail, where we can go into as much detail as we believe necessary to explain and justify; but in a space ad — especially in some of the more expensive print media — it can mean a lot of copy in a limited space.

One reason infomercials have been successful among seniors is the infomercial's extended explanation of the selling premise. The rule:

Don't make a long story short. It becomes suspect.

Motivating seniors to write or lift the phone

The 55-plus age group grew up with coupons. So response devices give them comfort. I suggest always including a coupon in any space ad sized ⅓ magazine page or larger . . . and allowing more than ample room to flesh out a reply card in a mailing.

Of all age brackets, seniors are most likely to mail their response instead of phoning. But don't assume this means you can abandon the toll-free number. As Alexandre Dumas said, all generalizations are false, including this one. Seniors are an *increasingly* polyglot group, and we're dealing in the broadest kind of averages when we draw any conclusion.

The AARP has listed as principal motivators: need, desire, solid information, and good price. The explanation:

"Older people will try very hard for a low or discounted price on items considered simply a need. If it is a desire, however, they are more apt to spend a great deal more. The trick is to know the difference. One person's need is another's desire. For example: One person may drive a 10 year old car; it gets them where they have to go (a need) . . . and spend a great deal on designer clothes (a desire). Another person will desire the latest, hottest car and spend on that while conserving on clothing, seeing clothing simply as 'a need.' "

So the two tricks are 1) to make a desire seem achievable; 2) to generate a need where none existed before.

Leaning on the old dependable motivators

I'll take a more brutal, more clinical position: We can lean on the standard "Great Motivators" — *fear, exclusivity, guilt, greed,* and *need for approval* — if we can tie them to psychological peculiarities generic to aging.

So we put a floor of credibility under every offer, because the older we get, the more we're aware of the P.T. Barnum Syndrome. Fear manifests itself as fear of being a sucker, rather than fear of some physical circumstance. Recognizing this, the more reassurance we put into the copy, the more credentials we bring into the arena, the more we emphasize and underscore the guarantee, the more we use comparisons between ourselves as "the guys in the white hat" and those other scoundrels out there, the more fear works for us.

Exclusivity is tricky for seniors, because it seems to work best with those still in the work force. Too, the ostensible offer of exclusivity can't allow itself to conflict with fear of being a sucker; that's why credit card companies have a tough time upgrading within this group, *unless it's free* . . . which changes the motivator.

Guilt works when it's tied to a carefully-mounted sales argument structured around the legacy for children or grandchildren; occasionally, too, one can build guilt based on the potential for personal image, or better yet, *loss* of personal image.

Of the five great motivators, the runaway winner with seniors is *greed.* Not *obvious* greed; bargain-based greed, the suggestion the reader or viewer or listener is getting a deal others won't get. (Actually, it's usually tops with all age groups. Test it for yourself.)

Scream "Bargain!" and your chance of sales goes up exponentially.

Scream "Bargain" tied to the suggestion, "You'll live longer or more comfortably or in a greater position of supremacy among your associates" and you can't miss — *provided the offer is credible.*

Not an easy task? If it were, we wouldn't have the competitive edge.

Can we scream "Bargain!" on every offer? Why not? Yes, this conclusion is cynical. Yes, too, it's erected on a substantial foundation of trying vainly to find another motivator that consistently can beat it. Certainly, if you're testing, make one side of the test a bargain-theme.

(Testing is always a good idea, especially because the senior market isn't homogenized, as I'm about to explain.)

Fragmentation Means Test, Test, TEST!

The marketer who regards ages 50 to 90 as a single entity is in for some nasty shocks.

One reason is Social Security and its accouterments, such as dramatic changes in health insurance and employee pension plans. Another is an attitudinal change toward the individual's position in the competitive workplace, a gradual metamorphosis as a worker reaches a pre-set retirement.

An example of the differential within the "senior" segment: 35 percent of the 55 to 59 age group has "discretionary income"; in the 70-plus age group it's 23 percent. The marketer who complains about how tough it is to get the over-65s to respond should ask the mirror: Have I transformed this offer into an apparent 1) necessity, which 2) I'm presenting as a supreme bargain?

A list company selling a "Mature Market Mailing List" makes this point in its promotional copy:

> "92.4% of all senior names are exact age coded. 76.8% have month and year of birth present for precise age targeting."

When I'm selling "continuity" programs (ongoing delivery of books, collectibles, videos, recordings, and the like), I prefer the under-65s to the over-65s, and not because of a greater availability of discretionary buying power; rather, the under-65s are less likely to be ready to discard books and collectibles than acquire them.

For insurance, considerable stroking and/or reassurance validates an offer:

- "You've driven safely all your life. Why should you pay the same rate as those who. . . ."
- "Do you ride a bike or play tennis or golf? Then you deserve the kind of coverage designed for active, vital. . . ."

We might as well learn the routines.

Certainly everybody reading these words is aware of the graying of America . . . and for that matter, of all first-world countries. The percentage of our targets who have passed the 65 barrier is increasing every year. Projections call for the median age of the U.S. population in the year 2020 to increase by seven years over its 1990 number. In the 30-year span between the long-gone 1990 and the not-so-far-away 2020, the under-50s will see a 1.5 percent drop in their numbers; the over-50s will see a 76 percent increase.

Equally significant: Both sophistication and spending power are expected to go up, faster than will be true of any other group.

But seniors have just one factor in common: age. Beyond that we'll continue to have fragmentation, and we'd better learn to live on our wits and test our way into and (for those of us still around then) through the twenty-first century.

This recognition that we'd better respect testing when approaching seniors isn't handwriting on the wall. Properly digested and used as marketing fuel, it's handwriting on buyers' checks made out to us.

Figure 16-1

This is a classic appeal to seniors: clear, specific, promising a bargain, and suggesting exclusivity because of age.

Figure 16-2

Discount coupons have a potent effect within the seniors marketplace, often doubling or trebling response to an ad.

17

Follow-up Mailings

"Thank you for being our customer this past year. To show our appreciation, if you place an order from this catalog before the expiration date. . . ."

"This Award Certificate is worth $10 toward any purchase of $50 or more from this catalog. It's our way of saying 'Thanks' for being our valued customer. . . ."

Follow-up mailings represent an extraordinarily low-cost way to re-reach customers and prospects. Whether as public relations cement or as a direct appeal, the opportunities too often are overlooked or misused.

Visualizing the power a marketer gains from a message as simple as the one quoted above — to a catalog customer, for example — is easy. All we have to do is visualize the same catalog without the message. Re-communication with existing customers or clients is such an obvious use of follow-up mailings it's bewildering that so many who do business on any level — consumer, commercial, or industrial — don't take advantage of this advantage.

The Low Cost Builder . . . of Business and Rapport

A follow-up mailing is a bond, a fastener, a reminder to the customer that the vendor recognizes him or her (or for that matter, the company) as a customer. Many mail order buyers forget the source of what they have bought. Marketers who are aware that the competitive playing field isn't level (someone who has bought from you before is seven times more likely to choose you instead of a competitor) exploit the relationship.

A parenthetical comment: Shrewd marketers treat prospects as though they are customers. Some perplexity may result, but so does some business.

For producers of computer software, follow-up mailings can be the principal source of revenue. Countless — and I mean *countless* — software companies will give away an early version of a program or sell it for just a few dollars. They depend on upgrades, sold through follow-up mailings, as their profit-generators.

The value of a "Thank you"

Sending a "Thank you" note can't damage a relationship.

On the other hand, unless the "Thank you" has some teeth, it won't help much either. That's why my own preference leans away from "Thank you" and toward "Congratulations" or "Welcome." The difference in psychological effect is obvious, even if the basic text of the communication is the same.

Preventing "buyer's remorse"

A follow-up mailing from a pest control operator splits the difference. On the envelope — which correctly uses a stamp, not postal indicia (I'd opt for a big commemorative stamp) is "You made the right choice!"

Inside is a table-tent-size folded card with "Thank You" on the front panel. The message inside begins:

> *Dear Valued Customer,*
> *I want you to know that you made an excellent choice when you selected Sears as your pest control company. Our revolutionary Once-A-Year pest control service provides. . . .*

And on it goes — a *re-sell*.

What's the value of a re-sell? It helps prevent "Buyer's Remorse," a ghastly syndrome that has become epidemic in the combatively skeptical, litigious marketplace of today. It helps the buyer justify what he or she has bought. And, assuming the welcome letter includes a secondary offer, it generates quick extra revenue. How much revenue? One veteran marketer tells me he anticipates a 10 percent response from an offer enclosed with a welcome letter, regardless of what the merchandise is, if it relates to the original purchase.

A cellular phone provider sends a packet of cards. On the front card is a welcome note which begins:

> *Dear Valued Customer,*
> *Welcome to Cellular Works! We thank you for your recent order and hope you are completely satisfied with both our customer service and your purchase.*
>
> *At Cellular Works we are committed to quality products, competitive prices, and complete customer satisfaction. We. . . .*

Reasonably standard stuff. At the bottom of this card is a "Special Offer":

> *For a Limited Time only!*
> *Call within 10 days of your invoice date and receive any Leather Case for $20.00. That's **30% off** our already low catalog prices!*

The concept is sound, although 1) capitalizing Limited Time unmasks any apparent altruism, and 2) unless the recipient has the company's catalog at hand, "Leather Case" is too generic to initiate a buying action.

Other cards in the packet do offer specific "Limited Time Only" discounts.

Credit card follow-ups galore

Issuers of credit cards are witnessing a slowdown in recruiting new cardholders. No wonder, with the huge volume of affinity cards joining the avalanche of solicitation mailings!

So, the next logical move is to intensify *within* the ranks of existing cardholders . . . to have those cardholders sign up for ancillary services, various types of loans and various types of insurance being the most common.

One credit card issuer — among the most aggressive in today's marketplace — has an ongoing schedule of communications with its cardholders. One mailing is a standard "credit card access checks" mailing with this curiously mild, ho-hum, motivationless, ungrammatical first paragraph:

> *We've designed your no annual fee MBNA® **Platinum Plus** MasterCard® to be a convenient financial resource. A wide array of services to help you do more with your MasterCard account.*

(Revisit chapter 3 of this book: An absolute rule of letters, whether a first solicitation or a follow-up: Fire your biggest gun first. Credit card issuers, please note.)

Another mailing from this same source has "Congratulations," followed by "You have been singled out for a NEW customer benefit" on its face. On the reverse side of the envelope is "Catch the Excitement!" a highly commercial catch-phrase damaging the "singled out" effect. Inside, "Catch the Excitement!" is the theme of a promotion to the bank's customers, offering prizes as an incentive to buy auto insurance from the bank's insurance services division. With frequent references to the preexisting relationship, the communication quite properly positions the offer as an extension of that relationship.

A competing credit card has on its envelope the single word "NOTICE" reversed out of a blue bar. I'd have settled for this, but the envelope continues with "Attention Optima® Cardmembers . . . Startling information that may affect your future travel plans."

The letter sells baggage delay and loss protection insurance, with a canvas sport bag as the incentive for quick action.

Never one to be left in the shadows, the American Express Platinum Card sends a follow-up to a follow-up.

On the envelope of the first mailing is, in tasteful type, "A feature of the Platinum Card® we invite you to use at your discretion." The letter begins:

> *As a Platinum Card® member, I cordially invite you to enroll in the Sign & Travel® Account, the payment option from American Express® that gives you even more flexibility with the Platinum Card.*

(American Express seems to hold the world championship for the number of "®" and "™" uses in a communication. This letter opening has a peculiar grammatical twist — "As a Platinum Card member, *I* " — suggesting that the writer, not the recipient, is the member. The same curse afflicted a follow-up from a software company, which begins, "As one of our valued customers, we want to keep you informed about our new products and services." If the whole concept confuses you, an easy way out is to start with "Because you're one of our valued customers, we . . ." or "We want to keep you, as one of our valued customers, informed. . . .")

The American Express follow-up mailing is in an identical envelope with identical envelope copy. So a question: Is repeating the envelope copy a sound or unsound technique?

My opinion: Unsound. The second mailing would be unnecessary if the individual had responded, so a more dramatic message is in order. Even "Did you misplace this?" or "Second invitation" probably would have more fingers at the flap.

The second letter begins:

> *Recently, I invited you to enroll in the Sign & Travel® Account. If you've already responded to my invitation-thank you, your welcome package should arrive shortly. If you haven't yet responded, I invite you to once again consider the benefits.*

I'm reasonably sure the production team meant to insert a dash, not a hyphen between "invitation" and "thank you," which, as printed, presents a bizarre effect — "my invitation-thank you," paralleling and unintentionally parodying the "Thank you, please" so many fund raisers use.

Another American Express second follow-up begins:

> *Not long ago, I invited you to participate in Privileged Assets®, a convenient annuity program offered by American Partners Life Insurance Company, an American Express Company. Privileged Assets enables you to accumulate substantial tax-deferred savings for your future.*
> *I'm writing today because I believe this opportunity is just too important for you to pass up without a close second look. . . .*

I'd have started with the second paragraph, then leaped into a competitive advantage. But that, too, is an opinion. The unassailable fact: Follow-up mailings are sound marketing procedures.

Astute Marketing

Always an astute marketer, Omaha Steaks has as one of its many follow-ups a folder with this incentive:

> *"Tell a friend about Omaha Steaks. When You Do, We'll Give YOU . . . 4 (5 oz.) Filet Mignons FREE with your next order!"*

I've written copy for Omaha Steaks. It's difficult to keep up with their inventiveness. No, I don't like the caps and lower case treatment, the automatic conversion from one-to-one message to pitch; but I do admire "FREE with your next order," which ties the venerable member-get-a-member approach to repeat business.

Consider your own customers and clients. Have you "milked" them as thoroughly as you might? It's flat-out impossible to overmail an existing buyer or donor.

Follow-Ups as Business Generators

From software to ice cream, from finance to fund raising, from phony surveys to video and record clubs, properly constructed follow-up mailings can generate business as few other direct marketing weapons can. Why? Because the marketer's announced assumption of dealing with "family" is contagious.

Have you been keeping tab on the follow-up mailings that come to you . . . and, more significantly, what your reaction is to them?

One follow-up worthy of comment is from the publisher of an expensive financial newsletter, who sent me a free issue. The mailing offers me a year's subscription for "the low subscription price of $595." Regular rate, it states, is $1075.

Just two problems with this follow-up:

1. The bill drives the communication. What leaps out of the envelope is an invoice, headed "IMPORTANT NOTICE — Your FREE trial subscription expires soon." Oh, there's a business reply envelope and a strange guarantee (I'm guaranteed "worry-free uninterrupted delivery"), but nowhere in this follow-up — and the follow-up to *any* free test is a crucial one — is there any warmth, any rapport, any "Look what you'll miss if you don't . . ." imperative.

Actually, the reason I didn't subscribe is that the free issue they sent me was dull and took second place in its nondescript envelope to a pitch for a financial seminar. But that isn't the point. What *is* the point? That this type of follow-up has to construct a heavy re-sell, or forget it. Even if the newsletter had been exciting, the follow-up would have leached the excitement out.

The First Rule of Follow-Ups

For subscriptions, for software upgrades, for any mailing suggesting status (and yes, I include fund raising in that category), I offer the First Rule of Follow-Ups, straight from Al Jolson:

Tell them, "You ain't seen nothin' yet!" . . . then prove it.

We're talking basic psychology here. We're talking "re-ups" here. We're talking re-initiation of the salivary glands here. Raw notices can't compete in this arena.

So a business magazine plays it right with this envelope copy:

Coming up: Salaries.
Is yours in line?

The pitch, explained quickly and dynamically, is that I'm going to miss the "Salary" issue if I don't renew.

It's the starter, not the fuel.

As I said, "You ain't seen nothin' yet" is a can't miss stimulus, bait we fish will gobble up as a reflex action. But use it as the starter, not as the fuel. Understand, please, if I may be arch: You have to follow up this opening of a follow-up with a follow-up that follows up. That means: If I ain't seen nothin' yet, what is it I haven't seen?

A premium ice cream, which shrewdly builds its database by including a name and address area on discount coupons in newspaper free-standing inserts, mails a booklet of recipes, which includes additional discount coupons for "new flavors and low-fat treats." That's using a follow-up the right way. Two minor carps: 1) Will premium ice cream lovers respond to an offer for low-fat? As a safety-net, why not include a coupon for the regular high-cholesterol stuff? 2) They didn't ask me, but I'd have mentioned the coupons on the cover of this booklet, since the names came from discount coupons in the first place.

A CD continuity "club" offers former members who have canceled their memberships 12 free CDs for reigniting their continuity engines. Well done! They obviously know, from experience or from a knowledge of basic psychology, the *Second* Rule of Follow-Ups.

The Second Rule of Follow-Ups: Don't be *Over-Assumptive.*

I'm in favor of assumptions. The mailing assumes, presumes, that the recipient wants the information or merchandise. Simple human indolence will account for many acceptances.

But don't let an assumption get out of hand. An assumption has to cleave to the Second Rule of Follow-Ups:

To be valid, an assumption must be congruent with the reader's experiential background.

That Rule may seem complicated because of the terminology. See how it works? If you *do* find it complicated, it's a violation of the Second Rule of Follow-Ups (except this isn't a follow-up).

The Third Rule of Follow-Ups

Anyway, the explanation lies in the Third Rule of Follow-Ups:

*Assuming a target-individual's background or education or personal history is dangerous **unless** the purpose of that assumption is to stroke and flatter.*

Got it? I can send you a mailing assuming you're bright and clever and well-read and a good swimmer and an award-winner and, if my own stature has any significance, my close buddy.

I *shouldn't* send you a mailing assuming you're adept at tight-rope walking or deciphering hieroglyphics or photorealistic painting or luge racing, unless I have prior information that you are.

The curse of overassumption

What happens too often is that an overeager mailer or an overassumptive list company says, "You bought a Red Flyer sled, so you're a luge racer."

That, in fact, apparently was behind a letterless mailing addressed to me as chairman of my company. The pitch, on a two-sided sheet:

Achieve both your Novell Certification (CNE) and Microsoft Windows NT Certification (MCSE) for less than you would pay for one at other training centers!

Huh?

I know what prompted this: I bought some software. But the *assumption* is wrong. I'm not approached as a software buyer; I'm approached as a trainee. The result of lumping me in a mass database of buyers could have been total disaffection, if I felt that without the training I couldn't achieve proper use of the software. (Fortunately, I have a terminal case of "Administrator's Ego" — I hire people to handle stuff like that.)

The mailer could have saved this by enclosing a letter explaining the value of certification. No one is exempt from useful education, and the higher up the corporate ladder one climbs, the greater recognition any useful education warrants.

Milk Your Customers.

Some companies recruit customers and members, recruit customers and members, recruit customers and members — and then, once they have them, they mail to them once or twice a year.

Opinion: Big mistake.

I've written copy for mailers who badger their buyers every two weeks. And it works, provided the mailings follow the Three Rules of Follow-Ups.

You may not have enough grist in your mill to maintain a schedule like that, but certainly you can find enough items and services fitting the Three Rules, even if they're third party endorsements, to schedule a mailing every two months.

A credit card company sent an almost-good mailing with this heading:

U.S. Department of Transportation reports 2,436,951 domestic baggage complaints in the U.S. last year.*

Okay, so it's a weak way of putting what should have been a strong opener. Okay, so the asterisk (not explained until the bottom of the reverse side — ugh) lists the source, an unnecessary interruption. Okay, so it's just a statistic. What partially saves this message is the powerful opening of the letter:

Frankly, I'm concerned about this alarming statistic.

I say "partially" saves because as presented the statistic isn't alarming. It needs personal relevance, some adjectives, and action verbs. That isn't the subject of this chapter, though. Lost baggage *is* a universal problem, and this credit card company has arranged with an insurance company to mail lost or delayed bag coverage to its cardmembers. A sports bag is thrown in as an incentive. It's handled well, except for copy and omission of the actual deal in the response device. (With those exceptions it parallels the old joke, "Except for that, Mr. Lincoln, how did you like the show?")

You can see: Even a nondescript follow-up mailing can connect if it follows the three Rules.

So what are you waiting for? Go thou and do likewise.

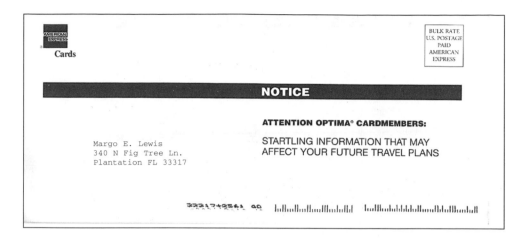

Figure 17-1a

Figure 17-16

The envelope from this mailing to cardmembers promises "STARTLING INFORMATION." The understated text and layout of the letter are out of sync with the word "STARTLING," the asterisk in the too-quiet overline is unconscionable, and not mentioning the actual charge in the response device suggests sneakiness. Follow-ups to active customers dare not lapse into either sameness or apparent equivocation.

```
Decisionmark Corp.
200 Second Avenue S.E.
      Suite 300
 Cedar Rapids, Iowa
    52401-1201
   800-365-7629
```

January 24

Dear Proximity Owner,

At the DMA conference in New Orleans, you received Proximity®, the powerful desktop mapping and marketing software from Decisionmark. Hopefully, you've already installed the program and find it to be an important part of your marketing efforts. If you haven't, I would encourage you to do so. Proximity came with a free year of technical support to assist you with any questions you might have. You can reach our technical support staff at 1-319-365-9924.

You can increase the effectiveness of Proximity in your marketing campaigns by overlaying census information at either the block group or the census tract level.

We are offering you the opportunity to purchase either census block group or census tract boundaries for $150 to use with Proximity! Census block groups are the smallest statistically significant census measurement available, allowing you to look at marketing campaigns in small chunks of 200-300 households. Decisionmark normally charges as much as $700 for the entire nation's block group boundaries. But through February 28, 1997, you can get this added marketing punch for only $150, a savings of over 75%!

To sweeten the offer and add value to Proximity, we'll throw in 34 census tables like Household Income, Age by Income, Age by Sex, and Race and Marital Status for just $99!

This is a time-sensitive offer which expires February 28, 1997. To help make this easy, call us toll-free at 1-800-365-7629 to order and we'll bill you! Or, you can e-mail us at sales@decisionmark.com or fax us at 1-319-365-9897.

If you have any questions about Proximity, or have other data, lists, or mapping needs, please feel free to call us directly.

Sincerely,

Jack F. Perry II
President and CEO

P.S. Don't delay. Call 1-800-365-7629 today to order your census boundaries and tables!

http://www.decisionmark.com
e-mail: sales@decisionmark.com

Proximity
FROM DECISIONMARK™

Figure 17-2

An apparently free software offer becomes a profit center when the company proposes upgrades to its distributed base. Some word processing programs have been through a dozen or more upgrades . . . and with each one, customer use intensifies because switching to a competing program requires greater re-training.

BellSouth Small Business Services
P. O. Box 100170
Columbia, SC 29202-3170

October 24
(954)581-0069

||ılılı||ılııı||ıllılıllı||ııılılılılılı||ıııılllılılı||ıllıllı||ılı||ıl

COMMUNICOMP
340 N FIG TREE LN
PLANTATION FL 33317-2561

Dear Small Business Customer:

Thanks again for choosing to do business with BellSouth Small Business Services.

If you have any questions, you can call **780-2800** from 8:00 a.m. until 6:00 p.m., Monday through *Friday and 8:30 a.m. until 4:30 p.m., Saturday.*

Enclosed is a chart with detailed information about your order, along with a "quick glance" contact card listing additional BellSouth Small Business Services telephone numbers.

Our goal is to provide you with reliable service, delivered by knowledgeable, courteous people, who create solutions based upon your *individual* needs. After all, our best communications solutions come from a thorough understanding of what's important to you.

Thanks again for choosing BellSouth Small Business Services. Call us again soon!

Your BellSouth Small Business Specialist

CRKYR434-2Y5VC4J-2019R-00691

Figure 17-3

This "welcome" letter reinforces the customer's decision and helps avoid Buyer's Remorse.

Norton Utilities™ 2.0 Lets You Make The Most Of Windows® 95 While Automatically Protecting Your Invaluable Information.

Discover the power of Norton Utilities 2.0 for Windows 95 now for the Special Preferred Customer price of only $59.95 ($79.95 value). Plus, we'll send you absolutely FREE "The ProductivityPak 95" CD-ROM that teaches the inside tricks needed to enhance your productivity with Windows 95 and other popular software.

Dear Symantec Product Owner:

As a **Windows 95 user**, you probably already appreciate the value of improved computing and are well aware of the importance of preserving your information.

But are you well protected? With more and more vital, and sometimes irreplaceable information (such as work files, personal finances, even your address book) all now stored on your PC, it is imperative that you consider some form of protection and recovery. And, as over 15-million users of Norton Utilities can tell you — there is no better software for this sort of safety than Norton Utilities 2.0 for Windows 95. In fact it's the number one Windows 95 utility program preferred by users today.

When you install Norton Utilities 2.0 for Windows 95, you will realize these powerful benefits:

- Automatic System tune-up and protection against crashes
- Automatic fixes for hardware and software problems
- Faster Windows 95 system operation
- Enhanced protection and recovery of your files

It's Like Always Having A Doctor In The House.

Once Norton Utilities 2.0 for Windows is launched, the System Doctor™ is always in, running unnoticed in the background, preventing crashes, scanning for viruses, and addressing small problems before they become big ones. It's like giving your computer a continuous check-up that automatically fixes any problem it detects. System Doctor also makes your system run faster and more efficiently by continuously monitoring your PC for optimal performance and information integrity.

System Genie™ Makes Windows 95 Everything You Wished For.

The more familiar you become with Windows 95, the more you'll discover small things you wish you could change. System Genie grants those wishes and makes Windows 95 work the way you always wished it could. System Genie's intuitive interface looks just like a Web Page and gives you simple point and click power to customize your Windows 95 system in a snap!

Stay Current and Stay Connected with Symantec's LiveUpdate™!

MIG/XGRD

Figure 17-4

Computer software upgrades are today's hottest follow-ups, because they have an irresistible "hook": Ignore them and you fall behind. This offer combines an improved product, a discounted price, and a bonus CD-ROM.

The Platinum Card®

Alfred F. Kelly, Jr.
General Manager

Herschell G. Lewis
340 N. Fig Tree Ln.
Plantation, Fl. 33317-2561

Dear Mr. Lewis:

Recently, I invited you to enroll in the Sign & Travel® Account. If you've already responded to my invitation-thank you, your welcome package should arrive shortly. If you haven't yet responded, I invite you to once again consider the benefits.

* **Sign & Travel gives you the ability to defer travel charges, should you choose.**
With a Sign & Travel Account linked to the Platinum Card, you'll have additional spending flexibility to vacation wherever and whenever you like. You'll enjoy the option of extending payment on airline tickets, hotel and resort accommodations, rental cars, cruises, and vacation packages you charge on the Platinum Card.

* **Of course, there's no pre-set spending limit.**
As always, your Platinum Card charges are approved based on your past spending and payment patterns, as well as your personal resources.

* **We've made Sign & Travel so inviting by emphasizing convenience.**
You never have to request Sign & Travel when you make a travel charge with the Platinum Card. Your eligible travel expenses will automatically appear in a separate Sign & Travel portion of your monthly Platinum Card statement.

* **You maintain control—absolutely.**
You decide each month whether to pay your Sign & Travel balance in full, or pay over time at a competitive interest rate. And as long as you continue to pay your balance in full when new travel charges are placed on your Account, you won't incur interest charges.

* **Please accept this invitation with our compliments.**
There is no fee to enroll. Simply sign and return the enclosed R.S.V.P. card by June 15, 1997.

It is truly our pleasure to provide our most distinguished Platinum Card members with even more spending flexibility. Please contact us at 1-800-525-3355, should you need any further information or have any questions. I look forward to your reply.

Sincerely,

Alfred F. Kelly Jr.

PD2X-2   AMERICAN EXPRESS TRAVEL RELATED SERVICES CO., INC., P.O. BOX 9819, FT. LAUDERDALE, FL 33329-9819
2-0023242

Figure 17-5

If a mailing or a follow-up mailing has paid for itself, a second mailing to the same target-group usually will be productive. This example typifies most second mailings: The first paragraph refers to the prior notification; the basic text remains unchanged. A more adventurous approach recasts the sales argument. In either case, envelope copy should emphasize that this is a follow-up — "Second notice" or "Final opportunity" or "Last chance" or "Did you miss seeing this?"

18

How to Use Testimonials

Wh5at's your opinion of testimonials as sales weapons?
Mine is almost universally favorable . . . especially if they're *user* testimonials, not paid-for celebrity endorsements. The qualifier, "almost," disappears if they're pointed, not loose and nonspecific puffery saying "I love you" without adding "because. . . ."

In the Age of Skepticism, testimonials add a dimension of verisimilitude whose power can be considerably greater than the "puff"-text around them. But beware! *Believability* is the key to an effective testimonial, even more than apparent enthusiasm.

When evaluating endorsements, as in any form of force-communication, a useful litmus test is: Specifics outsell generalizations.

And specifics can be emotional as well as mechanical. Compare these two testimonials:

Testimonial A — "Yesterday the romantic tribute I had carried in my heart for years became a reality."

Testimonial B — "Beautiful music, beautifully played."

Neither is 100 percent specific, but A carries the quick-sprouting seeds of specificity. B has no distinctive element to grab and hold the reader.

How to use testimonials in broadcast media

I use a hedge word — *credible* — when discussing testimonials in broadcast media. Testimonials have great verisimilitude *potential* in radio and television advertising. Introduction of a second voice into an announcement to deliver a testimonial is effective — if words and delivery are both credible. Less desirable, but safer, is the testimonial quoted by the announcer.

For television, showing a still photo of the person being quoted and/or having the announcer or another professional voice recite the testimonial may be preferable to having that individual deliver the testimonial poorly on-camera. We're dealing in human psychology here, and the still photo seems to have a CNN "news report" look, where a live, on-camera testimonial from an outsider would have to be in a location, require rehearsals which might only further infect the case of stage-fright, and look contrived because the subject, however sincere, has no stage presence.

Credibility unlocks the door of skepticism: The magical force-word "because"

The principal key to unlocking the door of skepticism that bars viewer acceptance is credibility — and credibility is as much in the hands of the writer as it is in the hands of the endorser. Do the words match the image? Does the delivery seem artificial because sentences are longer than one would expect from convivial conversation? Would a simple "I use it," "I drive it," or "I own one too" be a more convincing selling argument than pap- puffery?

These dimensions are the writer's call. Mine would be a "Yes, but . . ." call. I'll remove the "but" if "I use it" or "I drive it" or "I own one too" is followed by a credibility-enhancing phrase beginning with the word "because."

"Because" is a force-word leading to a specific. (If you're still unconvinced that specifics outsell generalizations, testimonials aren't for you.)

Why Pay When You Can Get It Free?

It's not unheard-of for a major advertiser to pay $1 million or more to a celebrity for an endorsement. Even in a global television campaign, I regard such an expenditure as questionable. And in fields of narrow interest or business-to- business marketing, I can't justify *any* payment to *any* celebrity whose celebrity status lies totally outside the area of immediate interest. If that seems obscure: I can endure beautiful women touting beauty products and muscular men touting muscle-building products or odd-looking athletic shoes. I can't accept the quasi-logic of hiring a movie star to endorse a soft drink or a sports celebrity with a brain-pan of questionable size endorsing computer software.

The more "vertical" the group — that is, the more coherent the group interest-level might be in what we're selling — the more logical it is to have user endorsements rather than celebrity endorsements. And they're easy to get.

No, I'm not referring to the illegitimate technique of having your out-of-town relatives be the source of your testimonials. I'm referring to an on-going flow of encomia from honest-to-goodness customers.

Two principal sources of user endorsements

Two of the principal techniques for gaining user endorsements are both logical and effective:

1. The follow-up phone call.
2. The follow-up questionnaire.

In both cases, the question asks for a comment . . . *not* for an endorsement. We discard the negative comments and use the positive comments.

Phone calls are the easiest and also the most dangerous, because unless you get written confirmation and permission from the endorser, you can qualify for the Woodrow Wilson Syndrome.

(President Wilson, whose actual first name — piece of trivia — was Thomas, is quoted as saying, "Every time I make a political appointment I make ninety-nine enemies and one ingrate.")

So when you get a positive comment over the phone, your own enthusiastic response is, "I can tell you, the head of our company will really appreciate what you said. Would you mind if we use your comment in our advertising?" *Not "our **promotion**"* — to many outside our orbit, "promotion" suggests sleaze.

Then send a copy of the quotation, with an "okay to use" release, to the individual. Send it by overnight courier and include a postage-free way to respond. It's worth it, because otherwise you'll lose more than half your testimonials. Including "A gift from our president is on its way to you for your kind words" locks in the individual as your permanent fan and probably will pay off in a higher volume of future orders.

If a written comment isn't quite targeted, call the individual and explain that you're so impressed with the comment you want to use it in your advertising, adding, "Can you elaborate a little? Tell us *why* you're so pleased." Don't be afraid to prompt the endorser if he or she asks for help: "Would you say because you have this, you . . . ?" A weak endorsement not only doesn't have the octane a strong one has, if you know how to handle endorsement-acquisition, a weak endorsement won't be in the mix because you'll have converted it to a powerful one.

What Not to Do

Don't oversimplify the technique. Three qualifiers assure you of getting what you want and not winding up in some newspaper's Action Line column:

1. Start your phone call or your questionnaire with a sincere desire to get *information,* not an endorsement. You really do want to get a reaction. And yes, that includes *negative* reactions, because you can head off a disaster by reporting to co-workers or management, after making ten calls or reading ten blistering questionnaires, "Hey, our packaging isn't doing our image any good" . . . or "We'd better rebuild that instruction sheet" . . . or "We should add some enclosures validating the price."

Your first questions should relate to circumstances in which the customer would be hard-pressed to formulate a negative: "What day did it arrive?" "Was the package in good condition?" "Have you *[tried, used, viewed, turned on, displayed]* it yet?"

Ease into the key question: If it's a call, "The head of our company has asked me to ask you what your opinion is. Is it good, bad, or terrible?" If it's a questionnaire, the questions are preceded by similar text signed by the head of the company.

Child psychology? Sure it is. Effective? Sure it is, because the person on the other end — even if, *had you not forced the question*, he or she would have offered negative thoughts — is hard-pressed to answer "Bad" or "Terrible."

2. Structure questions about the item or service so the answer has to give you a "why." A question such as "Are you satisfied?" is worthless: If you were reading a brochure or a space ad, would you be excited by a testimonial that said, "I'm satisfied"?

3. Don't be windy on the phone and don't be verbose in the mails.

You're an intruder. That's why sincere (or transparent) first questions set a mood. On the phone, capitalize on a positive mood quickly . . . and get out. Express surprise and regret when you sense a negative mood . . . and get out.

A mailed questionnaire doesn't have the one-to-one mood-sharpening potential a phone call has, but brevity not only will bring you more responses, it will bring you more *positive* responses.

Questions that force positive responses

Some of the questions that will bring you the gold you seek:

— Why did you buy your [WHATEVER]?

(Note, please: It's *your* whatever, not *the* whatever or *this* whatever. Assumption of ownership not only increases the possibility of a favorable comment, it actually might help prevent the horror of returned merchandise.)

— What, in your opinion, is the best feature of your [WHATEVER]?

— If you were selling it instead of buying it, what in your opinion would be the headline on an ad?

— If your [WHATEVER] has saved you time, trouble, or money, please tell us how.

— Compare your [WHATEVER] with a competing product.

You get the idea. Questions should stick your promotional head into the pot of gold, not into the lion's mouth.

Just What IS an Effective Testimonial?

The question is self-answering: An effective testimonial is one that helps convince another prospect of two points: 1) Your claims are true; 2) the item will be beneficial.

How to replace flab with power

Everyone in our business recognizes the power boiling in a testimonial that specifies *what* the testimonial is endorsing . . . and the flab softening the impact of a testimonial that substitutes a variation of "I like it" for a specific.

What we don't always recognize is *how* to cut the flab and start the pot of testimonials boiling.

Bringing testimonials to a happy boil is as easy as implementing two factors. The first of these is the eternal direct marketing principle that runs as a happy obbligato theme throughout this Handbook: Specifics outsell generalizations. The second is a Rule you already know. Reminder coming up shortly.

Two categories of marketing that literally demand testimonials are seminars and publications. Two categories that consistently represent the best and worst testimonials are seminars and publications.

I've puzzled over this dichotomy for years and concluded exactly what I concluded before I started puzzling: Some companies know how to ask for a testimonial and some don't.

Because seminars and conferences are such available targets, let's zero in on them.

How to ask for specifics you can use:

Every seminar of any consequence asks participants to fill out an evaluation form. Typical of these forms, along with ratings from 1 to 5 for speakers, is a structured question such as this (note that word *structured* because it's the key to a useless testimonial):

> *What is your overall opinion of this Conference?*
> □ *Excellent*   □ *Good*   □ *Fair*   □ *Poor*

Suppose 80 percent come in with the "Excellent" box tagged. So what?

Replace that with something *unstructured* such as . . .

> *What, in your opinion, is the best aspect of this conference?*

. . . or, moving up the specificity scale . . .

> *Which session was most valuable for you? Please tell us why.*

Integrity may call for another question asking what the participant might want to see changed (not "improved," please . . . why shoot yourself in the foot?). But these answers aren't for use as testimonials.

Wet-sponge endorsements

A "Global Conference" mailing included eight testimonials. Here they are, in their entirety (numbering is mine):

1. "Attending the Global Conference has changed our lives."
   D.W. - Florida
2. "Very impressive . . . informative and enlightening . . . I enjoyed it immensely."
   D.B. - Virginia
3. "The entire experience was magnificent."
   G.G. - Pennsylvania
4. "Great Speakers!"
   J.K. - Texas
5. "The Conference exceeded our expectations."
   S.M. - Ohio
6. "It's been a great experience! Never a moment when we didn't know what to do!"
   H.L. - California
7. "Stimulating and enjoyable."
   W.H. - Florida
8. "A remarkable experience. Thank you."
   S.W. - Michigan

See anything wrong with these? Oh, certainly everybody quoted seemed to have a good time. What's wrong is that not one of these gives us a specific to chew on. What we have here is the *second* line of a testimonial, masquerading as the first. Possibly the brochure writer threw away a specific that preceded some of these, because it just can't be that everyone who attended and remarked on his or her enjoyment avoided including a single specific.

The First Rule of Testimonials

So, we might consider The First Rule of Testimonials:

Either immediately before or immediately after you rave, explain why you're raving.

When should you rave first and explain afterward, and when should you explain first and rave afterward? Consider the difference between these two statements, based on testimonial number three:

a. "The session giving us three easy ways to train our employees in the art of greeting guests was alone worth *twice* the cost of the entire conference. The entire experience was magnificent."
b. "The entire experience was magnificent. The session giving us three easy ways to train our employees in the art of greeting guests was alone worth *twice* the cost of the entire conference."

For this endorsement "b" may be preferable, because it explains the rave. Had the rave been wordier (such as number one, for example), positioning the explanation before the rave would be preferable.

Trivial points, you say? Only if you've never wondered why your seminar or conference mailing didn't pull response the way it was supposed to.

Meat to chew on

Another conference mailing had an entire panel of testimonials — six in all. Each was from a representative of a different facet of the business world — a wise move. Now, take a look at the first sentence of each and decide which ones transmit attendance-ammunition for targets of this year's mailing (again, the numbering is mine):

1. "I enjoyed the full range of topics and the easy way to choose what I wanted to attend."
2. "Conference was very helpful to me as a person just beginning to measure customer satisfaction."
3. "Great conference to see where your company's processes and measurements compare against others."
4. "Another great conference."
5. "This was my first venture into the world of customer satisfaction, and I must say it was a very pleasant and rewarding journey."
6. "Conference was very enlightening."

Okay, which of the six is weakest?

Before we agree or disagree: If you think *any* of these is weaker than the others, you're accepting the existence of The First Rule of Testi-monials.

We probably agree: Number six has no specificity.

Now, read the entire text of number six and let's see whether or not we agree again:

> *"Conference was very enlightening. I found that my company has a long way to go as far as customer satisfaction measurement and deployment is concerned. Very interesting and helpful speakers — willing to share their expertise."*

Visualize this testimonial *without* that first sentence and you can see how much more powerful it is.

Combine the "Specifics outsell generalizations" principle with The First Rule of Testimonials and you'll never again be firing (in the mind of the reader) blanks.

The Second Rule of Testimonials

As we begin to complete the persuasional ensemble, let's add The Sec-ond Rule of Testimonials:

> *Transmit enthusiasm on a plane the reader instantly recognizes within his or her own experiential background.*

Simple stuff . . . but for some marketers who want to impress people in the office instead of recipients of the message, simplicity yields to a more brutal sibling: vapor rhetoric . . . gas as an ego-enhancing substitute for clarity.

Want to sell a book?
Don't leave the reader outside.

If you're wondering what vapor rhetoric is, here's an example from the envelope — the envelope, for God's sake — of a mailing selling a book about the way one's mind influences physical health:

> *"This is the best introduction to the mind/body approach and its potential for alleviating illness and improving health . . . compre-*

hensive, authoritative, eminently readable." — James S. Gordon, M.D., Clinical Professor Departments of Psychiatry and Community and Family Medicine, Georgetown University School of Medicine

Opinion, please: Despite that finial "eminently readable" claim, does this testimonial tell us this book is going to be easy to read? Does this quotation say the book is written for us, or is it a pedantic textbook?

Oddly, the mailing itself is well-written, clear, and aimed at a more universal target group; but I wonder how many potential book buyers discarded the mailing because they reacted negatively to the vapor rhetoric.

Compare that with a testimonial in a mailing for a marketing publication, quoting an advertising agency:

> *"Data you provided was enormously helpful in research for our first-ever magazine subscription package. Our copy test knocked that long-standing control for a loop, chopping net cost per sub by over 16 percent. Client has awarded us three new projects in a row."*

See the specifics here? See the terminology aimed at us, untainted by pomposity? That comment is pinpoint-targeted, obviously selected by somebody who (instinctively or deliberately) recognizes The Second Rule of Testimonials.

A publisher uses four testimonials to help sell a book titled *Stuck in the Seventies*. If space limitation forced you to cut copy, which of these four would you drop? (Numerals are mine.)

> 1. *"This book is hysterical and brings back lots of memories! These guys arc great!" — Cheryl Wells, Associate Producer, NBC's* Today *show*
> 2. *"The book is really fun." — Katie Couric, NBC's* Today *show*
> 3. *". . . an irreverent book that sends up and celebrates the decade of disco, smile buttons and polyester leisure suits." — The Boston Globe*
> 4. *". . . the book is funny. The five authors picked an easy target and they hit it." — San Francisco Examiner*

If your first impulse is to eliminate one of the *Today* show quotes, to avoid a "one string fiddle" look, you make an excellent point. It's not an easy choice, because although Katie Couric is a recognizable name, her recommendation is lukewarm.

The Third Rule of Testimonials

I'd certainly hang onto the newspaper quotes, not only because they're targeted, but because they exemplify The Third Rule of Testimonials:

An "official" endorsement outweighs a peer-group endorsement, provided it conforms to the first two Rules.

It worked for me so it should work for you.

One of the most powerful of all testimonials is the darling of those who sell franchises, business opportunities, and investments. It's any application of "It worked for me so it should work for you."

This type of testimonial is the backbone of infomercials, and with good reason: An infomercial viewer either identifies with what's on the screen or changes channels. (Considerable exposition on this in chapter 14.)

Bold and daring writers replace "should work for you" with "will work for you." The difference between conditional claims of "can" and "should" — and "will," an unconditional claim — can be tremendous. In testimonials, as well as standard sell-copy, some of those differences can have legal overtones.

A business opportunities ad for vending machines, in a business opportunities magazine, has a testimonial as the main headline and main subhead. The headline:

"Our First Machine Took In 4,072 Quarters, $1,018.00 The First Month!"

The subhead:

"It took us over 2 hours just to count all the money!"

Validating the claim is a picture of an "ordinary" couple, with this cutline:

"Jim McCarty, a pipe fitter and welder for over 30 years, retired only 4 months after starting his Wizard business."

Readers might interpret that word "retired" negatively and wonder about the relationship between "we" in the headlines and the absence of Mrs. McCarty from the caption. But most will see great verisimilitude here, because the testimonial has such specificity — "4,072 quarters," for example — and the photograph declares to the reader: "This man does exist."

If I were reading this instead of writing it . . .

Follow the Three Rules of Testimonials, and your response road is paved with gold. Add the spice of specificity and your gold sparkles.

If you wonder whether you've captured the essence of a potent testimonial, the answer comes from applying the same test you'd give any sales message: "If I were reading or hearing this instead of writing it, would it inspire me to lift the phone?"

Here's what your colleagues are saying about DMB

The highest ROI

"Spending 2½ days at this conference is equivalent to 2½ months of research. It's time well spent."
Wendy Hewitt, Fairchild Semiconductor

"This conference exceeded my expectations. There were many great sessions that tied direct marketing to the Internet."
Kristi Rinehart, Adaptec, Inc.

"This is the only worthwhile conference for direct marketing to business."
Lawrence Hefler, Boise Cascade Office Products

"The DMB Conference is the best way to condense months of searching and researching into three days."
John Rynecki, Sid Harvey Industries, Inc.

Real-world marketing insight

"Most useful professional seminar in direct marketing I've ever attended."
Tammi Wilson, Avid Technology

"Excellent opportunity to meet marketing leaders at blue-chip firms."
Richard Salmon, Colwell & Salmon Communications

"The DMB Conference is an excellent way to learn 'real world' how valuable direct marketing is now and in the future."
Fred Taft, Unisys Corporation

"Excellent presenters, timely topics, and a generally great learning and networking opportunity."
Sanford Grossman, AB & C Group, Inc.

Practical hands-on information

"The DMB sessions were outstanding. Right on the mark for our company. We will implement many of the ideas learned."
Brett Mulder, K Products, Inc.

"I was particularly impressed with the amount of practical information and tactics presented."
Noel Coletti, Acuity Imaging, Inc.

"Every minute of the conference was utilized with direct marketing information and ides I can put to work immediately. I was totally impressed."
Karen Lameier, Alabama CAD/CAM

"This is my 4th consecutive year, and there is always something I can take back and apply to my program."
Rob Reynolds,
Rockwell Automation/Allen-Bradley

Pure business-to-business focus

"One of the best conferences I have attended. You won't find this type of business-to-business direct marketing focus at any other conference."
Carol Koenig, Aladdin Synergistics, Inc.

"Because it is focused on business-to-business, the sessions use pertinent examples useful in day-to-day situations."
Peter Nill, Deluxe Corporation

"Solid information and actionable ideas for both business-to-business veterans and newcomers."
Ruth P. Stevens, IBM Direct

35

See Pre-Conference Workshops—pages 31-33

Figure 18-1

Evaluate this page of testimonials, for a business-to-business marketing conference, against the Three Rules of Testimonials. Which ones have strength? Which ones march in place?

19

Tips for Effective
Fund Raising

Sooner or later most people associated with advertising, marketing, or sales promotion are involved in fund raising campaigns. Fund raisers are in the vanguard of advertising, marketing, and sales promotion because theirs is one of the most competitive businesses.

So even if you aren't a fund raiser, the odds are you will be. The church, the library, the school, the college, the orchestra, the opera, the local chapter of a disease-preventing organization, the museum, the civic club, the youth center — someone will nail you; you represent an element without which no twenty-first century fund-raising activity can survive — *salesmanship.* "You're the hotshot marketer. Help us put this campaign together."

So you do. After all, you're the resident expert. Do you come up with the standard brilliant campaign ideas — "We need help"?

Sure. "We need help." Written, spoken, or screamed ("We need help!"), that was an effective call to action half a generation ago. Today it's burned out.

Traditional Forms No Longer Work

Techniques that worked 10 years ago are now *overwork*ed. What does bring response today? Why doesn't "We need help" have the punch it used to have?

Too many fund raisers have cried "Wolf!" at the same time. That's just one of the hair-shirts professional fund raisers wear as our juggernaut careens toward the twenty-first century. A more serious one is the devolving nature of society itself: Our targets have neither the attention-span their forebears had, nor the percentage of time available to us they themselves had even a few years ago.

This means our messages have to either a) strike home fast, b) grab and shake the reader within his or her own experiential background, or c) both.

Some old standbys seem to be tapering off.

I've had mixed luck lately with episodes ("Maria hopes you'll read this letter so one day she will be able to see"). Episodes used to be foolproof. So what has changed? In my opinion it's raw volume. Every fund raiser seems to have a Maria.

But I'll tell you what hasn't changed: *Victims outpull success stories.* Maria, whose eyes produce only tears, probably will generate more fundraising dollars than Esmeralda, who smiles because her eyes now produce bright, clear images.

What's the difference? A success story can say to the target-donor, "We triumphed without you."

Now, understand, please: Generating guilt is *not* parallel to the old standby "We need help" nor its more contemporary cousin "You can make a difference." The difference between a cry for help and having somebody feel ashamed or conscience-stricken is the difference between helpless casualty and master psychologist.

One area in which success stories do work

One area in which success stories wield great power: mailings to prior donors, in which you stroke them for making success possible ("Because of you, she can see") and present additional problems for the donor to solve.

Do spartan messages work?

A spartan message has one advantage: It costs less to produce, so the organization can mail more.

Let's suppose you have a tight budget. (*Suppose?* How long has it been since you experienced anything else?) You can mail 20,000 well-produced packages . . . or 40,000 bare-bones packages. Typically, for a cause of any worth, more bare-bones pieces in the mail will bring greater response than fewer well-produced pieces.

But be careful, please: Too naked an appeal says to the recipient, "You're one of the mob." The impression that you've blanketed the universe with millions of low-cost mailings doesn't jog the checkbook or get the credit card out of the wallet.

Our company received a mailing from the local branch of one of America's most respected fund-raising organizations. The sender: "West Broward unit." Opinion: Big mistake. "Unit?" Ugh.

This is the key message:

> *Your special gift to this year's Annual Fund is the* single most important way you can fight cancer *. . . and* save lives. *Please give what you can today. Thanks!*
>   *( )$200   ( )$300   ( )$350   ( )$_____*

Okay, they've done a couple of things right. They underline each word individually instead of having a single underline for the whole phrase. They say "Thanks!" And they suggest specific amounts.

How many mistakes did you spot?

They've also done a couple of things wrong. They underline too many words, so emphasis is diluted. They're a unit and they treat us as a unit. They don't justify the overused, abused word "important."

On a separate panel, a brief message tries to humanize the appeal, but the statements are boiler-plate:

> *Your gift is **urgently needed today** to make sure we can help your friends and neighbors struggling with cancer . . . expand critically important prevention and early detection programs . . . and continue the search for new cancer treatments and cures!*

"... to make sure we can help your friends and neighbors"? How about my family? *That* would have struck home. "Expand" is a business term. "Search" is a poor word, especially when "promising research" is right there in the keyboard. This part of the message has a typed-in signature, but no written signature — which would have been easy to include because blue is the second color.

So attempted personalization becomes impersonal. The impression is one of bulk, not individual. But they didn't ask me. If they ask you, give them directions.

"In-Group" Benefit and Drawback

The Opera Society has on its envelope: "Murder Mystery Party."

For 60 bucks I can attend this party: "Cocktails and Intriguing Hors d'oeuvres Followed by a Night of Clues, Fun and Excitement."

For an in-group, this is a welcome departure from the typical cultural fund-raising milieu. For an in-group, fun is a welcome substitute for dire predictions of no opera season if we don't kick in.

But what about those on the periphery — opera-lovers who don't know any of the people listed as officers and sponsors and who don't know what to expect at a "Murder Mystery Party"? The mailing needs a warmup for outsiders.

Assuming an individual will accept placement as one of the in-group is the right decision *if* prestige is involved. It isn't the right decision if the mailing is just another fund raiser.

I have a letter from a local university, one I never attended, never visited as a lecturer, and never had any other relationship with. The opening:

Dear Friends of FAU:

Florida Atlantic University is growing faster than ever before, and I invite you to join us on our journey into the 21st century. Your contribution to FAU and your investment in higher education will help prepare today's students to meet the needs of the new era.

Right away, that plural opening — "Friends" — tells me these people aren't of our world. That isn't the point; the point is the assumption that I accept the mantle of being part of their in-group.

My own school hasn't contacted me for years. I don't mind because the last time I visited the campus I was a stranger in a strange land — a homecoming homecomer who was ignored (except for a guy with a ring in his nose who handed me a fund-raising envelope). So I'm open to new affiliations. But the pitch here, "help prepare today's students to meet the needs of the new era," has all the appeal of a boil on the neck.

A mini-rule for fund raisers

I'll toss a mini-rule into this mixture:

> *The writer ALWAYS has access to a more specific noun than "needs."*

All this school had to do was test that line of copy in a telemarketing campaign. Someone asks, "What's the purpose of this call?" Would any fund raiser who doesn't have a cranium full of mashed potatoes answer, "Your contribution to FAU and your investment in higher education will help prepare today's students to meet the needs of the new era"?

The Provocative Question: Does It Provoke?

Whether in commercial advertising and marketing or in fund raising, two factors guarantee success . . . if they're properly executed:

1. Involvement.
2. Rapport.

Both of these factors depend on the writer knowing the reader's likes and dislikes. Obviously, that isn't fair to the writer of a mass message. So the professional communicator knows the likes and dislikes of *the typical* reader. That positively *is* fair, because if we aren't able to master even a primitive psychology, then we aren't professional communicators; we're technical writers, describers, word-regurgitators . . . not salespeople.

Tie those two to "You can make a difference" and the vaccination has to strike home, because the two keys open wide an emotional door "You can make a difference" can't budge without a key in today's skeptical, over-pitched fund-raising marketplace.

With that criterion, how does this opening rate?

Dear Mr. and Mrs. Lewis:

Doesn't it feel good to walk into a room full of friends and people you love during the holidays? Doesn't it make you feel happy, safe and secure?

Think about it. . . . Don't pets make people feel the same way? They bring comfort and joy. They keep everyday troubles in perspective.

Opinion: Nice try. The intention is there; the connection is weak, because the comparison isn't an emotional grabber. A "What if you . . ." or "When you really need a friend . . ." or "Heidi is hoping someone will come" might have a more powerful involvement/rapport factor.

A curious example is this one:

Dear Friend,
Will Sarah have her mother's eyes?
The answer to the question may be "Yes".
Because children who witness domestic violence in their homes . . . will often grow up to repeat the cycle of violence.
Unless there is early intervention and counseling.
Countless children like Sarah will flee with their mothers in the middle of the night this holiday season, escaping the unspeakable acts of abuse at home.

I don't get it, and not just because of the curious grammar nor the one-sentence paragraph artifice. "Will Sarah have her mother's eyes" could mean a) some sort of genetic hand-down or b) her mother has a black eye because of domestic violence. Neither of these connects with the message. The effect is muddy . . . And involvement/rapport dissolves in mud.

A Response-Enhancing Rule Would Have Helped.

Compare that message with this Johnson Box, preceding the opening of a letter (as described in chapter 3, a Johnson Box is a typed or printed message above the greeting of a letter, usually encased in a "box" of stars or asterisks):

In the few seconds it took you to open and begin to read this letter, four children die from the effects of malnutrition or disease somewhere in the world.

My opinion remains firm: a neat, centered Johnson Box isn't as effective an involvement/rapport device as a handwritten overline. My objection to this one is rooted in a different Fund-Raising Rule:

Examples outpull statistics.

Two damaging problems here: First, "malnutrition or disease" splits the impact. That word "or" can be deadly.

Second, "somewhere in the world" is not only unnecessary, it removes the reader from the arena. Involvement/rapport evaporates.

The letter itself opens with some strength:

Dear Friend,

No statistic can express what it's like to see even one child die that way ... to see a mother sitting hour after hour, leaning her child's body against her own ... to watch the small, feeble head movements that expend all the energy a youngster has left ... to see the panic in a dying tot's innocent eyes ... and then to know in a moment that life is gone.

Not bad — although you or I, recognizing the involvement/rapport equation, would have taken the water out of the story:

No statistic you or I might offer can express what it's like—a mother desperately holding her child's body against her own, trying to keep the flame of life flickering, only to see the light fade from a dying tot's innocent eyes ... and then to know in a moment that a precious life is gone.

Involvement and rapport aren't difficult to conjure up. What gets in the way of force-communication is one of two deficiencies: a) the writer's approach, too often analytical instead of empathetic; b) dependence on "You can make a difference" without linking that venerable concept to involvement and rapport.

Go Thou and Do Likewise.

Success lies in a recognition some fund raisers don't like: We're selling something, in a competitive marketplace.

Most people have a finite amount of money they'll dedicate to *all* causes. To get your fair share, don't assume "You can make a difference" is a failsafe stand-alone; identify and massage the fraternal twins Involvement and Rapport.

And, oh — don't forget to ask for the money. Rhapsody without a payoff is for poets, not salespeople.

For many women and children . . .

These are the colors of the season.

```
****************ECRLOT **C-002
Margo E. Lewis
340 N Fig Tree Lane
Plantation FL 33317-2561
```

Dear Friend,

Will Sarah have her mother's eyes?

The answer to the question may be "Yes".

Because children who witness domestic violence in their homes... will often grow up to repeat the cycle of violence.

Unless there is early intervention and counseling.

Countless children like Sarah will flee with their mothers in the middle of the night this holiday season, escaping unspeakable acts of abuse at home.

Because of your support, Sarah may not inherit her mother's legacy. Thanks to generous gifts from people like you, Sarah will have a safe place to stay, with care and counseling in a nurturing place here at Women In Distress of Broward County, Inc.

Because of what she has learned at Women In Distress, Sarah will know that domestic violence is not OK.

Our programs are effective in breaking the cycle of violence and abuse.

And that is why I'm writing you today. **We must make absolutely certain that every woman and child who has the courage to ask for help will receive it.**

By making a gift of $25, $50, $75, or $100 or more you can help bring peace at home to families like Sarah's right here in Broward County.

With a gift of $25 or more for the holidays we will send you our exclusive and beautifully wrapped "Peace at Home" tree ornament.

You may even want to have us send the ornament as a gift from you to someone you designate. We will enclose a card with the ornament stating that it is a gift from you and that it will benefit the families served by Women In Distress.

What a great gift idea!

With your help, we can change the colors of the season for Sarah and thousands of children like her.

Sincerely,

Have a Peaceful Holiday Season & Thank You for All Your Wonderful Support!

Bonnie M. Flynn

Bonnie M. Flynn
President and Chief Executive Officer

A United Way Agency

POST OFFICE BOX 676, FORT LAUDERDALE, FLORIDA 33302
HOTLINE: (954) 761-1133 • OFFICE: (954) 760-9800 • FAX: (954) 832-9487
Broward County's Only Comprehensive Domestic Violence Program

HRS

Figure 19-1

"Will Sarah have her mother's eyes?" The question is only mildly provocative, and the "may be" answer makes it even less provocative. The call to action doesn't clarify what this organization will do to help prevent domestic violence. Opinion: A more graphic example will bring a bigger response.

Mr. & Mrs. Herschell G. Lewis
340 N Fig Tree Ln
Plantation, FL 33317-2561

Dear Mr. & Mrs. Lewis:

Doesn't it feel good to walk into a room full of friends and people you love during the holidays? Doesn't it make you feel happy, safe and secure?

Think about it . . . Don't pets make people feel the same way? They bring comfort and joy. They keep everyday troubles in perspective.

We know . . . pets feel happy, safe and secure when they have special human friends in their lives. For them . . . it's a holiday . . . each time you walk into a room.

When you support the Humane Society of Broward County, you join good company. Thousands of good people . . . **like you** . . . celebrating their love of animals by supporting our shelter's efforts to bring people and animals together.

Unfortunately, **<u>some people think the work we do is not very important.</u>** They say that it is more important to help people than pets.

Well, when we fight abuse . . . we help people. When we teach compassion and responsibility . . . we help people. When our volunteers bring animals to comfort those in rehabilitation centers and nursing homes . . . we help people. Pets give people hope and a feeling that they make a difference in someone's life.

Now tell me . . . <u>isn't a pet very important to someone you know</u>?

The Humane Society of Broward County is self-supporting. We receive no funds from any governmental agencies or national affiliations. Our support comes from thousands of caring people. People . . . like you.

A gift of $20.00 or more **helps brighten the lives of both people and animals.** You don't have to give . . . but when you do . . . your gift extends the holiday spirit to the entire year.

Sincerely,

Arnold Grevior
President

P.S. There is no time limit on how long we keep animals. And we will find homes for more than 6,000 of them in 1997.

RECYCLABLE

2070 Griffin Road • Fort Lauderdale, FL 33312
North Broward - (305) 463-4870 • Central & South Broward - (305) 989-3977

Figure 19-2

When competing for an impulse donation for an organization dedicated to helping the helpless, whether human or animal, an episode has considerably greater "bite" than a calm narrative. This request might have been more powerful had it begun, "Heidi is hoping someone will take her to a warm, loving home for the holidays. In return, she promises many licks of affection."

Tonight, millions of Americans won't get enough to eat...

Meanwhile -- tons of surplus food are just out of their reach!

NATIONAL FOOD BANK NETWORK
▼▼▼
116 SOUTH MICHIGAN AVENUE, SUITE 4
CHICAGO, ILLINOIS 60603-6001

Dear Friend,

I have to tell you — I'm angry today!

Not at you, but at the fact that right now in America, millions of men, women and children risk hunger — and there's just no excuse for it. I know you agree: in the world's richest country ...

...no little boy or girl should have to go to school without breakfast — or to bed without dinner. No family should have to decide each month between keeping warm or buying groceries.

Yet every day, millions of people are suffering because they don't have enough to eat, while tons of surplus food that could solve their problem remains locked away.

That's right — the food they need is available, perfectly good edible food that our country's food manufacturers produce but can't sell to you or me because of simple processing errors.

And that is exactly why we created Second Harvest — to reclaim this lost harvest on behalf of our country's poor.

As America's only national network of food banks, we already serve nearly 50,000 local food pantries and soup kitchens. But with 39.3 million Americans still living in poverty, we need your help to do more.

For every $1 you can contribute to Second Harvest, approximately $68 worth of donated food that would have been thrown away will get to Americans who truly need it.

Will you help us stop the suffering and waste? You can with the gift you send to Second Harvest today.

Sincerely,

Christine Vladimiroff, O.S.B.
President - Chief Executive Officer

Figure 19-3

The combination of anger, logic, and specifics is the stuff professional fund-raising letters are made of. This is a good example of that magical blend.

20

How to Structure Response Devices (Order Forms)

Mail order litany says the response device should recapitulate the offer. If you follow this application slavishly, you could be costing yourself response. Here are rules for when you should . . . and when you shouldn't.

We've all heard, practiced, and taught the standard professional approach to order forms: Recapitulate the offer, because this verifies and validates what we've said in the text.

It's true, isn't it?

Well . . . sometimes.

The First Two Rules of Order Forms

"Sometimes" is in sync with The First Rule of Order Forms:

If your offer is strong and doesn't have any negatives, re-stating it on the response device adds that dynamic ingredient, verisimilitude.

But there's a heavy qualifier in that Rule, and that's why it's true *sometimes*. Other times, if we want to maximize response we invoke The Second Rule of Order Forms:

When your offer has exceptions, don't give those exceptions equal play on the response device. If you aren't asking for immediate payment, consider minimizing or even bypassing the exceptions on the response device.

Now, before you holler "Foul!" hear me out. I'm not in favor of duplicity nor deceit. I am in favor of smart salesmanship. You don't ask an attractive person out on a first date by saying, "I'd like you to join me for dinner at Lutèce. No drinks, though, and you'll have to put up with my false teeth and ill-fitting hairpiece and body odor and dull conversation, and you'll have to find your own way home after paying for your own dinner."

Those may be eventual conditions. You can soften them and, more significantly, justify them in conversation (the letter or the advertising text), but you don't blurt them out *as major factors* (the response device).

We have enough readership tests telling us a lot of readers jump from the overline and P.S. of the letter, or the headline of an ad, to the response device. There, exposed, naked truth can be heavenly or ugly.

Legitimate or Deceitful? You Decide.

An example of The Second Rule of Order Forms is a bind-in card adjacent to an ad in a business publication. (While I'm thinking of it: NEVER let the publication run your ad on a left-hand page if you're including a bind-in card.)

Heading on the card:

Get FREE software within 2 weeks and get free Internet access for one full year.

Is the statement true? *Partly.* If you read the full-page ad behind it, you'll notice the catch, hidden in the body-text: ". . . you'll get five hours of free Internet access per month for one full year, or enjoy unlimited Internet access for only $19.95 a month, as long as you're an AT&T residential or business customer."

None of this is on the card. And many, many people see, fill out, and mail the card without reading the small print in the ad.

So is this legitimate? In a perfect world, no. In our world, keeping score by the number of responses and assuming a telemarketing follow-up (the card asks for home and business phone numbers), it's congruent with the Second Rule.

Now, suppose the card headline had been:

Get FREE software within 2 weeks and get 5 hours of free Internet access per month for one full year.

Would response be as big? Or for that matter, as spontaneous?

Understand, please: I'm neither advocating nor criticizing. Rather, I'm calling attention to the technique. Ethics are a matter of corporate philosophy, and they aren't always complementary to The Second Rule of Order Forms.

I can justify The Second Rule easily enough, with a four-part rationale:

1. We keep score by the number of responses from those who have the capability of implementing a positive decision relative to our offer. The technique just described provides greater response than an offer with qualifiers.

2. Wording on the card contains no falsehoods.

3. No money will change hands until and unless all conditions are explained to the target-individual.

4. Many respondents will in fact have read the advertising text before entering information on the response device.

So you make the decision. My suggestion: Test it, counting total responses, net deals, *and percentage of negative reactions when the qualifications are clarified.*

Don't Load Up the Order Form.

I was the writer of a direct mail subscription package which tested a heavy-copy response device against an almost-no-copy response device. The test was easy because this was a "soft" offer (send no money now), so the commitment was only for a "free look."

The heavy-copy card was loaded with hyperbole, touting the brilliance and usefulness of the magazine. The spartan order card had a simple "Yes" box, plus initials — *not* a full signature. Both versions used a peel-off sticker as an action gimmick.

I'm not in a position to disclose exact results, but — no surprise, I'm sure — the simple card far outpulled the copy-heavy card.

We're talking cards here, not an order form in a catalog or a mail-order space ad. These demand a payment commitment, and The Second Rule doesn't apply.

On the other hand, too austere a response device can be a turnoff. Except for space for name, address, and phone, this is the entire message on a business reply card enclosed with a mailing:

YES! I WANT TO KNOW THE BENEFITS OF THE NEPTUNE PRE-NEED CREMATION PLAN.

Opinion: State one of those benefits on the card, please. Otherwise, it casts a ghoulish shadow.

And that brings us to . . .

The Third Rule of Order Forms

The Third Rule of Order Forms is the easiest of the rules affecting this most crucial element in a space ad or mailing:

*When you're asking for a commitment, emphasize a comparative benefit **before** recapitulating the cost.*

That's easy enough and logical enough. For example, a space ad for a book, in a business publication, has this text on the coupon:

*Yes, I want to increase my profits! Please send me **Grow Your Business with Desktop Marketing.** My check or money order for $19.95* — 20% off the cover price of $24.95, plus $3.50 for shipping and handling and any sales tax — is enclosed.*

(The asterisk indicates states imposing sales tax, plus that deadly response-killer, "Allow up to 4 weeks for delivery.")

One mistake here, aside from that wretched four-week delay in shipping: The wording suggests the $3.50 add-on includes tax. Put a comma after "handling" and change "and" to "plus," and clarity results. Don't ask me why this deal doesn't accept credit cards, which would gray down the tax add-on.

Diarrhea of the keyboard

Careful, please, to avoid diarrhea of the keyboard when re-stating benefits. Reader fatigue can translate itself into the conclusion that the deal is complicated.

Here is just part of the wording on a reply card in a "Special Introductory Offer" mailing for a travel newsletter:

> *YES, NOW, PLEASE! Start my subscription to **TRAVEL SMART** right away, as I've checked below. I'll receive each monthly edition of the newsletter, packed with tips, ideas and advice . . . plus immediate access to the travel service . . . plus "Travel Smarts," the book to make me a travel "insider" and save me money.*
>
> *I understand that my satisfaction is guaranteed or I can receive a prompt refund of my total payment! No Questions asked. TRAVEL SMART has been at it for 21 years — no one has complained yet.*

A couple of good things here: "right away" — yes! "No questions asked," although in the text "No" and "Questions" are capitalized and "asked" isn't. But this outpouring — added to a decision among three different subscription-lengths and various credit cards (this is to be enclosed in an envelope, so don't worry about exposing the credit card number) — heck, it's too much.

The simple solution to too many words

The solution is simple: Divide the card into two sections, the one on the left being "Keep this portion for your records." That's where you can list benefit after benefit without squashing the actual response portion.

If you do this, be sure to add a perforation between the two segments. And be sure the part they mail fits easily into the business reply envelope.

Accentuating the Positive

The response device isn't the place to have a burst of negative candor. Clarity, yes. Truthfulness, yes. Information optimizing, yes.

The amalgam of those three elements suggests making light of others the prospective respondent might regard as negative. An example:

SEND NO MONEY!
U.S. GOLF SOCIETY CHARTER MEMBERSHIP INVITATION
R.S.V.P.
I ACCEPT MEMBERSHIP in the USGS. Please mail my New Member Kit immediately, along with an annual statement for my $2 per month dues. If, at any time during the first year I change my mind, I can cancel and get a full refund no matter how much use I have made of Society benefits.

Some standard trigger-terms such as "Send no money" (I disagree with the exclamation point, which transforms the statement into a transparent pitch. Add to this a neat less-standard touch: ". . . an annual statement for my $2 per month dues." Mildly obfuscatory to some, I suppose, but certainly no organization can effectively bill $2 a month. So the dues are $24 per year . . . which is $2 per month, right? Now, what? When the individual gets the statement for $24, will he or she rise up in outraged wrath, saying, "You misled me"? Some may, but probably not in ratio to the increased response this wording generates . . . especially if this mailer rushes a "Congratulations!" acknowledgment before or with the invoice.

Compare that with this one, from an insurance company:

Free Information Request
There's no cost or obligation. Just complete this postage-paid card and mail today. An agent will contact you regarding this insurance.

Let's ignore "or" instead of "nor," because of common usage. And let's ignore the missed opportunity to use a trigger-word ("postage-free" instead of "postage-paid"). We'll focus on "An agent will contact you." Of course that's what happens, but why rub somebody's nose in it? Why not, "We'll get the happy details into your hands quickly"? Then, the agent can call . . . or send a letter saying he or she will call . . . or whatever.

The Fourth Rule of Order Forms

Actually, this is more a philosophy than a Rule, but it's probably more universally valid than any of the other rules:

Someone scared off by the response device doesn't even exist; someone lured by the response device does exist.

So this heading . . .

Sure, I'd like to save $27.

. . . creates a state of mind for the next line . . .

Send me a year's subscription (12 disks) for $79.95* — I'll avoid the hassle of ordering each month.

"I'll avoid the hassle of ordering each month" also works to put a positive spin on the expenditure. Many would just state the price. That's the difference between a salesperson and a clerk.

Without a promise, asking someone to request information is flat:

Find Out More About American's Newly Enhanced International Business Class.

No specifics. No structure.

The Fifth Rule of Order Forms

That brings us to The Fifth Rule of Order Forms:

Structured outpulls unstructured.

So this . . .

☐ *Send me my FREE checklist: "How to Avoid the Seven Critical Dangers to Your Network."*
☐ *I'd like to arrange a FREE TRIAL of Backup Express.*

. . . although not good copywriting, is superior to a loose call such as . . .

YES, I want to know more about the benefits of Backup Express.

How about Fund Raising?

That last Rule is a potent contributor to contributions. A structured response device not only usually outpulls an unstructured response device, it brings in more money.

So this . . .

☐ *$25*   ☐ *$35*   ☐ *$50*

. . . is likely to bring more response and more dollars per response than . . .

Amount I'm contributing: $_____.

Why do so many not-for-profit organizations bypass an emotional appeal at the moment of truth, the response device? Beats me. We see copy such as:

☐ *YES, I want to help support The American Museum and its many vital programs.*

Zero on three different scales: specificity, emotion, and structure. Compare it with this one:

No home . . . no job . . . no chance!
PLEASE HELP HOMELESS PEOPLE ESCAPE CATCH-22
☐ *YES! I want to build new lives for homeless people by helping them get permanent homes **and** jobs. Here's my tax-deductible gift to "The Partnership for the Homeless":*
☐ *$30*   ☐ *$50*   ☐ *$100*   ☐ *$_____*

Off the point of this chapter: Why put "The Partnership for the Homeless" inside quotation marks? It makes the group seem artificial.

And in Conclusion, Ladies and Gentlemen

Without discussion, because the percentage of mailed-in responses is constantly dropping when phone or fax options exist:

*If you have a toll-free phone option or a fax option, absolutely include the numbers **prominently** on the response device.*

Was this chapter necessary at all? You decide . . . after taking a look at your own order form.

Is it a turn-on or a turn-off? If you're not sure, grab the biggest benefit in the offer and use it as a header. Change "Tell me more" to a specific. Don't avoid the truth; just optimize it.

That's a good start.

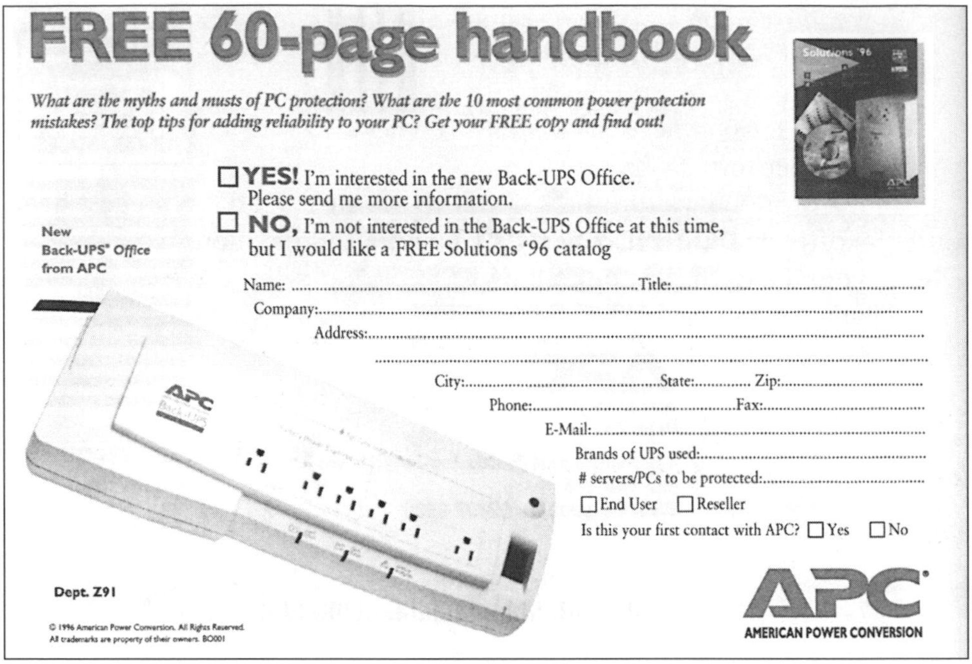

Figure 20-1

A venerable concept, often proved correct, is that a "Yes/No" option improves response. Here is an example, properly handled. A cold "No, I'm not interested at this time," is *not* what the concept means. This "No" keeps the prospect in the loop.

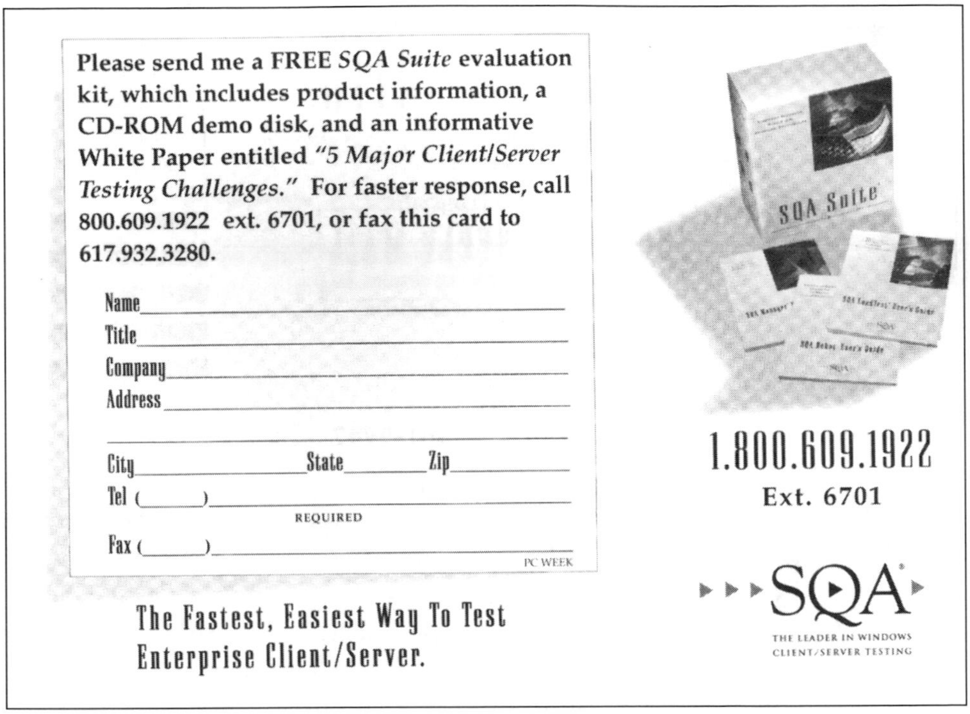

Please send me a FREE *SQA Suite* **evaluation kit, which includes product information, a CD-ROM demo disk, and an informative White Paper entitled** *"5 Major Client/Server Testing Challenges."* **For faster response, call 800.609.1922 ext. 6701, or fax this card to 617.932.3280.**

Name

Title

Company

Address

City   State   Zip

Tel (   )
           REQUIRED

Fax (   )
                              PC WEEK

The Fastest, Easiest Way To Test Enterprise Client/Server.

1.800.609.1922

Ext. 6701

▶ ▶ ▶ SQA ▶

THE LEADER IN WINDOWS
CLIENT/SERVER TESTING

Figure 20-2

A mail-in response device that also includes a toll-free phone number somehow increases response to both options. This clear, quickly understood card has only one problem: The size is 4¼" x 6", which makes the fax option — always a good inclusion — impossible on many machines.

Figure 20-3

The "Catch-22" ("You need a job to support a home. But how do you get a job when you don't have a place to live?") is explained in the letter, but it may be a little too flip to appeal to many prospective donors. The structure of this response device is sound, recapitulating what the organization will do with the money and suggesting specific amounts.

21

Want More Response? Tell Them What to Do, or Ask Them a Question

Don't just tell me you can "Solve my toughest marketing problems." Tell me what they are. And if I agree — which I'll do if you're a salesperson — you might make a sale. Two venerable rules hold true today more than ever. You've already seen the first one half-a-dozen times in previous chapters:

Specifics outsell generalizations.

Let's add another rule, one I wish more salespeople would observe — in person as well as in print or electronic media:

You're always safe being straightforward.

Don't Proclaim. Sell.

I don't know whether it's laziness, unfamiliarity with what they're selling, or an arrogant assumption that the reader will accept a proclamation instead of apparent fact, but I do know an epidemic has begun — or maybe it's a contagious infection — of half-baked sales arguments in cur-rent ads and mailings.

One example:

An envelope with the legend, "Solve Your *Toughest* Marketing Prob-lems in under 2 hours!" generated two questions. First, why did whoever wrote this drop the caps/l.c. approach halfway through the statement? And second, what *are* my toughest marketing problems?

What should have been on the envelope is the answer to that second question, not a loose generalization. Okay, we'll give these guys a chance. They'll tell me in the letter, won't they?

You decide. This is the way the letter begins:

> *Dear Customer,*
> *You already know what how powerful Business Insight® and Plan Write® are in helping your business to succeed — now we've taken our ten years of research and constant feedback from our loyal customers to create, **Quick Insight**™.*

Even if we forgive "know what how" and the extra comma, we're still at sea: What are our toughest marketing problems?

By studying the mailing — and I mean *studying* — we unearth hard, biting, salesworthy ammunition. This software claims to be able to predict whether a new product idea should be killed or funded, and, if funded, what its pricing strategy should be. Now, *there* are two marketing problems! Why not exploit them?

Aiming Above Your Target = A Missed Shot

A letter addressed to me has this overline:

> *The cable modem is here! And you need to understand how its proliferation will change your business.*

Somehow, I resent this overline. It might be because I really do think I can lead a long and useful life without understanding how proliferation of the cable modem will change my business, but it's probably because what we have here is a half-threat, poorly worded.

Suppose, instead of this wording, the overline were:

If the phrase "cable modem" means nothing to you, a suggestion: Read this report and change your mind.

A cemetery misses its mark by depending on a meaningless statistic instead of an emotional pitch. The heading:

72% of the People in America Today Believe It's Smart To Plan Ahead for Cemetery and Funeral Needs

Hard to think of a less-motivational opening, isn't it, especially when so many arrows with actual points on them exist in the sales-quiver, such as "Will your family have to undergo the pain of making critical decisions at a time of grief?" or "Give your family the comfort of knowing everything is planned according to your wishes" or "Will your legacy to your family be a pile of unpaid bills?" (Anyway, my guess at the percentage is 64 percent.)

How easy it is to operate inside the reader's experiential background instead of your own! All you have to do is ask the basic question:

If I were getting this instead of sending it, would it motivate me?

Some better examples

Some marketers understand the principles of marketing. Let's treasure them and hope they aren't a dying breed. Few examples could be considered "brilliant" writing, just as few effective salespeople could be considered brilliant talkers. In fact, brilliance too often calls attention to itself instead of what's being sold. Oscar Wilde probably would have been a less successful advertising copywriter than Elmore Leonard. Suggestion: If you have to choose between brilliant verbiage and effective communication, choose brilliance only if you're my competitor.

A newsletter sells itself with this opening:

Dear LANtastic User,
Do panic and confusion reign whenever your office network stops working? It's probably an all too familiar scene.

A mail order insurance company begins its message not with "Here's what we want you to buy" but "Here's the advantage for you," an old-time cliché that still brings results:

*This birthday message is being rushed to you so you'll have
a last-minute opportunity to get up to $3,000 worth of life insur-
ance at your lowest possible rate. And your ACCEPTANCE IS
GUARANTEED!*

Even those who are glutted with controlled circulation computer publications will open the envelope with this legend:

A No-Brainer!
A FREE Subscription Inside.

Visualize the drop in impact had the mailer omitted the first line
(which many, out of a misplaced emphasis on dignity, would have done).

Too much dignity = too little response

Too much awareness of dignity often accompanies too much awareness of vocabulary . . . and results in non-communicative openings, such as
this fund-raising letter:

Dear Friend,
      *I am writing to ask you to join me in a global humanitarian
campaign to help children whose lives have been traumatized by
war.*

Ugh.
Mailings for seminars traditionally are grist for critics. These self-
mailers too often assume an information base — which, if it existed, might
make the seminar too primitive for those who attend. For example, one
mailed to four different people at my organization is headed:

Customer
Segmentation
Techniques . . .
for business marketers exclusively

A question for this seminar company: Who, other than business marketers, would be interested in customer segmentation techniques?
Directly below the heading is this subhead: "Answer these critical
marketing questions . . ." Okay, what should come next? A critical marketing question, right? Here's the first question:

• *How do I get beyond segmenting by SICs and RFM?*

Maybe we're not quite with it, but even though we all knew what the initials meant, none of the four of us knew what the significance of this question was. None felt, regardless of the significance, it was "critical." It's a refinement, and refinements sell if they're pitched as a competitive edge, not as a "critical" marketing decision.

Who Is in Your Mirror?

A suggestion to marketers who feel generalizations might one day out-sell specifics and who think writing around a point might one day outsell getting to the point:

Your speculation is heading in the wrong direction. Patience no longer is considered a virtue. Clarity is *in*. Directness is *in*. Claims without proof are *out*. Showing off your gigantic vocabulary is *out*.

Don't believe me? Good. Let's have our ads and mailers go head-to-head.

Ask Me a Question . . . and You Have My Attention.

One of the always-available, but strangely underused (*never* "under-utilized" if you have genuine communications credentials), rhetorical tricks available to direct marketers is the *question.*

Questions trap the message-recipient in an absolute snare. That same reader or viewer or listener who can turn the page or toss the mailing or switch channels or click a mouse is stuck . . . on the tip of your punctuational rapier.

Okay, we've all known that for centuries. But how about this one, one of several Rules of Question Marks:

Transforming a command into a question not only dissipates latent antagonism, but promotes rapport.

That one isn't so easy to penetrate, but the principle becomes clear even with its first application. Two examples are the difference between these headings:

- *This is you!*
- *Is this you?*

You can see the difference between *assumption* and *apparent inquiry.* (The diplomat doesn't declare, "You're drunk." Instead, it's a question: "Are you drunk?") A comparable example:

- *Why I am sending you this message:*
- *Why am I sending you this message?*

The psychological impact of the headings is in no way parallel, even though the words are identical. The first is a proclamation from Mount Olympus; the second is a reader-involving challenge.

Who are you, relative to your target?

Choosing whether to proclaim or to question depends on who you are relative to your target. The dynamic statement might transcend antagonism if the reader *pre*-accepts you as an authoritative voice.

A mailing from a seminar company asks this question:

Sales and Use Taxes: Is Your Company Headed for Legal Trouble?

You can see the difference between this approach and:

Sales and Use Taxes: Your Company Is Headed for Legal Trouble!

You also can see why asking a question isn't always the most sales-worthy approach. In this instance the question forces the reader to think about a potential problem. For a mass communication, in media or in the mail, that's the safest course. But you also can visualize the power a direct statement can have: "You're headed for trouble!" can grab and shake readers — including executives whose response-ratio usually is nominal. A question *isn't* a universal problem-solver, especially if your target might answer the question with a "No."

Can they answer your question?

An envelope from the biggest software company asks: "What's the **real** story on the Internet?"

To whoever wrote that, I offer a mild suggestion: When you ask a question, ask one the recipient feels can be answered. This type of question is analogous to the semi-professional television interviewer who asks a hapless subject, "How does it feel to . . . ?" It's a non-question.

We open this envelope and see a bold headline above the greeting on the letter: "Separate fact from fiction." Yeah, I guess we should do that, but it's unrelated to the question the mailer asks on its envelope.

One of the many enclosures included with this mailing begins with another question:

> *How can you keep up with the latest development trends — games development, leveraging ActiveX controls, extending existing applications to the intranet and the Internet — when it all changes so quickly?*

Okay, friend, another suggestion: Don't formulate a question so loose and rambling the reader can't keep track of what the question is, even before you've finished asking it.

Questions don't have to be brutally terse. They do have to hit the reader (or listener!) in the emotional solar-plexus. One of the automatic benefits of a well-asked question is that it prevents dullness; so asking a dull question, or one that leads nowhere, blunts your own power.

Aggressive questions are "in"!

A suddenly pugnacious United States Postal Service mails millions of jumbo postcards. On the face of the card is cartoon art of the FedEx, UPS, and Priority Mail envelopes, with apparently comparable pricing. Copy, in its entirety:

> *What's Your Priority?*

I'd qualify this as an aggressive question because it's pure comparative advertising. It's a minor shame that the need to use the word "Priority" — and it *is* a need, because that's the name of the service — takes some of the steam out of what might have been a forceful question ("How much are *you* wasting?") . . . but probably postal decision-makers felt that coming out swinging might be too aggressive.

(I don't agree. In for a penny, in for a pound. If you see someone walking past your window and want to get his or her attention, you don't beat on the window with a sponge.)

A monitor service takes a more direct posture:

IS YOUR MAIL DELIVERED?
HOW LONG DOES IT TAKE TO BE DELIVERED?
IS YOUR LIST/DATABASE PROTECTED AGAINST UNAU-
THORIZED USE?

If we look at questions from the position of the questionee instead of the questioner, we often can insert rods and starch to eliminate limpness. "Is your mail delivered?" suffers from a lack of gauntlet-hurling. You or I would have written:

HOW MUCH OF YOUR MAIL IS ACTUALLY DELIVERED?

As questions gain *specificity* relative to the target, they automatically pick up power. We're back to one of the most venerable of all rules of force-communication:

Specifics outpull generalizations.

A loose-deck card from a computer supply house has this heading:

DROWNING
in keyboards & monitors?

The word-image is imperfect because no matter what the subject is, "Drowning" suggests something liquid. It's an attention-getter, though, which is probably more than adequate in a card deck. (Who decided to use that ampersand? Ugh.)

Card decks (see chapter 13) aren't regarded as hotbeds of brilliant copywriting, but they're especially well-adapted to the question headline. A company marketing standby battery backups for computers adds a dimension of reader interest with:

Who needs a **glitch** *in the system?*

Even better is the card headline that asks a one-word question, then answers it:

FUSES? YES.

Why Not Give It a Shot?

If that last subhead slid past you, unrecognized as a question, it's both good and bad: Good in that you're still reading without interruption, so maybe your recognition of (and response to) the question was subliminal, but it's there. Bad in that the question wasn't potent enough to gain recognition as what it was.

Anyway, we have this bit of ammunition. Why not take a look at some of your own headlines and openers? Why not write a question to replace one or two you acknowledge aren't as robust as they might be? Agreed? A question? Why not?

Do consumers use coupons to make a shopping list? You can plan on it.

Research indicates that 65% of primary grocery shoppers regularly use a shopping list. Another 53% say coupons play a big role in planning their list and in making their buying decisions.

Whatever your brand's objectives, Free-Standing Insert (FSI) coupons offer the right tactic to get your message home.

To learn more about the power of FSI coupons, call the FSI Council at (888) FSI-0881. And, remember, it's much easier to propose to her *before* she starts walking down the aisle.

FSI Coupons. Rediscover what they're worth.
CIRCLE 135 ON READER SERVICE

Figure 21-1

This ad asks a question, then answers it. As a straight statement, the message would be considerably less effective.

Figure 21-2

The heading on this ad, a question, doesn't lead to a forceful follow-up. If you ask a question, be sure the answer — one that benefits both you and your target-individual — is forthcoming.

22

Automatic Power-Enhancers

What do you do when your copy is due today, and you're sitting at the keyboard with your brain locked into neutral gear?

You can think of everything but a way to get your fingers rolling. You switch to the Solitaire game in Windows, waiting for a creative thought to grab you.

Somehow, the copy gets out. You're a professional, so your copy is always workmanlike, but does the true professional settle for "workmanlike"?

Not to worry.

Here are *40* automatic self-starters, to get you rolling in high gear on those days when the muse just isn't with you.

Understand, please: These are "boiler plate" openings, so you can't build a career on them. But understand too: *They work.* They work for ads. They work for brochures. They work for handouts. They work for broadcast commercials. They work for banners on the World Wide Web. They work for selective binding in publications. Letters? They *aren't* designed for letters.

Is a list of 40 "boiler-plate" headings, for jump-starting space ads and brochures, and broadcast commercials, and Internet banners and ads, *over-automating* the creative process?

What a fascinating topic for an academic discussion!

Ah, but we who toil in the creative furnaces can't often afford the luxury of academic discussions. The copy is due. What do we write, when our heads are full of mucus instead of ingenious ways to launch our sales spiel?

In my opinion, we can't over-automate. Lists of helpers are as venerable as Peter Mark Roget, whose thesaurus helped writers in the year 1852. What *this* list accomplishes is no more an intrusion into the creative process than looking up a word in the dictionary. Well, maybe a little more intrusive.

In a perfect world, the creative team takes one look at whatever they're selling and brilliance radiates through the room, striking in exquisite sequence just the right keys on the keyboard.

If this is your pattern, you can chuckle as you read these self-starter tips. The rest of us look at what we're selling and — as salespeople — ask ourselves, "What can I say that projects *benefit*? That's what they want to see."

If we were to separate these prefabricated headings into categories, the biggest category would be *benefit* . . . and that's as it should be, because that's what sells. You start with number 1 — "At last!" — or number 3 — "It's about time" — or number 6 — "Can your *[WHATEVER]* do this?" — or numbers 8, 13, 17, or most of the others from 20 and beyond — and you force yourself to follow with a benefit.

The second biggest category includes provocative headlines designed to get the reader into the message. That's okay, too.

It's your call. Recognizing that unlike letter openings, the dynamics of ads and brochures don't allow for hundreds of choices, your selection of these or one from your own sources follows an easy decision:

What will do the best selling job for me?

If you're a salesperson first and a creative writer second, you won't stumble. (A parenthetical note: The best advertising writers I know regard themselves as salespeople.)

A copywriter can pound the keyboard for a lifetime and never use any of these; another copywriter can pound the keyboard for a lifetime using *only* these. Is the one who says, "Everybody uses these so I'll use something else" a better copywriter than the one who leans on the old dependables?

Better? Not necessarily. More inventive? Probably. But the inventive copywriter who avoids headline wording "because it's been used before," runs the risk of having his or her imagination overpower a sense of salesmanship.

Suppose you're out to buy a new car. A salesperson confronts you. The old-timer swings into his standard sales pitch. The bright young innovator says, "Every car salesman says the same thing." So this revolutionary delivers the sales pitch in rhymed poetry . . . or sings it, playing the guitar . . . or emphasizes each sales point by holding up a printed card with a selling message on it.

From whom are you most likely to buy?

Don't discard innovation. But for the sake of the future reputation of advertising and marketing, don't be different just for the sake of being different. That doesn't require professional discipline.

Unless you tie innovation to salesmanship, you're showing off — a cardinal sin in selling. In every facet of selling, *cleverness for the mere sake of being clever may well be a liability, not an asset.* Don't fall into the "It's better *because* it's different" trap.

So, yes, look for approaches others aren't using. But for Pete's sake be sure your approach is designed to generate response, not to have others in the office applaud your cleverness.

While we ponder the philosophical differential, here are the self-starters. (Remember, while evaluating these: They're for components *other* than letters.) Use them as you like, with the single caution that you don't want to become an automatic self-starter junkie.

The first two are variations of a similar theme.

1. "At last," or "Now you can . . . ," or "It's about time!"

"At last" is the number one dependable, because this little phrase combines two salesworthy elements: First, it takes a swipe at all competition because the very phrase "At last" suggests superiority over anything that went before.

As I'll emphasize in the next chapter, I don't equate "At last" and "Finally" on equal terms. "Finally" has an exasperated feel to it; "At last" is exhilarated.

For the sake of everybody else in advertising, don't use "At last" and follow it up with nothing. We already have delivered a near-mortal blow to "Personal" by witless exploitation. Let's keep "At last" alive, so our children can enjoy it.

"Now you can" is parallel to "At last" in one powerful way: It damns all competition without apparently damning any competition.

Realize the variations available with this theme. "How often have you thought of . . ." and "When was the last time you . . ." are kissin' cousins within the "Now you can" family.

Even when your brain is racing flat out, "Now you can" is on a par with the most inventive openings. It's 100 percent reader-involving, and that's what any effective opening should be.

Power and danger are half-brothers. "It's about time!" has greater power than either "At last" or "Now you can"; its very aggressiveness can turn a neutral reader into an adversary . . . which suggests that this self-starter be reserved for either radical surgery or for assured communicative professionalism.

While you're at it, involve whoever chooses your media or lists in this one, to be sure the people you're reaching share your assertion that it *is,* really, about time that whatever it is you're selling happened or appeared.

2. Did you ever hope to . . .

Just as "It's about time" is harder-boiled than "At last" or "Now you can," this one is the softest-boiled of the Similar Two. "Did you ever hope to" doesn't demand an in-gear brain, because of its softness. But don't dismiss it on that ground, because it still forces out an immediately specific sales argument.

You have a wide selection of variations on this theme. One *very* serviceable cousin is "What if you could . . ."; another is "If I can show you how to. . . ." Each uses the concept of hope as surrogate for hard reality. Any career salesperson will tell you how potent such an approach can be, regardless of what you're selling. (Proof: salespeople who use this technique can swivel from one field to another, smoothly transferring their dominance to their next sales organization.)

The standard uses of "Did you ever hope to" and its clones end with a question mark. This is an extra attention-getting power-bonus for the writer.

3. The secret of . . .

Everybody wants to be in on somebody else's secrets. This provocative beginning is an exceptional "grabber" for space ads or any textual circumstance.

For the writer, "The secret of " unlocks the locked-up brain. Try it. Write "The secret of" and follow it up with either a) the principal use of what you're selling, b) the principal benefit of what you're selling, or c) just the name of what you're selling. Your fingers will be itching to continue.

Better yet, this opening will have *the readers or listeners* itching to continue. If you let them down, it isn't the fault of "The secret of. . . ."

4. The most unusual guarantee you've read all day

This heading combines three winning elements, and the synergy crackles with appeal.

The first winner is the word "Unusual," a curiosity-grabber. The second is "Guarantee," which, without explanation, suggests benefit.

The third is "You've Read All Day," which adds just a touch of tongue-in-cheek wit to the mixture. And why might we want this often-questionable component? Because in its usage here, the phrase disarms skepticism aimed at the first half of the headline.

5. How much are you paying for [WHATEVER]?

"How much" is a universal *and intrusive* question. So, "How much are you paying?" combines two attention-getters — the very nature of a question and the specificity of an intrusive question.

What makes the heading even stronger is the context. One can't *physically* approach a stranger and ask, "How much are you paying for the prescriptions you're taking?" or even "How much are you paying for temporary office help?" The level of intrusion, on a genuine one-to-one level, is intolerable. But once removed, in media or mail, the question becomes provocative without crossing the border into impertinence.

6. Can your [WHATEVER] do this?

Number six is valuable as a comparative, especially for product introduction. Two factors have to be in place:

 a. The reader has to have prior knowledge of the product phylum.

 b. Whatever yours does that others can't do has to be quickly recognizable as a benefit.

Comparatives are strong medicine, which makes this self-starter a potent sales weapon for space ads, envelope copy, and/or a descriptive brochure.

7. Confused about . . . ?

What a versatile opening this is!

"Confused about" has an educational overtone without the usual negative "preachy" image. Want to introduce a product? Upgrade a product? Damn the competition? Establish quick rapport (by admitting you're confused too)? Half-explain an abstruse concept? "Confused about" works in every one of these circumstances.

A suggestion — and it's only that, not a requirement:

Follow "Confused about" with either an anecdote or a narrative, *be-*

fore attacking and solving the cause of confusion. Reader comfort breeds clarity of understanding. Jumping on the coattails of "Confused about" too quickly with a hard sales pitch is a betrayal of your role as a confusion-dispeller.

8. Try this and you'll never again settle for . . .

This one follows one of the venerable rules of force-communication: It begins with a positive imperative and uses a negative for reinforcement.

As is true of all these automatic self-starters, "Try this and you'll never again . . ." is an outline, not a specific. The writer has, literally, hundreds of "Try this" varieties from which to choose.

For example, tack onto the beginning a "When you" opening (an assumption, a psychological trick); or "If you" (weaker but to some target-groups more palatable); or replace "Try" with "Grab" or "Demand."

9. You won't believe this!

Obviously this opening doesn't apply when you want to project a dignified image. It's showmanship in action, the carnival barker shrewdly stopping passersby and hustling them into the tent.

Don't assume, though, that this opening damages legitimacy. Legitimacy depends on the comparison that follows. This headline will stop the eye . . . but in inexperienced hands, it becomes a kamikaze dive if the reader concludes, "You're right. I *don't* believe this."

"You won't believe this!" is one of the patriarchs of a family of credibility-strainers that includes "Good News!" and "Have I Got a Deal for You!" and "You're One of the Lucky Few." What these have in common is their dependence on willingness to suspend disbelief.

So they share a common danger: In the hands of a hit-and-run copywriter who can't or won't or doesn't know how to justify the claim, they damage the credibility of all advertising. (Examine your own skepticism of advertising claims: Isn't most of it the result of an opening such as this, its effectiveness weakened and diluted by an ineffective or obviously self-serving follow-up?)

10. The true story of . . .

When space limitation isn't a major problem, this can be more than a self-starter; it can be a major winner.

"The true story of " combines two wonderfully salesworthy elements: the delicious suggestion of *confession,* which everybody wants to read, and revelation, which suggests revisionist information.

Understand, please: You don't have to follow this starter with a confession or even with a revelation. It's simply a sound mechanical device to get fingers moving crisply on the keyboard.

11. Take a trip with us to . . .

Here we have a versatile tool. For nostalgia, it's "Take a trip with us back to . . ."; for product introduction, it's "Take a trip with us into the future"; for travel, it's "Take a trip with us to an exotic land"; for books and recordings, it's "Take a trip with us — an easy and enjoyable trip — into a world limited only by your own imagination."

And so it goes.

Why "with us"? Because telling the reader to take an *unaccompanied* trip generates as much rejection as it does acceptance. Depending on the thrust of the ad, or if this is a signed mailing, "with me" not only is a surrogate for "with us," it's preferable because it's more one-to-one.

12. Enjoy

"Enjoy" comes in two flavors: with and without an exclamation mark. "Enjoy!" is a stand-alone, and you have to follow it with a subhead-statement of apparent benefit or it's another one of those deadly unexclaiming exclamations. Without the exclamation point, you have to follow it with a noun that stimulates the salivary glands. "Enjoy the benefits of . . ." or "Enjoy the advantages of . . ." are workmanlike, but for a pow! effect you need greater imagination: "Enjoy the Moon"; "Enjoy Sex"; "Enjoy Your Loot." (Of course, if you had greater imagination that day, you wouldn't need a headline-helper.)

The two benefits of "Enjoy," with or without an exclamation point, are a) the absolute implication of positive result, and b) the epidemic effect it has on the entire sales message that follows.

"Enjoy" also works well in combination with number 13, coming right up.

13. How would you like to . . . ?

"How would you like to . . ." grabs the reader because it combines three irresistible elements: challenge, promise, and provocation. This opening is especially useful when what you're selling is exotic, unusual, or self-improving.

You can see how well "Enjoy" dovetails: "How would you like to enjoy . . ." is a double whammy.

14. Special offer for (or to) . . .

"Special offer to . . ." implements the realization that exclusivity is not only one of the great motivators, but also is the easiest to implement.

We're salespeople, not bemused observers of the human scene. Still, even though most "special offers" are cynically-inspired — because no bulk offer is really special — our sense of logic, if not ethics, suggests that what follows this heading do its best to convince the reader that, yes, he or she *is* getting a special offer.

One easy way to prove the "special offer" claim is to follow it with qualifiers: "If you" or "If you're." This says to the reader, "We think you're special, but we aren't quite sure; you'll have to qualify yourself for this." It's a primitive but still effective bit of child psychology.

If you think "Special offer to . . ." requires personalization, which limits it to direct mail or online, think again. It can be a special offer to any target group.

15. It's 10 o'clock. Do you know where your . . . is?

"It's 10 o'clock" is an all-purpose performer, effective because it's both barbed and light-hearted. If you're selling perishables or gifts, it works. If you're selling fear, it works. If you're raising funds, it works. If you're selling seasonal or timely items, it works.

Here we have a recognizable phrase, based on a warning to parents. This gives "It's 10 o'clock . . ." an extra kick, because it places the reader in a parental — i.e., decision-making — position. The reader is less likely to reject the offer by making the claim, "I'm not the one who makes decisions about this matter."

Suggestion: Don't strain to tie the selling argument to this headline, beyond "Whether it's 10 a.m. or 10 p.m. . . ." or "Whatever the time of day . . ." or another generic follow-up. Tortured ties are far, far greater reader turnoffs than no tie.

16. Introducing . . .

This list already has included two serviceable introductories . . . "Can your *[WHATEVER]* do this" and "Confused about . . . ?" Those two aren't custom-designed for product or service introduction; this one can't be anything else.

Now, then: What do you introduce? Newness has a universal appeal, and for electronic devices, computers and software, appliances, products with yearly model changes, and items relating to health, the logic exists.

Just one caution:

Almost universally, "Introducing . . ." is weaker than *something* else. What, specifically? If your imagination is in gear, you won't need a list of surrogate beginnings.

So save "Introducing . . ." for those brain-dead days when even your own intellect recognizes the weakness of the opening but also recognizes the copy deadline.

17. It's easier than it's ever been to . . .

Here's a natural for product improvement or for an upsell. Brilliant? Absolutely not. Serviceable? Absolutely.

"It's never been easier to . . ." reads better; but, "It's easier than it's ever been" is superior to "It's never been easier," not only because it avoids the negative, but also because the suggestion of action, to a first-time user, is stronger.

"It's easier than it's ever been" has a natural tie to an "If . . ." opener such as number 18.

18. If you ever . . .

Not all "If " clauses are equal. The power lurking in "If " is the power of having the reader, viewer, or listener think you haven't pre-judged, while actually you have. "If" gains strength, then, just by being a far more negative opening word than the more action-suggestive "When"; but "When" has its problems, too, being *assumptive* ("When you drive this car, you'll . . ."). Some of the smarter salespeople begin with "If" and gradually switch to "When," shifting into overdrive as they close with a second switch from "When" to "As soon as."

As an opener, "If you ever . . ." begins a natural parallel with "Then you'll. . . ." That's why it effortlessly slides into number 16. Example: "If you ever dreamed of *[WHATEVER]* your time has come, because it's never been easier to. . . ."

19. Why should you (or Why you should) . . .

"Why" is a reader-involving word. Everybody knows this; that, probably, is why it's overused.

But then, so are "Free" and "New," and they're still churning along on all eight cylinders.

The difference between "Why should you" and "Why you should" is the difference between a question and an imperative. Each has its strengths. The writer's decision to use a question or an imperative hinges on these factors:

a) Who is the target? Are we projecting an image of superiority or authority? Then an imperative is in order. Analysis of the list will give us a quick answer here.

b) Are we masquerading as the exponents of rational thought? Do we want the reader to think he or she has formed a conclusion from a previously plastic position, a conclusion that couldn't be achieved by an outside push? Then a question is in order.

20. *Why are we (or Why we are)* . . .

Don't assume "Why should you" is parallel to "Why are we." The effect on the reader is totally different. "Why are we" either results in a revelation, or it's a flop. Usually that revelation is supposed to explain an impossibly favorable deal: "Why are we making this *[WHATEVER]* available to you for only $5.00?" Or, "Why are we giving away these nationally-advertised *[WHATEVER]* for only $5.00?"

Okay, why *are* you doing this? If you can't figure out a way to justify the question, don't ask it; use another opening.

"Why should you" projects a patently rational case; "Why are we" projects a shrill, high-pressure case. The decision of which one to use, if you're evaluating the two, depends on both target and medium. In a space ad, a free-standing insert, or a broadcast commercial, I'd use "Why are we"; in an upscale publication, I'd use "Why should you." In the mail, I'd let the list tell me which one to choose.

21. *If (or When) you do that, you need this.*

Here's another example of the difference between an "If " opening and a "When" opening. Which is more likely to irritate the reader? "If you want to make money, this magazine is a must," or "When you want to make money, this magazine is a must"?

Right! It depends on who your target is.

"When" is more positive than "If," but that doesn't make it an automatic choice.

Want more proof? Reader rapport has to override any factor other than clarity when you're choosing between "If " and "When."

Or should the previous sentence be: Reader rapport has to override any factor other than clarity *if* you're choosing between "If " and "When"? In a letter, I usually prefer to open with "If " so the reader doesn't feel threatened, then gradually switch to "When" because the word suggests the reader *will* respond; but this technique is for letters, not headlines. A headline is too terse to allow a switchover, so the choice has to be based on long-distance mind-reading: How familiar, how skeptical, how eager for improvement or ease is your target?

22. We're solving this problem:

The benefit of a problem-solving heading is the targeting. Those who recognize the existence of the problem are likely to read the piece with an anticipatory attitude.

That's the *three*-edged sword of this opening. Sword one: We impale those who recognize the problem. Sword two: We leave uninterested both those who have the problem and *don't* know it, and those who might respond to a heading linked to a positive advance instead of a negative circumstance. Sword three: After that heading, we have to thrust home immediately with the solution. No subtlety (which usually doesn't work anyway), no sluggishness in getting to the point. "We're solving your problem of too-high overnight delivery costs . . . and here's how we're doing it."

A regional telephone company has this heading on its brochure:

We're talking to small businesses . . .
We're listening to their needs . . .
We're responding with solutions.
Here's the solution to your overburdened phone . . .
and how to capture business you may have been missing.

Raw opinion, please: Good or bad?

In my opinion the first three sentences have zero impact. This would have been stronger starting with "Here's the solution," plus replacing punchless words such as "overburdened" and "capture" with action words.

23. Answers to your questions about . . .

This one is my all-time favorite, because it combines two "can't miss" reader-involvers — "you" positively related to the subject at hand, and "question," a primitive psychological trick suggesting the reader isn't your captive.

That word "about" is the key. You have two choices: a) the field or area of interest; b) the name of what you're selling. Examples:

- *Answers to your questions about computer graphics.*
- *Answers to your questions about CorelDraw 8.*

Some enhancement usually is in order:

- *Straight answers to your tough questions about CorelDraw 8.*

("Tough" dictates using the name of what you're selling rather than the field of interest, because the suggestion of implicit skepticism makes more sense when aimed at a vendor than at a universe.)

24. What *[WHATEVER]* can do for you:

This opening works well when limited space prevents considering it as a *sub*-head. It starts in high gear . . . no preamble, no buildup, no brand-puffery. So the writer needs less space to launch the pitch.

Two variations: "Here's what . . ." and, reversing the second and third words, as a question.

If you use this opening, remember why you used it — to get into the meat of the matter quickly. The way to do that is simple enough: Tell them what *[WHATEVER]* can do for them. Don't get lost in a rhetorical labyrinth. A marvelous overall rule of force-communication is:

Get to the point.

25. What trouble I had until I discovered this!

The exclamation point is optional, but the statement has to be exclamatory.

After all these years of battling the great unwashed public, I'm still surprised by the number of non-revelations people seem to exclaim as testimonials. We see statements such as, "Now I'm in touch because I read this magazine!" or "Since I started using this I feel a lot better!" or other generalized nonsense.

Usually the fault lies with whoever collects these endorsements. We do have ways to force specifics out of our buyers (see chapter 18).

26. Turn this *[NEGATIVE ILLUSTRATION]* to this *[POSITIVE ILLUSTRATION]* with . . .

Number 26 requires graphics, usually a "before" and "after" photograph. But it doesn't have to be a photograph; it can be an artist's depiction of "problem situation" and "problem solved."

Some varieties use the power phrase "How to" — "How to turn this. . . ." If you use "How to," discard the word "with" and what would follow without "How to" and substitute *procedure* for product name:

How to turn 600 dpi to 1200 dpi for $25.

I'm looking at a space ad which is headed, "Turn This" — with a drawing of a truck labeled "Shipping Costs" on an upward incline — "Into This" — with a drawing of a truck labeled "Shipping Costs" on a downward incline. The payoff line, immediately below: "Increase Your Profits With CTC."

Notice anything? "Increase your profits" is a thin payoff line, because it suggests that profits already exist. "Slash Those Delivery Costs with CTC" seems more potent. (This comment reflects on the execution, not the concept.)

27. Announcing something for you . . . and only you.

Targeting is in, as well it should be. One-to-one is becoming easier, more practical, and cheaper in every medium. Success on the Web is founded on one-to-one.

An ad in a retirement publication has this heading:

AARP Group Health Insurance Is Designed For One Group And One Group Only. AARP Members.

Quite properly, the ad sports a big coupon. The more *direct* a message is, the more it should emphasize *response*.

When you use this opening, be sure to include two elements: a) A reaffirmation of the exclusivity; b) the logic behind the exclusivity.

28. The [fastest, easiest, newest] way to . . .

If you're sure your target matches your offer, this is an excellent lead-in for an upgrade, advancement, or replacement. It has great power when tied to personal improvement, pleasure, or satisfaction.

A brochure for a computer program has this heading:

*Discover The Fastest, Easiest & **Most Enjoyable** Way To Learn Spanish, French, German, Italian, or Latin!*

I'm not sure about that word "Discover" in this context; and a headline this long is probably more readable without all those caps/lower case words forcing the reader to re-start after each word. It's a good use, though, of this opening, even though it uses that wretched ampersand.

29. Stop doing this. And here's why.

This is a cousin of number 8, "Try this and you'll never again settle for. . . ."

The difference is one of force. Number 8 is a suggestion; number 29 is a command.

You can see the danger. Fifty years ago, we (that is, our forerunners) could command our readers and expect a "Yes, sir," or "Yes, ma'am." Today, we're just as likely to generate "Who the bleep do you think you are?"

So "Stop doing this" has to be tied to what appears to be unassailable logic; and we dare not deliver a "You fools!" ultimatum. Structure the wording to imply the end of an ongoing predicament or obstacle, not the end of the reader's stupidity.

This heading satisfies our requirement, in its intent if not in its grammar:

Stop Waiting On Your Windows Application to Print!

Need I add the obvious? If we tell them to stop doing this, we then tell them what to do instead.

30. Here's the [WHATEVER] that accomplishes [WHATEVER].

The word "Here's" is optional, but the decision of whether or not to include it shouldn't be a casual or thoughtless one. One criterion: The more familiar the message-recipient is with the subject, the more logical the use of "Here's" becomes.

Don't make the mistake too many writers make when they use this heading. The "accomplishment" is either trivial or inconsequential. I'm looking at a brochure selling a weekly schedule planner. The heading:

The business gift that works hard for you . . .

(The ellipsis is the writer's.) Had this writer posed a self-question — *How* does this gift work hard for you? — the answer might have dictated a more salesworthy heading.

Mitigating the weakness of this heading is the adjacency of a picture showing the schedule planner. So the combination of graphic and copy assures us that the description is clear enough. Clarity is paramount; tie it to creative salesmanship, please.

"Here's the *[WHATEVER]*" isn't like number one, "It's about time," which fits almost every situation. Trying to bend a circumstance to fit this heading is far less productive than choosing a heading which fits the circumstance.

31. Because of this your *[work, life, appearance]* just got easier.

We're used to the near-cliché, "The best just got better." This isn't the same, because it adds the dimension of specificity. The very word "this" demands either a description or an illustration.

A descriptive sheet for a computer "interface" has this heading:

With this interface, your workday just got easier!

Good or bad?

Opinion: Neither. If you or I had been on the creative team, we'd have asked, "Hey, how does this interface make your workday easier?" The answer to *that* question, whatever it might be, is a better heading because it replaces the generality with a specific . . . and we all know The Specificity Rule:

Specifics outsell generalities.

Incidentally, some artists to whom I showed the sheet asked, "Is this interface a software program, or a card you have to insert in the computer, or what?" For them — for many — this message fails because they're not on the same information-plane.

32. Announcing . . .

I really didn't want to include this one, because it's the weakest, the schlockiest, and the least dynamic of all 40. It's also the most common. So rather than look down our noses as though this opening belongs in intellectual ghetto, it's here with others whose impact would flatten it, head to head.

Ah, head to head. But what if you don't want impact?

"Announcing . . ." has its uses. It makes no statement of superiority. It makes no claim. It has no imperative overtones. For that reason it removes itself from the competitive arena and assumes the mantle of statesmanship: If you want it, here it is.

Typical of this heading is a mailing from a theme park:

Announcing an Evening of Fun
[SUBHEAD] Eat, drink, and be merry until the wee hours, with
a healthy dose of fun.

That word "dose" bothers me, and I'm also bothered by some of the copy, which writes *around* the subject.

33. Now!

Don't assume we're repeating a version of number one, "Now you can. . . ." or "Now's the time to. . . ." "Now!" is an exclamation and those others aren't. If you don't follow "Now!" with a call to action you've wasted it.

"Now!" has two benefits: Timeliness and terseness. Follow it with an action verb such as "Get" or "Grab" and you have that call to action. "Now you can . . ." tells you it's possible, but makes no demands. That's the difference between the two.

A complex self-mailer has just two words on its cover: "Go ahead." We dismiss this, because it's marching-in-place. Inside is the main heading:

NOW: Get a $100 Instant Rebate on every Starter-Pack You Buy!

Before you criticize the mundane aspect of this heading, visualize it without "Now:" and you'll quickly see how much weaker it would have been.

34. Your guide to . . .

Here's an all-purpose workhorse nobody can object to because it steps on no toes. It's also flexible enough to cover every circumstance I can think of, from publications to hardware.

This very flexibility can make it a second-best choice. So when using it, a suggestion: Don't use the words "Your guide to . . ." but, rather, the *concept* "Your guide to . . ."

An example is a mailing from a publication:

Whether it's just around the corner or years away . . . The publishers of Consumer Reports show you HOW TO PLAN FOR A SECURE RETIREMENT

Only on analysis do we recognize this rhetoric as "Your guide to. . . ." That's a tribute to the versatility of this old war-horse.

35. SAVE!

How can you miss with this one? "SAVE!" appeals to the number one 1995 motivator — greed. "Save!" has many faces, from "Buy one, get one free" or "2 for the price of 1" to "Special rebate!" (A parenthetical note: I don't like the word "rebate" as a motivator because it plays up the time-gap between spending money and getting some back.)

"SAVE!" is combinable with other headings, adding spice and strength.

Look through today's paper. Look through a week's mail. You're bound to find a batch of "SAVE!" headings. One I'm looking at right how has this heading:

SAVE 60%
ON OUR DOUBLE STRENGTH HIGH QUALITY COMMER-
*CIAL & INDUSTRIAL **TRASH BAGS***

Here's another:

SAVE 15% UP TO $750*
Sears Authorized Premium Vinyl Siding

I wouldn't saddle "SAVE!" with an asterisk, but that's part of another set of opinions.

36. Free

I didn't suggest any punctuation after "Free" because this is probably the most adaptable opening of any we can consider. "Free" works with or without an exclamation point; it works as a stand-alone or as one of many words in a headline.

Usually, if "Free" is the key word we should give it special type-treatment so the reader's eye flashes to this key word.

We don't need examples of the word's use; we do need to help the survival of this beleaguered motivator by our own use of it: If we advertise something as "Free," please, please, please be sure it really is free. Thanks.

37. Exclusive

The magic formula, "Only you . . . only from us" survives despite cynical misuse. It's parallel to "Free," because the jackals have discovered the word and eaten away at its vitals. That the selling power of "exclusive" survives is due to the occasional offer that really is exclusive.

In our society, we're used to the word used wildly without factual backup. Like "Free," if you're in the Word Preservation Movement, do your bit by avoiding a hit-and-run use. Don't say "Exclusive" unless a nearby bit of copy validates the claim. The claim doesn't have to be exclusive for the reader; it also can mean the supplier has an exclusive.

Example: I'm looking at a Christmas mailing. It's carefully die-cut in the shape of a Christmas stocking, and the heading is:

EXCLUSIVE HOLIDAY OFFER INSIDE

I open the stocking, and I see the "Christmas Pop-Up Collection." And what, you ask, makes this exclusive? Reversed out of an oversize red oval are the words "NOT AVAILABLE ANYWHERE ELSE!"

Fair enough. Or *almost* fair enough. True fairness would have called for the explanation to be on the front of the stocking, not inside. Why? Because without a qualifier the reader always interprets exclusive to mean him or her, not you.

38. You've never had it so good.

This one is an amalgam of others. Take a look at the list and you'll see what I mean. But without the blend into this statement, no other makes quite the same statement.

I like the one that begins:

NEVER WILL YOUR BED HAVE FELT SO GOOD!

Yes, it's a bit off, the result of mixing future and past tense. But consider: You'll find it almost impossible to start with a "You've never had it so good" opening and not emphasize a highly personal benefit. And highly personal benefits are the Kingdom of Heaven in our business, aren't they?

39. Are you doing it wrong?

Wow, power surges through the arteries of this opening! A reader can regard it as accusatory, which can be a turn-off; on the other hand, it can turn *on* a reader who's too jaded to respond to any other opening.

Obviously, if you ask the reader "Are you doing it wrong?" you then have to explain, in a non-accusatory way, how to do it right.

A heavily-produced direct response space ad is headed:

Are You Relying on A Primitive
System To Sort Small Items?

Capitalization is as shown here, including "A" and "To" — which you or I wouldn't have done. In fact, this is the kind of headline that in modern usage capitalizes only the first word.

Illustration is an old wood-cut of a primitive tribe grinding grain on stone slabs.

This is too esoteric for my taste, but it's much in keeping with the spirit of "Are you doing it wrong?" It also exemplifies a danger: Some readers will think you, not they, are foolish.

40. Are you still stuck in the twentieth century?

I'll cover (and dismiss) this one with one sentence: If you use it, use it after the millennium.

Try Some. Add Some.

Why not, before moving on to the final chapter, dig out 10 of your own? Ten? Another 40? One hundred? Why not? It's possible, because the cosmic supply of "stock" headings is unlimited.

23

A Potpourri of Response-Enhancing Techniques: Before I Forget

You're writing a piece of copy. Uh-oh — here's the word *receive.* Will your message be stronger if you substitute *get*? And here's a guarantee. Should you replace *Unconditionally Guaranteed* with *Unconditionally 100% Guaranteed*?

Every dinky change should have a purpose. Purpose has to link itself to response. Dilettantes play with words; professional wordsmiths build and cement their sales arguments with words. We tolerate no rotting boards, no powdery or dried out mortar, no second-rate bricks made without straw.

The core of any successful marketing strategy has to be the ability to convince the reader, viewer, or listener. That ability stems from astute word-choice. The writer who doesn't ask, "Why did I make that change in words or punctuation?" is throwing away tiny nuggets that could be beneficial throughout a professional lifetime.

Here are some of this writer's personal nuggets. The professional communicator should regard these suggestions as "seeds." Cross-pollinate with your own procedures to begin a personal file of power-enhancers your competitors are unlikely to match.

Analyze: Why Is This Way
Stronger Than That Way?

Every one of us who earns a semi-legitimate living as a "professional" copywriter stumbles upon golden rhetorical nuggets.

We usually entertain a fleeting "Hey, how about that!" . . . insert it in our copy . . . and then forget what we've done. Our nugget becomes a one-time flash instead of part of a communications wedding ring.

So before I forget, I'll share some of my nuggets. If you're reading this and feeling benevolent, maybe you'll do the same.

Don't expect any "Eureka!"-type revelations. Instead, expect to think, "I more or less knew that." Listing some of the power-additives we all have, hidden somewhere in our brains, not only helps us have them at hand when an opportunity to use them occurs, it also helps dislodge others that may have been stuck in our cerebral mud.

I don't apologize for picking nits. For every direct marketing revelation equal to Einstein's Theory or Newton's Law we have ten thousand minuscule discoveries that help us improve the vigor and conviction our words display.

Some writers think of word and punctuation changes as pennies lying on a muddy sidewalk. Why get our hands dirty picking them up?

I'd rather think of them as upgrades from "economy" to "first class" — we get to the same destination, but we get there in a far more spirited manner.

So Before I Forget . . .

• "You can count on us" isn't as powerful as "Count on us." Why? Because "Count on us" has no qualifier.

• What is the difference between . . . "We are the first to be awarded this honor" and . . . "We are the first to earn this honor"? Simple: An award is recognition; earning is accomplishment.

• The difference between . . . "If you are among those who . . ." and . . . "If you are one of those who . . ." is the difference between being one of the mob and being singled out.

• How to "hedge" a positive statement: Instead of "I'm convinced that . . ." use "In my opinion. . . ."

• The difference between *"We don't have apples but we do have pears"* and *"We have pears but we don't have apples"* lies in the conclusion the reader or listener reaches. The first sentence leaves the reader with a positive conclusion; the second sentence leaves the reader with a negative conclusion.

• Which is more salesworthy?

If you'd like to continue receiving our catalog

or

If you want to continue receiving our catalog?

In almost every instance, the conditional is weaker than the declarative; so, "If you'd like to" is less compelling than "If you want to." Tens of thousands of advertising messages suffer impact-loss from "would/should/could" usage in place of definitive words. Understand, please: conditional words are neither useless nor obsolete, but they're weak competitors in a dynamic playing field.

• Don't use positive words for a negative effect. "Tired of that big, spacious house?" . . . "As the rebels opened fire, the Rwandan children scampered into a ditch" . . . "If you've been protected by regular homeowners insurance" . . .

The reader can't envision anyone being tired of a big, spacious house; he or she *can* envision being tired of daily maintenance of an immense fuel-gobbler. Scampering children aren't in danger; fleeing children are. Those who are protected by regular homeowners insurance are secure; those who are at the mercy of old-fashioned insurance aren't.

The point of this nugget: Words have to match, or your message loses conviction. If you're going to damn, *damn.*

• A "touchstone" is more colorful than bald recitation of fact. Example: "We were in business four years before George Washington was elected president" draws a better word-picture than "Founded in 1784."

• Direct the thought: What is the difference between . . .

"Do you want to live to be 100?"

and . . .

"Don't you want to live to be 100?"

Each suggests a different challenge.

• Singular suggests exclusivity. Collective nouns suggest universality. Example:

> • *You'll save on anything you see in these pages.*
> • *You'll save on everything you see in these pages.*

• (Here are two little words that not only can improve response by a huge percentage, they can literally make you rich.) The easiest way to force yourself to be specific:

"For example:"

• What is the difference in the effect generated by

> "*. . . has never looked better*"

and

> "*. . . will never look better*"?

"*. . . has never looked better*" has no timely implication. It suggests a completed, stabilized circumstance. (Use this construction for image-building or image-retention.) "*. . . will never look better*" implies immediacy and impermanence. (Use this construction to suggest fast action or the situation might change, so for maximum response tie in an expiration date.)
• The difference between

> "*It might be easier for both of us if . . .*"

and

> "*It might be easier for us both if . . .*"

exemplifies the difference between the casual wordmonger and the master wordsmith. So not only shouldn't you use the two interchangeably, if you have been using them interchangeably, don't admit it! And before reading on, check your semantic equipment for synchronicity with this apparently complex but genuinely simple deduction:

> "*Both of us*" is a separator, suggesting different benefits.
> "*Us both*" is a combiner, suggesting identical benefits.

- What is the difference between

"If we bill you once a month"

and

"If we were to bill you once a month"?

Anyone who understood and agreed with the previous point will understand and agree with this one. *"If we bill you once a month"* is more straightforward, less conditional, and, therefore, "harder" than *"If we were to bill you once a month."*
- If you have a price which requires a counter-qualifier, such as "plus tax" or "if available," *don't* use a comma before the phrase.

"$9.95, plus sales tax"

draws more attention to the tax than

"$9.95 plus sales tax."

Eliminating the comma makes the qualifying phrase more of a throw-away, by eliminating the pause before the eye moves to it.
- Consider replacing "into" with "to" . . . books on grammar notwithstanding.

"Into" is more complex movement than "to"; "into" suggests more penetration than "to." So "Into" seems to be a more difficult action.

"Bring your coupon to our store" is less work *and less of a commitment* than "Bring your coupon into our store."
- The word "of" can add stature to a title, profession, event, or assemblage:

"A collection of fine art" has greater stature than *"A fine art collection."*
- To carry the previous point one step farther: Using "of" enables the writer to place the noun before its qualifier. Placing the noun before its qualifier adds strength to both words.
- Beware of imperatives that imply a power-mad attitude.

"You must . . ." can generate more antagonism than *"You have to. . . ."* We're salespeople swimming in the Age of Skepticism. Naked commandments sit poorly with those who are best able to respond to our offers.
- The word *"even"* adds uniqueness to your offer:

"We'll even refund the cost of shipping" adds octane to the standard *"We'll refund the cost of shipping." "Even in these difficult times we still . . ."* makes you more heroic than *"In these difficult times, we still . . ."*

• Here are three little words that can be pure gold when we want to sidestep reader skepticism or antagonism:

"We both know . . ."

• If you've been using "be" and "become" interchangeably, consider the difference between "be" and "become":

"Be" suggests status: *"You can be a member of this unusual group."* "Become" suggests change: *"You can become a member of this unusual group."*

To exalt, *be.* To mutate, *become.*

• Have you considered the difference between "un" and "not"? Of course you have. Of course you acknowledge what that difference is:

"Un" seems inadvertent: *Unmarried . . . unimpressed . . . uncertain. Not* seems more intentional: *Not married . . . not impressed . . . not certain.*

• Danger lurks! You can generate a *competitive* reader reaction when using words considered self-enhancing:

"I'm perfectly aware" may seem competitive.
"I'm very much aware" doesn't have this problem.

(See the difference between the self-enhancing "perfectly" and the neutral "very much"?)

• Okay, a mini-quiz: When would you choose:

"This is our most popular model" . . .
"This is our most sought-after model . . ."?

Don't read on until you've analyzed the difference between "popular" and "sought-after." Staring at these words parallels staring at one of those puzzles that seems to be out of focus and then forms an image. In this case, the image clears to . . .

Popular suggests mass acceptance, but no exclusivity. This means safety.

Sought-after suggests upscale, harder to get. This means exclusivity.

So the more upscale you want your image to be, the more you'd eschew "popular" and lean toward "sought after."

• You probably will generate more response by substituting *reply* for *respond*, because *Please reply* implies no commitment; *Please respond* implies a commitment. That's why we *respond* to a complaint and we *reply* to an offer for free details.

• If you've been using "At last" and "Finally" interchangeably as an opener, you might want to drop "Finally" from the competition. "At last" has more pep than "Finally." Why? Because "At last" implies a beginning. It hasn't happened before. "Finally" implies an ending. It's the end of an era. Yes, certainly the reader (or for that matter, listener) will know what you mean, but we're discussing power, not comprehension.

• Why is "try it at our risk" less threatening than "examine it at our risk"?

For the same reason "reply" is less threatening than "respond" . . . or "discover how to" is less work than "learn." Trying something doesn't suggest *effort* nor *commitment*. Examining something suggests effort plus the *need for expertise*.

• In selling copy, *enablement* outsells *granting permission:*

"This makes it possible for you to correct mistakes in your credit report" is more dynamic than "This lets you correct mistakes in your credit report."

Oh, it's a minor point . . . but *everything* that isn't obvious, in every facet of life, is a minor point. Minor discoveries, in wordsmithy or in electronics, tend to blossom into major discoveries when the principles behind them begin to clarify.

Think it through: Which is more valuable, if you were paying dollar for dollar? Something that says to you, "Here's everything to get you up and running" . . . or something that says to you, "Here's the starter; you supply the engine"?

• Readers react to danger more positively than they react to threats. So "Look out!" is more likely to generate a response than "Warning!"

We're on the edge of subtlety with this one, especially since the line dividing "Look out!" and "Warning!" is a ragged one. The rationale lies in the skepticism we've generated over the last 30 years toward all imperative messages. We don't want the reader to sneer, "Says who?" We don't want the reader to match wits with us. A warning has its place and we all use it (often as a "Don't miss out" clincher), but no one can claim "Warning!" is a rapport-builder.

So the cry of "Wolf!" penetrates apathy more readily than the cry of "You fool!" That's one reason stick-on notes have become so powerful: They can transmit a "Look out!" message quickly and brightly without corrupting the core message.

• "It was . . ." followed by a *predicate nominative* adds historicity to fact:

"It was an amateur astronomer who made the celestial discovery of the decade"; "It was Robert Tyler who discovered how to achieve high gloss on recycled paper"; "It was a victory the likes of which wouldn't be seen again for 100 years."

How does "It was . . ." add historicity to fact? In this use, it says *revelation* is coming up. Without the predicate nominative, "It was" is just another opening weakened by the nondescript pronoun "It"; tied to the noun (or even pronoun), "It was" is a suspense-builder. The writer might want to add some monosodium glutamate by padding the suspense with an intermediate "teaser" line before total disclosure.

But a warning (word used advisedly . . . why not "look out"?): If you hold suspense too long it begins to melt. Should you decide to use this device for letters, don't match it against a more potent rule: *Fire your biggest gun first.*

• Write what impresses the reader, not what a bookkeeper might enter in a ledger.

> *Wrong:* "While supplies last"
> *Right:* "Until our limited allotment is exhausted"

Bookkeeper mentality differs from salesperson mentality in a crucial interpretation. The bookkeeper keeps stock, and all amounts are equal. An item is either in stock or out of stock; an account is either current or past due. Much of a bookkeeper's value is dispassionate, non-emotional analytical reporting. The difference between "allotment" and "supply" is trivial.

The salesperson doesn't think, "They still have some stock so I won't approach them again until they're out of stock." Smart salespeople seize onto the difference between "allotment" and "supply" as an indication of rarity, justifying "Look out!"

A suggestion: Before reading on, think of one additional word-pair to be used differently by bookkeepers and salespeople. Do this once a day and you'll add a surprising amount of octane to every sales message you create. Make today the watershed day.

• "Not any" — *as a statement of opinion* — is more decisive and authoritative than "No":

"I don't see any problem" bestows more authority on the message-transmitter than "I see no problem." The difference is the dissimilarity between *inability to perceive* ("I see no problem") and *informed decision* ("I don't see any problem").

• Adverbs affect an action more powerfully than adjectives. So for more power, use the adverb. For a throwaway, use the adjective. Example:

Temporarily provides relief

versus

Provides temporary relief.

(The word "provides" is itself weak.)

If you're still skeptical, replace temporary with permanent. Which is stronger, "Provides permanent relief" or "Permanently provides relief"?

• Adding words between promise and payoff can subtract impact:

Enjoy the benefits of being a Citrus Groves Preferred Member loses some of the impact of the tighter contruction . . .

Enjoy the benefits of Citrus Groves Preferred Membership

"And in Conclusion, Ladies and Gentlemen . . ."

The purpose of the mini-series in this chapter has been to remind us all that intensification of messages is always within our control. No, we can't control the offer; no, we can't control bad list selection; no, we can't control non-delivery by the post office nor impossible placement in media. But we do have some control over the reaction our message engenders in the plastic brains of those to whom we send it.

So what's the point of all these? To those whose dedication is filling space, they're a curio. To those whose dedication is maximizing response, they're mini-keys to the Kingdom.

Now it's your turn. Before you put this book aside, write down at least one similar tip you've discovered (not "learned") as you've wandered through your own career as a force-communicator. Believe me, not only will at least one be there, lurking in mental limbo ready for plucking, but yanking loose that one will open a gate that can yield surprising results.

But be sure to write it down. Then use it, to lock it in your forebrain. You're off and running!

Start amassing your own pile of "Before I forget" power-additives and, as you use them, watch response start inching up.

"That's All, Folks!"

Oh, no, it's not!

The human mind can be a wondrous or a rusted implement.

Don't let yours rust. Add, to whatever of these principles that may be of value to you, your own list of precepts and procedures.

The world of communications is NOT static. Nor should be your approach to it.

—HGL

Index